HANDS-ON STRATEGY

NEW DIRECTIONS IN BUSINESS

New Directions in Business books provide managers and business professionals with authoritative sources of ideas and information. They're designed to provide convenient and effective ways to upgrade your skills in today's fast-changing world of business.

New Directions books cover current topics that leaders in every business need to know about. They focus on applied techniques that can be used today and are written by authors with academic and professional experience.

New Directions in Business titles

Hands-On Strategy: The Guide to Crafting Your Company's Future by William C. Finnie

The New Competitor Intelligence: The Complete Resource for Finding, Analyzing, and Using Information about Your Competitors by Leonard M. Fuld

New Product Success Stories: Lessons from the Leading Innovators by Robert J. Thomas

The Smarter Organization: How to Build a Business That Learns and Adapts to Marketplace Needs by Michael E. McGill and John W. Slocum

Touchstones: Ten New Ideas Revolutionizing Business by William A. Band

HANDS-ON STRATEGY

The Guide to Crafting
Your Company's Future

William C. Finnie

JOHN WILEY & SONS, INC.

New York · Chichester · Brisbane · Toronto · Singapore

Copyright © 1994 by William C. Finnie
Published by John Wiley & Sons, Inc.

Library of Congress Cataloging-in-Publication Data

Finnie, William C.,
    Hands-on strategy : the guide to crafting your
company's future / William C. Finnie.
        p.   cm.
    Includes bibliographical references and index.
    ISBN 0-471-04586-1
    1. Strategic planning.   2. Industrial management.   I. Title.
HD30.28.F564   1994
658.4'012 – dc20   94-6808

Printed in the United States of America

10 9 8 7 6 5 4 3 2

DEDICATION

I am blessed with both challenging work and a wonderful family. My parents, Thomas C. and Evelyn W. Finnie, gave me a firm foundation. This book is dedicated to my wife, Glenda, and my two sons, John and Steve. Glenda is the most caring person and one of the more remarkable managers I have known. It's been a great marriage for the past 26 years. While my father is a hard act to follow, my sons are a wonderful Act III. They and their friends give me confidence in America in the twenty-first century.

PREFACE

Consider these new realities:

- The pace of change in technology, politics, economics, and life-styles accelerates every decade.
- The rise of global trade means there are no more "protected" domestic markets. Every business faces high-quality competitors from industrialized countries and low-cost competitors from developing countries.
- The increased competition has created more sophisticated and demanding customers. Good quality at a good price no longer sells. Value today means great quality at a low price.

These realities make the need for solid business strategy obvious. Strategy is about controlling your destiny—increasing your control over forces that affect you and responding more effectively to those you can't control. Organizations must pay special attention to strategy when their environment changes faster than their ability to adapt to it through informal methods.

Given this greater need for strategy, you would think that it would be high on the agenda of every CEO. Yet, it's not. This unprecedented need for strategy has arisen just when the use of formal strategic planning has begun to decline.

What is the cause of this paradox? Is it because strategy tools and techniques have been inadequate to the demands of this brave new world? The answer is yes and no. Yes, in that the strategy techniques so uncritically embraced by the business community in the 1960s and 1970s turned out to have had major deficiencies. And no, in that strategists since 1980 have invented powerful approaches and paradigms that can give a company significant advantages in today's complex, competitive environment. Unfortunately, once burned, twice shy—and many of today's disillusioned CEOs simply shun all efforts to develop a long-term strategy.

Let's look at this gap between the great potential of these tools and their limited adoption. The dominant paradigm in strategy today is "strategic thinking," which, in the words of Steven Schnaars, is "a way of thinking about consumers, competitors, and competitive advantage."[1] The emphasis is on understanding the complex forces acting on a business so that you can control or create the future through strategy, not simply forecast it. Most thinking about strategy since 1980 reflects this concept, with Michael Porter's seminal *Competitive Strategy*[2] being the most influential single work.

Strategic thinking deals with the complex forces acting on an organization and with providing exactly the right approach for developing its long-term strategy. Still, its successes have been modest compared with its potential, for several reasons:

- As it has been presented, strategic thinking is not results oriented. It is strong on analysis, providing insight and understanding, but is weak on direct linkages with higher sales and profits.

- Strategic thinking has come to encompass dozens of separate paradigms and analyses. Little has been done to develop a coherent framework in which these concepts work together.

- Strategic thinking focuses primarily on customers and competitors, but again the linkage to shareholder value is unclear. Meanwhile, finance continues to drive planning in most companies.

[1]Steven P. Schnaars, *Marketing Strategy, A Customer-Driven Approach* (New York: The Free Press, 1991), p. 27.

[2]Michael Porter, *Competitive Strategy* (New York: The Free Press, 1980).

- Strategic thinking addresses long-term strategic concerns, with little to say about short-term implementation. It does not directly address bottom-up involvement, commitment, and accountability.

- Effective strategic thinking requires creativity and a multi-disciplinary approach to develop a winning vision and strategy, and these are precisely the weakest areas in U.S. business education.[3]

As a result of these limitations of strategic thinking concepts as they have been put into practice, most companies do not use the new strategy tools. Small companies either do no strategic planning or resort to motivational speakers and simplistic cure-alls like management by wandering around or becoming a one-minute manager. Larger companies are likely to use concepts from the 1982 bestseller *In Search of Excellence* or to rely on management approaches like Total Quality Management (TQM). Meanwhile, planning continues to be driven more by finance and internal needs than by the key to financial success—beating competitors in meeting customer wants.

This book bridges the gap between strategic thinking and its practical application to the real world of competitive business. It is about developing and implementing long-term business strategy, not about planning as many people think of that term. It does not belittle planning and in fact devotes one chapter to the critical importance of annual planning to successful strategy implementation. It is written for CEOs and would-be CEOs who want to dramatically improve the effectiveness of their organization's control over its destiny.

The purpose of this book is to encourage and enable companies to use strategy to increase their sales and profits. To do so, the book

[3]The most recent in-depth analysis of business education in the United States found two major shortcomings at the undergraduate, graduate, and continuing education levels: insufficient emphasis on generating "vision" in students and insufficient emphasis on integration across functional areas. Lyman W. Porter and Lawrence E. McKibbin, *Management Education and Development: Drift or Thrust Into the 21st Century?* (New York: McGraw-Hill, 1988), pp. 64–65.

exploits the considerable strengths of strategic thinking and directly addresses its weaknesses:

- It integrates strategic thinking concepts to *provide a solid foundation for an effective long-term strategy.*

- It uses the "interactive planning" techniques developed by Russell Ackoff. Like other strategic thinking concepts and tools, interactive planning focuses on creating rather than forecasting the future. It also provides the tool of "idealized design" to release an organization's creativity in order to *design a desirable future and a challenging but feasible strategy for achieving it.*[4]

- It uses a mission statement and a continuous improvement program such as TQM or Customer Satisfaction to *promote teamwork throughout the organization* so everyone is working together toward the same vision.

- It resurrects valuable but neglected "predict-and-prepare" techniques and three-cycle annual planning to *keep the strategy fresh and action oriented.*

- It uses bottom-up goals and action plans to *produce involvement and commitment and drive strategy implementation.*

Most of all, this book moves strategy from being finance driven to being customer and competitor driven. It is grounded in the belief that shareholder value is the ultimate objective. Most companies have done their financial engineering toward that end. Today and tomorrow, the real key to creating shareholder value lies in beating competitors in meeting customer wants. This book will help you do that.

St. Louis, Missouri   WILLIAM C. FINNIE
August 1994

[4]Russell L. Ackoff, *Creating the Corporate Future* (New York: John Wiley & Sons, 1981). Reflecting Ackoff's seminal role in systems analysis, interactive planning includes a total approach to strategy development and implementation. It begins by using a "reference forecast" to create awareness of the need for a new strategy. It produces a superior strategy through idealized design, which uses multidisciplinary approaches to relax self-imposed constraints and release creativity. It also addresses such issues as organizational design, resource planning, and implementation and control.

ACKNOWLEDGMENTS

The strengths of this book rest on three foundations:

- Dr. Russell L. Ackoff, my doctoral advisor at the University of Pennsylvania and long-time consultant to Anheuser-Busch, taught me how to structure complex problems so that organizations can address them effectively. Many fundamental concepts in this book originated with Russ, the most creative person I have known. I also want to thank Russ for his detailed and valuable comments on this book. My debts to Russ just keep increasing.

- August A. Busch III and other senior executives at Anheuser-Busch consistently stretched me to 100 percent of my ability from the time I got a summer job in 1965 until I left the company to form my own consulting firm in 1991. My peak experiences came from taking responsibility for units that were operating significantly below expectations and bringing them up to standard within two or three years. These experiences included managing consumer research in 1976–1978; directing alcohol, tax, and other issues in the office of industry and government affairs in 1981–1985; and directing nonfinancial strategic planning in the office of corporate planning in 1986–1991. August Busch and the policy committee of Anheuser-Busch have a commitment to planning and strategy that is unsurpassed in U.S. industry. They are unwilling to separate planning from decision-making and have always maintained a disciplined focus on consumer expectations and shareholder value (which may be the key reasons that the stock increased from $1.90 to $53 per share, adjusted for splits, during my 26 years).

- Teaching strategy to second-year MBAs at Washington University in St. Louis since 1978 has honed my approach to planning and strategy. Since 1988, the course has combined lectures on the theory of planning and strategy with "real world" cases. The class is divided into groups of about five students, and each group develops a strategic plan for a business. The students benefit because doing strategy is the best way to internalize the theory. The organizations also benefit significantly from their involvement. Seeing how these concepts can transform all types of organizations influenced my decision to write this book and form a consulting company to take the approach to a wider audience.

I want to thank four Anheuser-Busch people — August A. Busch III, Leon Pritzker, John H. Purnell, and Robert S. Weinberg — whom I have worked for and with since the mid-1960s. I also have deep appreciation for four people at Washington University's Olin School of Business. Tom Kirk, Charlie Wirtel, and Tani Wolff each helped me teach my strategy course for several years and helped me better understand strategy and business. Robert L. Virgil, dean of the business school from 1977 through 1993, provided continued support and demonstrated how to transform a nonprofit organization through a strategic vision.

Finally, I want to thank Jim Fullinwider, who helped me with this book. The book's structure and content are mine. Jim deserves much credit for its readability.

W.C.F.

CONTENTS

HANDS-ON STRATEGY

1

CONTROLLING YOUR DESTINY

The Concept and Nature of Strategy

In 1981, General Electric (GE) was a success by most measures, widely admired and frequently emulated. Founded in 1879 by Thomas Edison, the inventor of the electric light bulb, GE virtually invented the modern standard of living. In addition to Edison's electric lights, the company brought to market the phonograph, radio, and television; the electric fan, toaster, refrigerator and freezer, cooking range, clothes washer, and steam iron; jet engines; nuclear power plants; and a host of other products. A century after its founding, GE had grown into the eleventh largest U.S. company, with a market value of $12 billion.[1]

But in 1981, GE's new CEO, Jack Welch, and its board of directors were less impressed with past successes than with future threats—both internal and external. They saw a company whose success had rested on a strategy and culture no longer adequate for the future. GE had become a company made slow and unresponsive by its massive bureaucracy—a company without a vision and a strategy for the new era of global competition.

GE had evolved into an extraordinarily diverse collection of businesses, most of whose products had become commodities in markets whose growth had peaked. Moreover, the company held a leadership position in only a few of its markets and was actually losing share in many of those.

When Welch became CEO, he compiled a list of principles he used to guide both his personal and business affairs. His six rules of life and business were:

1. Control your destiny, or someone else will.
2. Face reality as it is, not as it was or as you wish it were.
3. Be candid with everyone.
4. Don't manage, lead.
5. Change before you have to.
6. If you don't have a competitive advantage, don't compete.[2]

Two of these, "Control your destiny, or someone else will," and "Change before you have to," were particularly relevant to the situation he inherited in 1981.

Buoyed by those precepts, Welch set out to revolutionize GE's strategic direction and corporate culture. His new strategy for growth demanded that every GE business be number one or two in its *global* market. GE would "fix, sell, or close" any of its businesses not in that market position, carrying out his principle, "If you don't have a competitive advantage, don't compete."

Initially, Welch concentrated on the "hardware" of strategy—restructuring, acquisitions, and divestitures. Within the first four years, he eliminated 125 businesses, including old-line ones that manufactured small appliances and TVs, as he began a series of divestitures that would amount to $11 billion by 1992. At the same time, he started a program of acquisitions that would eventually total $21 billion. He restructured 350 separate businesses into 13 coherent units, while reducing the total work force from 420,000 to about 280,000.

After five or six years of focusing on the "hardware," Welch turned his attention to the "software"—people and values. He launched a war on bureaucracy. When he became CEO, GE had up to nine layers of management between the CEO and the shop floor. Welch reduced that number to as few as four. He instituted what

GE calls "work outs," "New England–style town meetings" in which employees openly assault such bureaucratic burdens as excessive reports, unnecessary paperwork, and multiple approvals. Employees now organize ad hoc work outs as needed to solve problems. Sometimes their supervisors hear about the work outs only when they are presented with the solutions.

This revolution in strategy and culture has renewed GE as a growth company. The proportion of its businesses in growth industries, just one-third in 1981, had become two-thirds by 1992. During the same time, GE's share price grew fivefold. At $67 billion market value in April 1992, GE had moved from the position of eleventh to that of third most valuable company in America, and to fifth most valuable in the world.

Few companies have the anatomy – "head, heart, and guts," in Welch's terms – to attempt even much smaller change, especially when they are at what appears to be the peak of success. Many other companies like General Motors (GM), Westinghouse, and IBM, who in the early 1980s all faced the same external forces and competitive future that GE faced, are changing only now – when they have been forced to.

Staying ahead of a changing business environment by keeping your strategy fresh and relevant is the way to keep control of your destiny. The long-term and sustained performance of any organization – whether business, academic, charitable, social, or otherwise – depends on the relevance of its strategy to market conditions and on the effectiveness of its implementation. Together, strategy and implementation mean superior performance. If you have lousy strategy, you'll have lousy performance. If you have lousy implementation, you'll also have lousy performance. Implementation is much better in organizations with a clear strategy. People work harder, they work smarter, and, most importantly, they work together.

Strategy has become more important in the past 20 years, precisely because of the fundamental shifts in the marketplace that Jack Welch responded to:

- *Emergence of global competition.* In 1970, most companies had to worry only about domestic competitors. Today, they also compete with high-quality competitors from Japan and Europe and low-cost competitors from developing countries. Global competition has also made domestic competitors tougher.

- *Big-company competition.* The largest competitors once tended to focus on the biggest segments of a market, but now they compete in all segments. In the U.S. beer markets of the 1970s, for example, Anheuser-Busch and Miller fought over the premium-beer segment. Today, each brewer also has low-price brands. There's hardly a safe niche any longer, as the big companies target *all* market niches.

- *More demanding customers.* Two decades of growth in both segmentation and positioning have caused today's customers to expect a product that precisely meets their needs. Moreover, the increased competition of the past decade and the frequent resort to price promotions have made today's shoppers extremely price sensitive and brand *dis*loyal. If you don't give them high quality at the lowest price, they know somebody else will.

In the early 1980s, Jack Welch was ahead of most of his business colleagues in recognizing the fundamentally altered competitive environment, and he was way ahead in doing something about it. But the changes have just begun, according to Welch: "If you thought the 1980s were tough, the 1990s will make the 1980s look like a cakewalk. It will be brutally competitive."[3] To survive and prosper in the 1990s, you'll need a superior strategy. Fortunately, strategy tools developed since 1980 are available to help you beat competitors in meeting customer wants. Controlling your destiny through strategy is what this book is about. This chapter starts the examination of the strategy development process by looking at two issues:

1. The concept and nature of strategy.
2. The value of strategic planning.

THE CONCEPT AND
NATURE OF STRATEGY

What is strategy? What it's *not* is "one-minute management." Some things just can't be done in one minute, or even one year. Strategy is designed for the long term.

Strategy isn't "management by walking around." It is important that managers "walk around," that they be visible and involved up to their elbows in the work of their associates, but that's not strategy.

Strategy is not Total Quality Management (TQM) or Reengineering. As important as these tools can be in focusing efforts and improving efficiency, strategy is still something more.

Strategy is not just "being close to your customers." No one will deny the importance of that, especially in the 1990s. But if each of your sales people is out making different promises to your customers, if each has a different notion of what you are trying to accomplish, you sure don't have a strategy. You have chaos.

Nor is strategy the same as planning. Planning is the process of developing, updating, and implementing strategy, action plans, and budgets. In too many companies, planning has become bureaucratic. It has become more concerned with the quality of the rain dance than with producing rain. Chapter 9 shows how to use annual planning to help drive strategy implementation. But planning is not strategy.

The concept of strategy is military in origin. Coined in the time of Napoleon, the term comes from the Greek word for "generalship." Strategy is what generals do in developing broad plans for winning a war. It guides them in determining which battles they should fight and which ones they shouldn't. In the military, strategy is a battle plan to gain superiority at the point of contact. Tactics, by contrast, addresses winning the battle with your resources once it starts.

Business strategy is similar. Strategy is a long-term direction that says what you are trying to accomplish and how you are going to do it. Strategy is concerned with developing long-term objectives, devising a coherent set of plans for achieving them, and then allocating the resources needed to carry out those plans. In business, strategic decisions are long term and difficult to reverse, require major resource commitments, and involve many functional groups and multiple objectives. Tactical decisions are simpler on each dimension.

The purpose of strategy is victory. That, however, does not always mean war. Even for generals, a superior strategy sometimes avoids battle. "To win without fighting is best," said the great

Chinese general Sun Tzu 2,500 years ago. Strategic victory means controlling your destiny and achieving your goals. The State Department and economic development are often more important than the Defense Department.

The reason you need strategy is the existence of competition. All organizations, including business and government monopolies, eventually face competition. The decline of the Catholic church during the Protestant Reformation and the fall of communism show that even the most dominant monopoly will fail if it is unresponsive. The decline of IBM and GM in the late 1980s shows that unresponsive businesses decline very quickly. No organization is totally free from competitive forces and the consequent need for strategy.

"The essence of strategy is the *interdependence* of competitors," says Robert Grant.[4] "Because actions by one player affect outcomes for other players, each player's decisions must take account of other players' expected reactions." Grant distinguishes games of strategy (e.g., chess) from games of chance (bingo) and games of skill (archery).

Grant illustrated the concept of strategy through the cases of three superior strategists: Beatles' manager Brian Epstein, North Vietnamese General Vo Nguyen Giap, and America's Cup winner Dennis Connor. These winning strategies are summarized in Exhibit 1.1.

Grant saw three key elements common to the strategies of each: (1) long-term, simple objectives, (2) a profound understanding of their customers and competitors, and (3) an objective appraisal and effective use of resources. The approach to strategy used throughout this book is a bit more detailed and comprehensive, but there's no doubt that these three elements are key to every successful strategy.

As in these three examples, the *objective* must be motivating to the entire organization and personally embraced by each participant. Thus, it must be simply stated, intensely inspiring, and thoroughly consistent with the values of those who implement the strategy. Frequently, a business will state its objective in terms of shareholder value. There's little question that the ultimate objective of a business is maximizing shareholder value, but stated as such, that goal doesn't inspire many people. Financial success (shareholder value) certainly was Epstein's objective, but his stated goal of making the Beatles "bigger than Elvis" was a lot more motivating.

	The Beatles	North Vietnam	Dennis Connor
Long-term, simple, agreed *objectives*	To be "bigger than Elvis"	Expel Western powers from South Vietnam; implement communism	Recapture the America's Cup
Understanding of customers and competitors	Music and image to appeal to teens	General Giap understood the battlefield and his enemy	Seamanship and technology
Effective use of *resources*	Developed a sound and style which exploited their youth, humor, and irreverence	Protected against weakness in arms; exploited commitment of troops	Recognized his sailing skills; obtained technology
Implementation	Different styles, but all demonstrated enthusiasm, involvement, commitment, and unity of purpose. Appropriate organizational structure. Used specialist skills through effective coordination and communication.		

Exhibit 1.1 Effective nonbusiness applications of strategy.

The *competitive environment* is the focus of strategy in the 1990s. For virtually any product and service category you can think of, global competition is becoming the norm, and there will be no going back to simpler, less competitive times. Americans in particular but also many Europeans failed to understand the nature and portent of Japanese competition in the 1970s and 1980s. The lesson is clear: The key to business success is the development and execution of superior strategies—strategies that beat competitors in meeting customer wants.

Effective use of *resources* means you need to know the strengths and weaknesses of both your competitors and yourself. Even if you have fewer resources than your competitor has, you do not have to lose. A superior strategy often compensates for inferior resources.

However, your objectives and strategy must be consistent with the resources available to you.

Effective and Ineffective Strategies

A superior strategy usually makes the difference between success and failure in a competitive situation. If you have no strategy or an inappropriate one, you have virtually eliminated yourself from the competition. You are actually playing a game of chance, and when was the last time you won a lottery?

Exhibit 1.2 illustrates some effective and ineffective strategies. Wal-Mart's experience shows that a well-executed low-cost strategy can work beautifully. By contrast, Microsoft used a differentiation strategy to dominate the market for personal computer software. But each had a clear and relevant strategy and executed it well. The

	Wal-Mart	Microsoft	Sears (in the 1980s)
Generic Strategy	Low-cost mass marketing, initially in rural Southeast	Dominate PC software; originally DOS, now all PCs and Macintosh	"Caught in the middle"; neither low cost nor differentiated on product attributes
Customer perceptions	Everyday low prices; friendly, good variety, clean	Excellent application software; Windows makes DOS OK	Bad service. Old-fashioned. Still good quality in durables
Employee perceptions	Good feedback; good culture; glad I bought stock	Lets me work 16 hours a day doing great stuff. Rich from stock options	It's a job. I hope I don't lose it when they cut costs
Stockholders	Great company	Great company	It's been a disaster.

Exhibit 1.2   Effective and ineffective business applications of strategy.

disastrous strategic error is "being caught in the middle." In the 1980s, Sears did not have low costs and prices or products with distinctive customer appeal. With no clear long-term direction from the top, but strategy changes every year or two, Sears was neither low cost nor high quality. It was "caught in the middle" and consistently lost share to competitors.

With an effective strategy, all the primary stakeholders in a company win. Likewise, customers, employees, and stockholders all lose with a poor strategy.

Poor strategy leads to unhappy employees. Their productive skills and potential are not fully utilized, while great demands are placed on their less-than-productive political instincts. The lack of a clear direction causes them to devote their energies to defending turf and building empires instead of meeting customer wants. However, a vision shared by everyone in the organization causes people to work to 100 percent of their ability. That is the number one ingredient in the quality of work life. Without it, your best employees leave, often joining your competitors and thereby further weakening your ability to compete.

Poor strategy leads to dissatisfied customers and lower sales. Without a clear vision and direction, you will not be able to position your products or services in the minds of customers as having special value for them. Actual product quality and service also suffer. The result is lower repeat sales.

Finally, stockholders suffer from poor strategy. Unproductive employees and weak sales cause poor profitability from existing products. Investments for new products also produce low returns. For example, General Motors had $65 billion in capital expenditures in the 1980s, but the company had a market value of only $50 billion in early 1993. Similarly, IBM's slow response to personal computer innovations produced enormous costs in an industry where 90 percent of the profits are earned in the first six months of a new product generation.

If organizations once could get away with mediocre strategy, they no longer can. Today, poor strategy sets off a downward spiral that ultimately produces failure. Recently, the world has seen the sad results of this downward spiral in several American companies that were once inspiring role models. Twenty to thirty years ago, it was common to find an ambitious startup company that set a goal of becoming "the IBM of the popcorn industry" (or whatever industry). Three decades ago, many Americans agreed that "what's good for General Motors is good for the U.S.A." But few today care to model themselves on GM and IBM. How could two such giants in their industries, such paragons of business success, be brought as low as they are today? The answer: bad strategy.

THE VALUE OF STRATEGY

Businesses have always been concerned with strategy, ever since the world's second stone tool and weapons maker set up shop across the dirt path from the first. But strategy was to businesses somewhat the same as prose was to Moliere's bourgeois gentleman: "For more than forty years I have been speaking prose without knowing it." Illiterates in fact speak prose all their lives, but those who have studied a little grammar, composition, and the principles of rhetoric sometimes do a better job of it. The same goes for strategy. Those who become versed in the art and science of strategy have an advantage over their "unschooled" competitors.

The Evolution of Business Strategy

Strategy, along with systematic business planning, has become a distinct formal concern of business enterprises only since World War II. The war experience stimulated interest in formal strategic planning. To conduct such a complex and massive enterprise, the U.S. and British war departments invented management and analytical techniques that were the precursors to postwar management science and operations research—the application of scientific and quantitative techniques to the analysis and implementation of complex systems.

From that experience emerged the first era of formal business planning, with a heavy emphasis on budgeting and cost control and a lesser emphasis on what would today be considered true strategy. Exhibit 1.3 summarizes this planning era and subsequent ones.

The most famous case of wartime planning brought to business was Ford Motor Company's planning department under Robert

Era	Primary Characteristic	Approach	Objective
1950s	Budgeting and management science	One-year; bottom-up	Improve efficiency; provide top-management control
1960s	Long-range planning	5-year "predict-and-prepare" planning	Bottom-up functional plans based on corporate planning forecast
1970s	Formula planning	Financially driven formula planning	Experience curve and low-cost strategy; growth-share matrix for managing business units
1980s	Strategic thinking	Market-driven, competitive advantage	Develop strategy consistent with 4 Cs (climate, customers, competitors, and company); create your own future
1990s	Goal-oriented strategy	Design a desired future and develop a strategy to achieve it	Incorporate strategic thinking into an action-oriented planning framework

Exhibit 1.3   The evolution of strategy.

McNamara and his "whiz kids," all of whom had gained their planning experience during the war. The postwar boom in America created even larger and more complicated business enterprises that stood to benefit from the management science focus on systems analysis and budgeting. Efficiency greatly improved, and top management gained more effective control of their organizations.

In the late 1950s, new long-range "predict-and-prepare" planning techniques gave birth to the second phase of planning that came to maturity in the 1960s. The basic approach was to predict the future and then develop action plans to exploit the inevitable. In the economy of the time, market growth and the periodic ups and downs of the business cycle were reasonably predictable, making five-year forecasting generally accurate and reliable. Once the forecast was agreed on, top management could then ask for bottom-up functional plans to achieve the predicted sales and income targets.

The dominant theme of planning in the 1970s was "formula" or "portfolio" planning, ideally suited, it seemed, for the conglomerates that had been assembled in the 1960s and early 1970s. Perhaps with too much cash in hand and too great a sense of control through the planning systems of the previous 10 to 20 years, executives of many corporations went on a diversification binge. Putting together a portfolio of cyclical and countercyclical but unrelated businesses, so the thinking went, would level out the effects of business cycles.

Formula planning became the gospel preached by the new high priests of planning, the young MBAs who flocked to the consulting firms. They propagated the view that a group of businesses could be managed much like a portfolio of stocks, and they put forth a variety of financially based formulas for planning and managing these businesses. Similar to other formula planning approaches, the most popular one analyzed companies on two dimensions—rate of industry growth and market share of each business unit. When the businesses in the portfolio were plotted on a growth-share matrix, the CEO could determine which ones were "stars" (high growth, high share), which ones were "dogs" (low growth, low share), which were "cash cows" (low growth, high share), and which were "question marks" or "problem children" (high growth, low share). Accordingly, the CEO knew which ones to manage for cash, which to invest in, and which to divest.

This is all very rational and comforting in theory, but overly simplistic and not always so effective in practice. Many top managers were frustrated by the inability of formula planning to help them beat competitors who were doing a better job of meeting customer wants. Moreover, many senior VPs had a tough time swallowing dictation from 30-year-old hotshot MBAs who'd never met a payroll. Finally, the oil shocks of the 1970s and the unpredictability of the growing global competition put an end to what little faith remained in long-range quantitative forecasting. A reaction set in against all strategy and planning.

The fourth phase in the evolution of planning and strategy placed heavier emphasis on strategy as such. Since 1980, the "strategic thinking" theories of academics and consultants like Michael Porter and Russell Ackoff have dominated the literature on strategy.[5] Moving away from financial strategies and focusing more on markets, they developed a series of valuable tools for understanding industries, competitors, customers, and the broader climate businesses operate in.

Meanwhile, American and European managers found themselves scrambling to cope with the loss of market share as global competitors breached the walls of their familiar domestic markets. The only strategy many of them currently pursue is survival planning—restructuring, downsizing, divesting, and other cutbacks in an effort to get in better financial shape to take on the competition.

Most of the restructuring in the West is over, and both the thrivers and the survivors will have to focus on new kinds of strategies in the 1990s. In this new era, the smartest CEOs will develop "goal-oriented" strategies using the analytical tools developed in the 1980s. But their focus will be results, not analysis. The successful executive will use strategy development processes, such as the Four-Cycle Strategy Planning Process presented in this book, to design a desired future, to develop a strategy to achieve it, and to drive implementation. In Jack Welch's terms, the executive will take charge of the company's destiny, lest someone else does it.

Approaches to Strategy and Planning

Companies that don't take control of their destinies and plan for the future may eventually find that they have no future. Many individuals and organizations will be forced to change their traditional attitudes and approaches to planning. Protected organizations such as schools and government agencies, which have faced little competition and therefore have given little thought to planning and strategy, will also find the 1990s a different world.

Russell Ackoff has identified four approaches organizations have traditionally taken to planning and strategy (Exhibit 1.4).

The *inactive* approach has been the usual response of protected organizations—such as government bureaucracies, schools, unions, some corporate staff departments, licensed professions (e.g., medicine), and regulated utilities. Their attitude is to resist change. If it

	Inactive	Reactive	Preactive	Interactive
Attitude toward change	Avoid change	Respond to it as it occurs (muddle through)	Anticipate and exploit (predict and prepare)	Create your own future
Top-down vs. bottom-up	Neither (avoid change)	Bottom-up	Top-down	Top-down and bottom-up
Typical organization	Subsidized, bureaucratic	Industry follower; current U.S. political system	Most companies	Leader in a complex environment

Source: Adapted from Russell L. Ackoff, *Creating the Corporate Future* (New York: John Wiley & Sons, 1981).

Exhibit 1.4 Types of planning.

comes at all, it is forced on them from above and only as a last resort.

The *reactive* approach[6] may be the most common, especially among corporate staff groups and small companies. People in these organizations deserve sympathy. They accept change and try to deal with it, but they spend their time and energies responding to the crisis *du jour*. They fight fires. They do the best they can do, but they seldom thrive. The basic problem is that big success requires exploiting opportunities rather than reacting to threats.

The *preactive* approach is the classic American predict-and-prepare planning of the 1960s. While this alone is not adequate to the competition of the 1990s, it still has a valuable role to play. For those few businesses in highly stable and predictable industries, preactive planning may in fact be all that's needed. You will also see that it is a valuable tool for *annual* planning. However, long-term strategy requires more.

The *interactive* approach, in Ackoff's words, is "the design of a desirable future and the invention of ways to bring it about."[7] Interactive planning shares the strength of "strategic thinking" in stressing the importance of understanding the complex forces acting on your industry and reflecting them in your strategy. Interactive planning has two additional strengths. First, Ackoff's concept of idealized design leads to a clear vision that excites and motivates everyone in the organization. Second, it has explicit linkages to bottom-up action plans, implementation, and control.

The goal-oriented Four-Cycle Strategy Planning Process discussed in this book relies on (1) interactive planning and strategic thinking concepts in developing long-term strategy and (2) predict-and-prepare preactive planning techniques in annual planning. Companies that rely on these methods will survive and flourish in the 1990s. Organizations that rely on inactive and reactive approaches will find survival in the 1990s difficult. They will be a source of market share for companies using goal-oriented planning.

Inactive and reactive organizations, with few exceptions, will find survival difficult in the 1990s.

The Time for a New Strategy

Strategy is important when the environment changes faster than an organization's ability to adapt using informal methods. Recognizing the changing competitive environment and then making the appropriate strategic adjustments are especially important for the industry leader. A leader with the right strategy will remain the leader, with followers adjusting their strategies accordingly. A leader with a wrong or outmoded strategy allows a strategy void to form, and there will always be a shrewd follower to fill the void and seize the lead.

Not all strategies are created equal. What was adequate for one time and circumstance is not necessarily so for another. Leaders of organizations need to know when a new strategy is called for. Sometimes the need is clearer than at other times, but even when it is most urgent, the obvious is not always easy to recognize.

Four situations, which typically happen every three to ten years, create the need for a new strategy, or at least an in-depth strategy review:

1. *A new chief executive officer.* Often, the new CEO is brought in because the strategy of the old CEO wasn't working. But even if the predecessor was an excellent strategist, the evolution of the

industry makes a thorough review desirable at this time. Also, during the new CEO's "honeymoon," he or she has an excellent but limited opportunity to put a personal leadership stamp on the organization. If a new strategy is needed, this is the best time for the new CEO to get the right strategy adopted. If the old strategy is still valid, the formal review and reaffirmation at this time lets the new CEO gain ownership of it.

2. *A major internal change in the business.* A change in ownership, a leveraged buyout, a restructuring, or a downsizing usually calls for a new strategy. Restructuring and downsizing are survival strategies that should last only about three years or so; after that, a new market-oriented strategy is needed. Major growth or a significant acquisition can also require a reassessment of the overall corporate strategy.

3. *A major external change in the industry or business environment.* A new competitor with a "new rules" strategy (e.g., Philip Morris' buying Miller and introducing sophisticated marketing to the brewing industry) or intensified international competition (e.g., Japanese cars and consumer electronics) requires new strategies. New technology could force strategic changes, as the development of the personal computer fundamentally changed the rules of the computer market. The deregulation of airlines and telecommunications in the United States called for fundamentally different strategies. The rise of Southwest Airlines and the demise of Pan Am and Eastern demonstrate the importance of fitting strategy to the changing business climate.

4. *Organizational inertia.* Finally, it's time for the CEO to initiate a new strategy whenever the organization is performing significantly below its potential. When drift, lethargy, or malaise overtake the organization, when the organization becomes complacent and fails to respond effectively or quickly enough to opportunities and competitive challenges, or when an internal focus and political infighting predominate, it's time for a new strategy.

The first two situations—a new CEO or a major internal change—are easy enough to recognize. They tend to be discrete events. The other two, however, are sometimes downplayed or ignored until it is too late. The cost of waiting increases exponentially with time. It's stupid to wait until you're on the edge of bankruptcy, as did the Chrysler Corporation before Lee Iacocca became CEO and the federal government bailed the company out in 1980.

Ineffective Strategic Planning

It's neither good strategy nor sound management to count on a government bailout, and companies that have reached that point can probably be associated with one or more of the common failures in strategic planning shown in Exhibit 1.5.

Failure to Adopt a Top-Down Strategy. This is usually a problem for bureaucracies, nonprofit organizations, and small companies which tend to be inactive or reactive. Big companies can fail this way too, but most often they fail because of a bad top-down strategy or because they stayed with a strategy long after competitive conditions demanded change. Even governments can fail because of lack of a top-down strategy. President George Bush never got around to the "vision thing" and squandered the highest level of public support of any president in modern history.

Ineffective Strategic Planning	Effective Strategic Planning
• Failure to adopt a top-down strategy	• Led by the CEO
• No effective planning cycle	• Top-down *and* bottom-up
• Lack of full commitment of the CEO	• Qualitative, quantitative, and creative
• Process-oriented instead of goal-oriented planning	• Action oriented
• Poor contingency planning	
• Lack of a feedback or improvement process	

Exhibit 1.5 Characteristics of ineffective and effective strategic planning.

Many business gurus today preach that being "close to the customer" is enough, but top management needs to provide a vision and strategy so that being close to the customer pays off in profits rather than in the conflict and chaos that result from lack of clear direction.

No Effective Planning Cycle.   Even when there is some top-down direction, irregular or unsystematic planning can result in failure. Sometimes a top-down strategy gives rise to new programs, but if the strategy is not regularly and systematically reviewed, these programs can drift on forever in the wrong direction. Governments commit this sin all the time. Too often, startup ventures with too-deep pockets endlessly discuss strategy without ever implementing anything. A planning cycle needs "bombs away" deadlines.

Lack of Full Commitment of the CEO.   If the CEO is not interested in strategy, forget it. Even if the organization does have a strategy development process, staff people typically develop the strategy and operations people view it as ivory-tower and off-target. Then, nobody takes it seriously.

Process-Oriented Instead of Goal-Oriented Planning.   Most people think of themselves as goal or results oriented, but how many times have you been through a planning process where there was more concern for the rain dance than for the rain? When a CEO doesn't see strategy as *the* tool for leading the company, planning meetings become presentations instead of the interactive process of developing winning plans. After two or three years of this time-wasting exercise, everyone is relieved when the CEO deemphasizes planning.

Poor Contingency Planning.   All good strategic planning accommodates change, both that which is probable and predictable and that which is unlikely but possible. That means contingency planning. Companies that rely only on preactive predict-and-prepare planning fail to account for external change. Just as soon as the forecast on which the plan is based becomes invalid, which it will after about three months, the plans get shelved and everyone reverts to an undirected reactive mode.

Lack of a Feedback or Improvement Process.   Planners should be responsible for improving the planning cycle and planning systems, such as forecasts, financial plans, methods for developing objectives, and so forth. Every year there should be incremental improvements in the process. Every three to ten years, when there's a major change in strategy, planning systems and processes should undergo fundamental review and revision.

Effective Strategic Responses

Fortunately, there are ways to avoid these common failings. Organizations should have effective strategic plans if their planning process has the characteristics listed in Exhibit 1.5.

Led by the CEO.   The process must be led by the CEO and senior managers, since they have the best knowledge of the industry and the company. However, they should not do it in isolation. Talking to all levels of their organization and to customers, suppliers, and others outside the company will temper their superior understanding with fresh and valuable perspectives.

CEOs should lead the process because strategy is the key mechanism at their disposal for implementing and controlling change in the organization. Jack Welch used a two-stage strategy, focusing first on the "hardware" and then on the "software" to transform GE from a sluggish industrial giant into one of the world's most agile and powerful enterprises.

When led by the CEO, the strategy development process uses staff planners and consultants as they should be—as facilitators who do analyses, recommend agendas and schedules, and develop first drafts of plans using input from senior management.

Top-Down *and* Bottom-Up.   The CEO and senior management develop the vision and long-range strategic direction. Then, functional managers develop functional strategies and bottom-up action plans to realize the vision. Without bottom-up planning, you can make the kind of mistake General Motors made in the 1980s. When the CEO decided to spend billions on robots, the money was largely wasted because GM's engineers were not ready to use them effectively.

Qualitative, Quantitative, and Creative. Good strategy development is qualitative in order to capture the directional forces affecting the industry and company. A long-term strategy requires this, and excellent tools for qualitative analysis now exist. Good strategy development is also quantitative, since "running the numbers" eliminates many superficially plausible theories. Moreover, what gets measured is what gets done. While long-term quantitative forecasting has limited value today, *annual* planning and implementation should be rigorously quantified. And good planning requires creativity to move beyond incremental change to a breakthrough strategy and a motivating vision.

Action Oriented. Good strategy development should not be a passive process, during which everything is on hold until the plan is promulgated. An action orientation is the glory of a superior planning process. At Anheuser-Busch, for example, management has for years made major decisions during planning meetings and used the resulting strategy in their decision-making throughout the year.

CONCLUSION

Effective strategy development and planning, then, is your organization's most powerful means of controlling its destiny. After the changes in the competitive climate of the past two decades, there should be no doubt of the value of good strategy. There's also no reason to doubt Jack Welch's observation that if the 1980s were tough competitively, just look at changes coming in the 1990s.

Strategy is simply the management of change—the intelligent adaptation to external circumstances and the conscious creation of a desired future. Without a systematic, formal strategy development process, the quality of strategy is likely to be hit or miss, and more often the latter, since it depends solely on the instincts, judgment, and guts of the business leader. One should not belittle these qualities; nothing can ever replace them. But they alone are not sufficient. You also need a good long-term strategy. Only then will your business win by beating competitors at meeting customer wants—which is what controlling your destiny is all about.

2

CREATING THE FUTURE
The Four-Cycle Strategy Planning Process

Every business has a strategy, even if by default. If your approach to planning is inactive, reactive, or preactive, you're letting your competitors impose a losing strategy on you. They will recognize and exploit opportunities and keep you on the defensive. However, if you rely only on the "strategic thinking" tools developed since 1980, implementation will be poor; you're unlikely to get bottom-up commitment and effective action plans.

Strategy development is a responsibility of top management and requires strategic thinking. Implementation is the responsibility of everyone and requires predict-and-prepare preactive planning. Strategic thinking is glamorous. It's like the passing game in football. Preactive planning is quantitative and focused. It's the ground-control, running game. Successful football teams use both passing and running games. And successful strategy requires both strategic thinking and preactive planning.

THE FOUR-CYCLE PLANNING PROCESS

The Four-Cycle Planning Process, shown in Exhibit 2.1, incorporates both strategic thinking and preactive planning for superior strategy development and implementation.

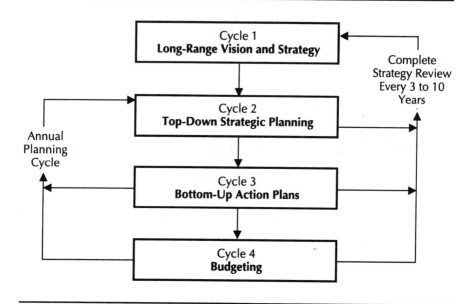

Exhibit 2.1 The Four-Cycle Strategy Planning Process.

The Four-Cycle Process works for every type of organization:

- Small and large organizations (but it is much simpler for small organizations).
- Makers of industrial products, suppliers of consumer goods, and service industries.
- Industry leaders and followers.
- High-growth, mature, and declining industries.
- For-profit, nonprofit, and government organizations.
- Corporations, business units, and staff groups.

Cycle 1 uses strategic thinking tools to devise your company's long-range vision and strategy. Although the Cycle 1 strategy will be reviewed and revised each year, the basic strategy will last for three to ten years or longer. Even in a fast-changing industry like personal computers, Compaq maintained the same differentiation strategy from its founding in 1982 until a price shakeout required shifting to a low-cost strategy in 1992.

The annual planning process – Cycles 2, 3, and 4 – uses predict-and-prepare preactive planning techniques. Cycle 2 uses an in-depth review of your business environment to revise goals and fine-tune the long-range strategy.

Cycle 3 produces bottom-up action plans. Each operating division and staff department develops plans consistent with the top-down strategy to achieve goals set in Cycle 2. This gives each person his or her marching orders. Cycle 4, budgeting, becomes a piece of cake once the first three cycles have been completed.

Winning in the real world with the Four-Cycle Strategy Planning Process is what this book is about. This chapter reviews the total process, giving emphasis to Cycle 1, the foundation of the other three. But the chapter has a dual purpose:

1. To give you an overview of the book, and

2. To help you start your own long-term strategy process.

As you read through this chapter, especially the material on Cycle 1, you'll come across some fundamental issues and questions. You should apply each of these to your business, pausing as you go to jot down your answers to those questions. By the time you finish, you should have two to four pages that become the basic material for a *tentative strategy*, which will form a solid foundation for your Four-Cycle Planning Process.

The Four-Cycle Process differs in four ways from most current approaches:

1. It produces *goal-oriented* strategy rather than strategy "analysis." The purpose of strategy is to help organizations increase sales and profits, not to produce intellectually appealing paradigms.

2. It relies on a planning *cycle*, which is an essential element in applying strategy to the real world. The planning cycle identifies threats and opportunities and prevents drift. It also leads to bottom-up involvement and commitment. Few strategy books since Abell and Hammond in 1979 and Lorange in 1980[1] discuss planning cycles.

3. The *four-cycle* approach is superior to the three-cycle planning process – annual strategy, action plans, and budgeting – devel-

oped by Lorange. The three-cycle approach implies that strategy is completely reinvented each year. But completely reinventing your strategy each year is a prescription for confusion. It takes two or three years for employees to understand and implement a new strategy, and even longer for customers to understand it.

4. Preactive planning tools are essential for sound annual planning. Most strategy theorists since 1980 have focused on strategic thinking techniques, downplaying or ignoring quantitative predict-and-prepare techniques. Both are important. Strategic thinking tools are critical for long-term strategy development; preactive planning provides clear targets, quantitative rigor, and bottom-line linkages that are essential to effective implementation.

CYCLE 1: LONG-RANGE VISION AND STRATEGY

Cycle 1, which drives the Four-Cycle Process, should be done every three to ten years. At some point during that time, your organization will probably confront one or more of the four situations that create the need for a new strategy—a new CEO, a major change in your business, a fundamentally altered industry or business climate, or simply the realization that your organization has become unresponsive. And if you get to ten years without a new Cycle 1, you'd be wise to trigger one anyway, whether you think you need it or not.

Cycle 1 has three parts, as shown in Exhibit 2.2:

1. *Tentative strategy*, which provides broad direction.

2. *Strategy analysis*, which provides in-depth understanding from several perspectives.

3. *Mission statement*, which moves the process from complexity and analysis toward simplification and implementation.

Developing the *tentative strategy* is the responsibility of the CEO or corporate office. The process is initiated when an annual planning "environmental analysis" or one of the four precipitating

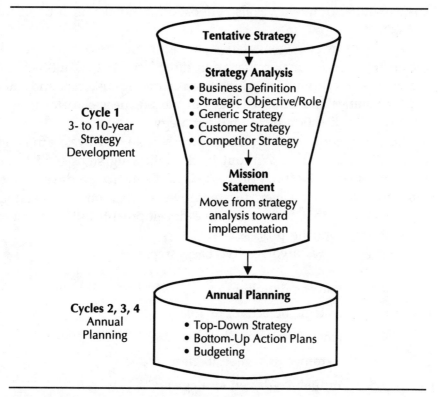

Exhibit 2.2   Overview of goal-oriented strategic planning.

events mentioned previously shows the need for a new Cycle 1. Perhaps your current strategy is incapable of exploiting an important opportunity or countering a competitor's potentially superior strategy. Perhaps industry trends and life-cycle phase point to long-term decline, even though current results seem satisfactory.

Gaining support for changing to a new strategy requires "unfreezing" the organization from its current strategy. Sometimes the need for a new strategy is painfully clear to everyone in the organization; at other times, the need is less obvious. In the latter case, the CEO faces a major educational and selling job. In one form or another, a reference forecast[2] can show that the current strategy will lead to disaster (or at least to performance far below the organization's potential). A clear demonstration of the threat of raiders, activist shareholders, or foreign competitors can "unfreeze" many in the organization. Research showing that competitors have lower costs or superior quality is also effective for mobilizing support for change.

A two- or three-page tentative strategy from the corporate office makes the case for major change in direction. First, it outlines the threats or opportunities resulting from changing customer and competitor realities and other changes in the business climate. It then suggests the direction of the new strategy.

Such a document allows each successive step in Cycle 1 to build on a solid foundation. Without it, the following steps tend to be mechanical and the final strategy is unlikely to produce breakthrough results. However, the tentative strategy must be seen as provisional, so that further creative development and refinement occur throughout the process.

Strategy analysis involves five basic steps:

Step 1.   Business definition.

Step 2.   Strategic objective, or role.

Step 3.   Generic strategy.

Step 4.   Customer-driven strategies.

Step 5.   Competitor-driven strategies.

The business definition tells you what business you are in, which is not always as clear as you might think. The strategic objective, or role, states the single critically important goal you are trying to achieve over the next three to ten years. Generic strategy states how you will achieve your strategic objective. Customer- and competitor-driven strategies turn the generic strategy into marketplace strategies for beating competitors in meeting customer wants. These five steps of strategy analysis focus on the three external Cs: Climate, Customers, and Competitors. They provide a solid analytical foundation for the strategy.

The *mission statement,* the final step of Cycle 1, takes into account the internal fourth C: the Company and its culture. It uses a process called "idealized design" to help the organization make a creative leap to a vision of a challenging but achievable future. This provides the foundation for the strategy for achieving the vision, which is expressed in a single-page mission statement that guides and motivates everyone in the organization for the duration of the strategy.

Tentative Strategy

When you start the task of strategy development, you will have prior notions about your business and your markets. These amount to a tentative strategy. The better you articulate it at the start, the better your strategy will be in the end. Your tentative strategy should define your business and customers and show how you will beat competitors in meeting customer wants.

Exhibit 2.3 outlines sources of tentative strategy for the purposes of the Four-Cycle Process. The discussion here will look at the last three sources, in order to (1) do a situation analysis of your business

Source	Benefit of Source	Rationale
The previous long-term strategy	Provides overall strategy	Judgment changes to old strategy based on changed environment provides good starting point.
Business definition	Starting point for Cycle 1	Customer wants, mechanism for meeting wants, and vertical integration are basic decisions.
Porter's five competitive forces and five external climate forces	Provides threats and opportunities and long-term drivers of change	Indicates direct and indirect customers and competitors and long-term drivers of change.
Judgment-based "perceptual maps"	Customer- and competitor-driven strategy	Leads to solid segmentation and positioning strategy.
Four Ps of marketing	Provides product, price, promotion, and place (distribution)	These are the basic elements of how you will beat competitors in meeting customer wants.

Exhibit 2.3   Sources of tentative strategy.

and market, (2) locate you in relation to your customers and competitors, and then (3) develop a rough plan of how you will meet customer wants better than your competitors.

Situation Analysis: Competitive and Climate Forces

What are the forces impinging on your business? Every day you are beset by two sets of external forces, as shown in Exhibit 2.4, which is based on Michael Porter's discussion of competitive strategy.[3] Five climate forces are shown outside the circle. The forces inside the circle are five competitive forces you face daily. It's clear how the competitive forces affect business, but business leaders sometimes

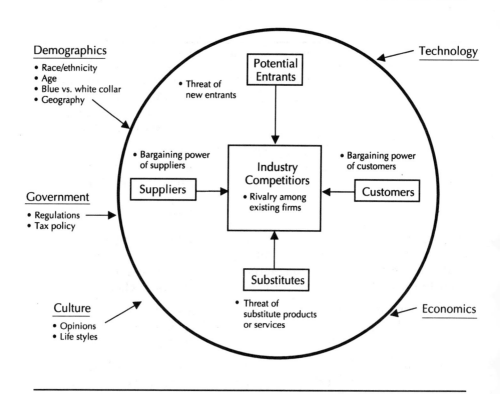

Exhibit 2.4   Porter's five competitive forces embedded in the five climate forces.

tend to slight the climate forces. That's a mistake. Changes in the climate forces cause changes in the five competitive forces.

A little thought will show how these climate and competitive forces affect your business. Use Exhibit 2.5 to develop the "threats and opportunities" you face from each of these forces.

Market Position: Perceptual Maps

Next, where do you stand in relation to customer wants and your competition's efforts to meet those wants? To answer this question, you can use a *perceptual map*, which is a two-dimensional representation of customers' perceptions of products and benefits sought. Marketers find them especially useful in positioning products and companies in the market. These maps, which are discussed in some detail in Chapter 6, often rely on large amounts of consumer research data and highly sophisticated statistical processing.

For now, it is not necessary to conduct a lengthy and costly customer survey. Instead, you should create a *judgment-based* perceptual map of your industry and marketplace, using your own extensive knowledge and experience.

On a piece of paper draw two axes. The horizontal x-axis is the primary customer want or market characteristic (high price vs. low price, style and status vs. utility and functionality, etc.), and the vertical y-axis is the second most important want or characteristic. Next, think of where your customers would locate your competitors on that map, and then where they would put your own products. This should give you a rough but useful picture of where you are positioned in the marketplace.

This can be illustrated with a perceptual map of the world of business consulting (Exhibit 2.6). The primary axis relates to cost. The secondary axis is a strategic/tactical continuum. Plotted here is a range of business consultants, including functional specialists, CPAs, public relations firms, strategy consultants, and others.

This map can suggest many conclusions about the market for business consulting. One is that strategy consulting is largely limited to the Fortune 500 companies. There is no major strategy consulting firm occupying a low to midway position on the cost

Force	Threats	Opportunities
Demographics		
Technology		
Economics		
Culture/lifestyle		
Government		

Exhibit 2.5a Threats and opportunities due to the five climate forces.

Force	Threats	Opportunities
Industry competitors		
Customers • Channel • Consumers		
Substitutes		
Suppliers		
Potential entrants		

Exhibit 2.5b Threats and opportunities due to Porter's five competitive forces.

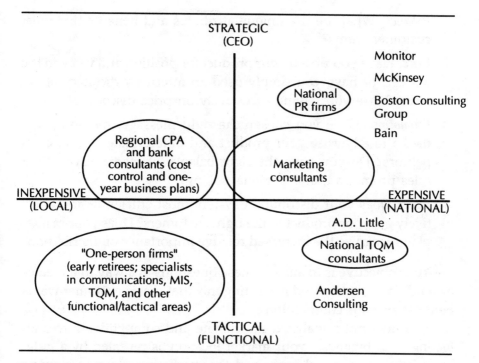

Exhibit 2.6 Perceptual map of consulting firms.

axis, and a large unserved market seems to exist. This suggests a potential niche for a Wal-Mart of the strategy consulting business.

Using a judgment-based perceptual map to help clarify your mental "picture" of your market and business position is valuable, even necessary, preparation for Cycle 1. Of course, an unrealistic, myopic, and distorted understanding of your business and market can result in a map that actually reinforces that distorted view. Be honest with yourself. Even better, get several others, inside and outside your company, to use their judgments to position you on a perceptual map.

Meeting Customer Wants: The Four Ps of Marketing

Finally, how are you going to meet the wants of your customers better than your competitors? Consider how you will use the Four Ps of the marketing mix to gain a competitive advantage:

1. *Product.* What are the unique attributes and benefits that meet customer wants?

2. *Price.* Have you priced your product for position and value in the market, or have you simply used an internally dictated rate of return? Are you relying excessively on price discounts?

3. *Promotion.* Have you chosen the right message, methods, and media to advertise your product and differentiate it from competitors? Do you have the right balance of media advertising, sales promotion, and personal selling?

4. *Place.* Does your distribution system most efficiently and effectively get your product to the right customers? Does your market plan recognize the increased relative importance of distribution?

Your objective is to answer these questions in a way that creates a coordinated, integrated marketing mix that meets customer wants better than your competition.

You now have analyzed the climate and competitive forces affecting your business, your market location as revealed by a judgment-based perceptual map, and the marketing mix you need to meet customer wants. These materials are the beginning of your tentative strategy. They provide a solid starting point for developing a Cycle 1 strategy that gives you competitive advantage for three to ten years. You will complete your tentative strategy by the end of this chapter.

Strategy Analysis

Step 1: Business Definition

The classic statement of the importance of business definition was Theodore Levitt's 1960 article on "marketing myopia."[4] He argued that the decline of American railroads was rooted in their limited business definition. They saw themselves in terms of traditional hardware—rails and rolling stock—when they should have defined their business in terms of customer wants—transportation. Seeing themselves as being in the transportation business would have led to expansion beyond railroads into trucks and airplanes—and continued growth instead of decline.

A strategy can be no better than the business definition it's based on. A little history of the automobile industry illustrates this. At the start of this century, automobiles were mainly toys for the rich. As transportation, they were still less reliable than horses. As novelties and status symbols, they worked just fine.

Henry Ford, however, saw a different definition of this fledgling business. He believed the horseless carriage could become basic transportation for everybody—"a universal car [to] meet the wants of the multitude"—not just a plaything of the elite five percent. He set out to build a simple, reliable, and above all affordable car for the masses. The result was the Model T, priced at less than $365 at the peak of its popularity—"one dollar, one day, one year, one Ford."

To keep costs to the absolute minimum, Ford designed a basic car with no frills, introduced assembly-line mass production, and integrated his business all the way back to rubber plantations in South America and iron ore fields in Minnesota.

His low-cost strategy and minimum-cost competitive advantage created the modern automobile industry. Between 1908, when the Model T hit the market, and 1923, when Model T sales peaked, total industry annual sales grew 5,600 percent, from 63,500 cars to 3.6 million. In the process, Ford gained more than 50 percent of the market.

But in the early 1920s, Alfred P. Sloan of General Motors developed a superior business definition, as shown in Exhibit 2.7. Ford had defined customer want as basic transportation and met that want with a low-cost strategy. GM slightly redefined the want as basic transportation *plus* style, and opted for a differentiation strategy.[5] GM still offered basic transportation, but now customers could choose from a range of colors, a line of models to fit every price segment, and a list of options for each model. In addition, GM inaugurated annual model changes.

GM strove to be "best cost," not lowest cost. For example, the flexibility required by frequent model changes caused GM to incur slightly higher costs to avoid the rigidity of vertical integration. Outside suppliers could respond better to GM's changing needs.

GM's slight revision in the definition of the automobile business made a huge difference in strategy, in competitive advantage, and ultimately in market share. Ford continued to hold to his basic

Four dimensions of business definition*	Early Cars	Model T	General Motors
Customer	The elite 5%	Everyone	Everyone
Wants	• Status/novelty • Transportation	Basic transportation	• Basic transportation • Style
Mechanism	High craftsmanship	Mass production	Mass production (but greater flexibility)
Vertical integration	None	High	Low
Strategy	• High price • Low volume	• No options • Low cost	• Line of models • Differentiation
SCA	None	Minimum cost	• "Best cost" • Flexibility

*The four dimensions of business definition lay the foundation for your strategy to gain sustainable competitive advantage (SCA).

Exhibit 2.7   Business definition for the early car industry.

definition and strategy until 1927, but by then the momentum was all GM's. Ford's high-water market share of 55 percent in 1921 declined during the next decade to 21 percent in 1933. There it remained.

The lesson here is that no business definition is forever, no strategy is forever.

As you can see from Exhibit 2.7, business definition should take into account four dimensions:[6]

1. The customer (Ford and GM = everyone).

2. The customer's wants (Ford = basic transportation; GM = transportation plus style).

3. Mechanism (Ford and GM = assembly-line mass production of cars).

4. Vertical integration (Ford = yes; GM = no).

When you analyze and incorporate these dimensions into a proper business definition, they provide a foundation for your strategy to gain sustainable competitive advantage. This is discussed further in Chapter 3. For now, you should write out your business definition using these four dimensions. Smaller businesses often completely omit the vertical integration dimension.

Step 2: Strategic Objective or Role

In an ultimate sense, there is only one objective for a business—maximizing shareholder value—but that statement doesn't provide much guidance or motivation. So you need to derive other, more actionable objectives. In Cycle 1 you determine your *single most appropriate long-term objective or role* for the next three to ten years, the one which best reflects your situation and balances your sales targets, return on investment (ROI), and free cash flow. Then each year, in Cycle 2, you set quantitative *annual goals* for sales, ROI, and cash flow.

One way of defining business roles, popular in the 1970s, sorted businesses into "cash cows," "stars," "question marks," and "dogs," depending on relative market share and rate of industry growth.[7] Exhibit 2.8 summarizes the roles of businesses described by this system, which was developed by the Boston Consulting Group (BCG).

		Market Share (Business Position)	
		High	**Low**
Industry Growth (Industry Attractiveness)	**High**	*Stars* Increase share (maintain good margins)	*Question Marks* Double share or divest
	Low	*Cash Cows* Supply cash to other subs (maintain share)	*Dogs* Supply cash, harvest, or divest (depends on strength)

Exhibit 2.8   Roles of businesses according to BCG's Growth/Share matrix.

Although now largely out of favor, matrices similar to this have some value for businesses whose ROI and market share are in "equilibrium." For ROI, equilibrium simply means that your ROI is about what it should be, based on industry attractiveness and your business position. For market share, equilibrium means that your share is not expected to change dramatically over the next five or ten years, given the continuation of current industry trends and market conditions. In BCG terms, "cash cows" and some "dogs" (those that should maintain market share and generate good ROI) are in equilibrium. "Question marks," most "dogs," and many "stars" are in a state of "disequilibrium."

Many companies' ROIs are not in equilibrium—that is, their ROIs differ significantly from those predicted by such variables as capital intensity, market share, and quality. For example, health care reform will cause the projected ROIs of many hospitals for the mid-1990s to fall far below their cost of capital. Survival requires that they restructure and take on the role of improving their ROIs to a reasonable equilibrium level.

Similarly, some companies' market shares are not in equilibrium. Home Depot's current market share, for example, is far lower than it will be in ten years if all of its competitors maintain their current strategies. Wall Street believes this strategy will allow Home Depot to increase sales 300 percent by the year 2000, a confidence reflected in Home Depot's price-to-earnings ratio of 40 in May 1994.

Home Depot then should have a role of only maintaining its current "good" ROI while aggressively increasing sales and thereby consolidating the industry.

Exhibit 2.9 shows what your role should be in various situations where your ROI and/or your market share is in disequilibrium. If your business is now in a state of disequilibrium, one of these roles may be appropriate for you.

Step 3: Generic Strategy

After you have settled on a role and strategic objectives for your company, the next step is to determine *how* you will achieve this objective. That requires developing a generic strategy.

Disequilibrium Situation	Appropriate Role
Expected ROI* below cost of capital	*Restructure:* Divest and downsize to become financially viable.
ROI significantly below expected ROI (but above cost of capital)	*Reduce costs:* Divest low-potential businesses and "reengineer" both production and overhead.
Market share significantly below equilibrium**	*Increase share:* Exploit your strategic advantage by, for example, holding prices below the level that maximizes short-term profits in order to consolidate the industry.

* Expected ROI, given your industry attractiveness and business position, can be approximated using the PIMS data base (see Chapter 4).

** Your current market share is significantly below where it will be in a few years if you and others maintain current strategies (e.g., Wal-Mart in 1970s and Home Depot today).

Exhibit 2.9   Roles for businesses in disequilibrium.

"Generic strategy," as conceived by Michael Porter,[8] is a broad strategic approach to creating a defendable position in an industry, that is, a strategic competitive advantage. Porter identified four generic strategies, shown in Exhibit 2.10.

These generic strategies derive from two variables: the source of strategic advantage (low cost or uniqueness of product features) and the strategic target (the broad market or a specific product or customer niche). These variables produce four generic strategies:

1. *Low-cost strategy.*   This strategy targets the broad market and uses price as the key marketing variable. It is usually appropriate for commodities, like oil, grain, or personal computers, where the similarity of products makes it difficult to differentiate them. This is also the strategy used by Wal-Mart and other discount department stores.

2. *Differentiation strategy.*   This strategy also targets the broad market but emphasizes nonprice differences among products, such as image, quality, and reliability. Branded products like beer, soda, and clothes often rely on heavy advertising to create the perception of uniqueness.

		Source of Strategic Advantage	
		Low-Cost	**Differentiation**
Strategic Target	**Broad (Industry-wide)**	*Low-Cost* Selling a comparable product or service at a lower price	*Differentiation* Appeal to customers based on nonprice variables (e.g., image, quality, attributes, service)
	Focus (Segment only)	*Cost-Focus* Focusing on price *and* wants of a particular segment	*Differentiation-Focus* Uniqueness makes your product or service significantly better than competitor's

Exhibit 2.10   Porter's generic strategies.

3. *Differentiation-focus strategy.*   This is similar to differentiation except that the target market is a niche. This is the strategy of mall stores like The Limited and of luxury goods like Rolex watches and Mercedes-Benz automobiles.

4. *Cost-focus strategy.*   This is the strategy of niche marketers who sell on price: "new rules" marketers like Southwest Airlines, which has eliminated frills like meal service; specialized large-volume discounters like Home Depot, whose massive purchasing allows lowest costs; and small fringe operators in a differentiated market whose only advantage is low price.

Some businesses create a sustainable competitive advantage through specialized marketing and sales approaches that don't quite fit into Porter's classifications. These strategic approaches, or generic strategies, can apply to either the broad market or to a niche. They are as follows:

5. *Sales strategy.*   This is appropriate when the key to success is quantity and quality of sales calls. This is the approach often required for products that one "ought" to have but doesn't necessarily "want"—life insurance, for example.

6. *Guerrilla strategy.* This is an opportunistic approach in which the marketer quickly takes advantage of temporary conditions: shifts in supply, like stores that depend on manufacturers' close-outs; or shifts in demand, like candies or cereals named after an animated character in the latest Disney cartoon or movie.

A company must avoid being "caught in the middle." Throughout the 1980s, Sears was neither low cost nor, except for hardware, high quality. The lack of a clear strategy confused Sears' employees and customers and was a major cause of its decline. Contrast Sears with Wal-Mart. It is widely known that Wal-Mart has everyday low prices. Because this strategy is so clear and widely understood, Wal-Mart spends only 0.5 percent of sales on advertising, compared with 2.5 percent for other discount department stores.

Your generic strategy, further discussed in Chapter 5, will be determined by answers to four questions:

1. What is, or should be, the source of your strategic advantage— low cost or differentiation?

2. Should your strategic target be the broad market or a niche?

3. Is the key to success the number and quality of sales calls?

4. Is the key to success responding quickly to changing supply or demand curves?

Your generic strategy provides you with a defendable position in your industry. Now you should review your strategy to ensure that it will allow you to beat competitors in meeting customer wants.

Step 4: Customer-Driven Strategies

Successful customer-driven strategies rely on two processes—segmentation and positioning. These are designed to identify attractive groups of potential customers for your products and to help you develop products and marketing programs designed to precisely meet their wants.

Segmentation. Your first step in developing a customer-driven strategy is segmentation, dividing the total market into groups of customers who have similar wants and buying behavior. The market can be segmented in many ways, but every good segmentation approach has two key features:

1. The segments are large enough to justify a targeted marketing program.
2. Each segment consists of customers who have similar wants and who respond similarly to marketing stimuli—so you can develop a marketing program to meet the precise wants of the segment.

Obviously, the most attractive segments (1) are large, growing, and profitable and (2) do not have strong competition.

Positioning.   The next step is to develop coherent marketing strategies to meet the wants of each target segment. You need to develop products to meet the wants of each target segment and then use price and promotion to create a perception among customers in each segment that your product meets their wants better than any competitor's product.

Positioning is based on the fundamental belief that consumers will purchase the product that best meets all of their wants. Hence, you need to develop a marketing mix of the four Ps (Product, Price, Promotion/advertising, and Place/distribution) that allows your product to precisely satisfy the wants of customers in each segment.

Step 5: Competitor-Driven Strategies

Meeting customer wants is essential—but not enough. You will lose if you cannot beat competitors in meeting your customers' wants. For example, in the late 1960s, GE, RCA, and Xerox all took on market leader IBM in the mainframe computer market. They lost, not because their products were inferior to IBM's but because they were not significantly better in meeting customers' wants. Thus, your marketing strategy must take into account your competitors' strengths and vulnerabilities in the market.

Marketplace competition often resembles *warfare*. Competitors resort to offensive and defensive strategies similar to those developed by military strategists over the past 3,000 years. Several principles of warfare and a range of offensive and defensive strategies are covered in Chapter 7. For now, consider a couple of general statements:

- Only the market leader should engage in defense. (Defense does not mean passivity; all good defenses are aggressive.) All other competitors are on the offensive.

- The least successful offense is a head-on assault upon the leader. The least successful defense is that of staying in place and defending a stationary position.

If you are the leader, move into all segments on your flanks. If you are a follower, attack the leader's unguarded flanks; if none exist, look at other markets.

Not all competition should be characterized as warfare. *Strategic intent* is a form of competitor-driven strategy practiced particularly well by Japanese and other Asian businesses. It is a way of leveraging your resources over a long period to beat much stronger competitors. Competitors following strategic intent are as likely to build strength through cooperative ventures as through warfare, at least while they are so small that warfare would mean certain defeat. For example, many Japanese consumer electronics companies initially became low-cost manufacturers for dominant American companies. This way they developed key competencies, improved quality, and built critical manufacturing mass. Only then did they challenge the Americans for the leadership positions.

In a mature industry, peace is usually more profitable than war, not only for the market leader but also for smaller followers. In this situation, the leader can use a strategy of encouraging peace through carefully measured responses to competitors' pricing moves. Peace is especially important to consumer product companies that run the risk of becoming locked into price-promotion wars.

In Chapter 7, you'll consider specific competitor-driven strategies. For now, think about the following:

- Are you the market leader? If so, you should develop a strategy for defensive warfare.

- Are you a significant enough follower that you should engage in offensive warfare?

- Are you very small and have ambitions out of proportion to your size and strength? You should think about strategic intent.

- Are you the leader in a mature, consolidated industry? It may be in your interest to shun war and encourage peace.

Mission Statement

The next step after strategy analysis is development of an inspiring mission statement, which is the public expression of your organization's role and strategy for the next three to ten years. The mission statement is both the end and the beginning – the culmination of the Cycle 1 process and the first step toward implementation of your long-term strategy. It has a single purpose – to keep everyone in your organization, from top to bottom, motivated and focused on achieving the common vision.

The mission statement process involves the following, as illustrated in Exhibit 2.11:

- Analysis of your company's culture.

- "Idealized design."

- The one-page mission statement.

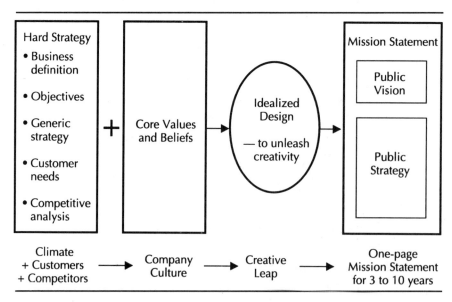

Exhibit 2.11 Developing the mission statement.

Analysis of Corporate Culture

Your *corporate culture*, its "soft" soul, must be factored in with the "hard" strategy elements you've derived from an analysis of the first three of the four Cs—Climate, Customers, Competitors, and Company. You should make a list of your organization's 10 to 15 most important core values and beliefs—not what they *ought* to be but what they actually *are*—what you hold in your gut.

Many companies have developed a brief statement—such as a company motto—that expresses these core values, usually in the form of an enduring purpose. For example, there is Merck's "We are in the business of preserving and improving human life," and Disney's goal "to make people happy." You'll see other examples in Chapter 8.

Your core values will heavily influence the way you express your mission and strategy. Your organization is not likely to adopt and implement a strategy in conflict with its corporate culture.

Idealized Design

The next step is Russell Ackoff's concept of *idealized design*. This process allows you to make the creative leap from all the analytical statements of definition, objectives, strategy, and corporate culture to the final statement of a mission that excites, motivates, and directs everyone in the organization.

Idealized design (or more appropriately, redesign) leads to the ". . . conception of the system that its designers would like to have right now, not at some future date. Therefore, the environment in which the system would have to operate need not be forecast; it is the current environment. . . . There are three properties required of an idealized design of a system: it should be (1) technologically feasible, (2) operationally viable, and (3) capable of rapid learning and adaptation."[9]

Idealized design often leads to breakthroughs because it (1) explicitly focuses on meeting wants in the current environment and (2) rejects self-imposed constraints that too often limit creativity.

The Mission Statement

At this point, you are ready to draft the *mission statement*. Since it must guide and inspire your organization, its presentation—format and style—are critical. To be usable, its length should be one page or less. You don't have a coherent strategy, anyway, until you can summarize it in one page.

In a simple phrase, you should state a "public vision"—a challenging but attainable goal that can be realized in the next three to ten years. A classic example is President Kennedy's 1962 challenge to NASA to "put a man on the moon by 1970." The rest of the page will be the "public strategy"—a distillation of the business definition, objectives, and strategy, all expressed in terms compatible with your corporate culture.

In the Four-Cycle Planning Process, you will have completed Cycle 1 with the mission statement. For now, you should have the elements of a tentative strategy. This well-expressed tentative strategy is essential preparation for your formal Cycle 1 strategy process. Chapters 3 through 8 guide you step by step through development of your Cycle 1 strategy.

ANNUAL PLANNING: CYCLES 2, 3, AND 4

Chapter 9 covers annual planning—Cycles 2, 3, and 4 of the Four-Cycle Process. There are two purposes of annual planning. First, the annual review keeps the long-term strategy fresh and action oriented. Second, the annual planning process ensures that the long-term strategy is implemented (i.e., turned into near-term goals, operational strategies, and action plans that get results).

Annual planning is highly quantitative. Cycle 1 uses many of the qualitative "strategic thinking" techniques developed since 1980 to set direction. By contrast, three-cycle annual planning uses quantitative predict-and-prepare techniques to set concrete, measurable goals.

Cycle 2: Top-Down Strategy

While developing a new strategy, Cycle 1 obviously replaces the annual strategy review. But during each of the next three to ten years, you and your top management should review and revise the long-term strategy to maintain its validity and vitality. This is Cycle 2 of the Four-Cycle Process.

In a large company with several businesses or product lines, Cycle 2 may take 10 to 15 days of management's time spread over six months. A small or single-product company might be able to do Cycle 2 in two or three days spread over a month or two.

Cycle 2 has three parts:

1. Review the broad business environment and specific changes in customers and competitors to identify threats and opportunities.

2. Revise goals to reflect the changed environment and to counter threats and exploit opportunities.

3. Review and revise strategies for achieving these goals.

Cycle 3: Bottom-Up Action Plans

Armed with approved goals and strategies, business unit heads initiate the process of developing action plans. They communicate the top-down strategies to their organizations. Managers then meet with their units to put together functional goals, action plans for achieving the goals, and rough budgets—all consistent with the overall strategy.

Effective action planning requires input from everyone from the bottom up. This is important to create full understanding of the strategies and of every individual's role and responsibility for implementation, to gain full commitment from all employees, and to create accountability. Once the action plans and the cost estimates are reviewed and approved by business unit management and then by corporate management, you are ready for Cycle 4.

Cycle 4: Budgeting

With approved action plans, developing realistic budgets is relatively easy. This process can be done mostly on paper, with every manager completing a form with a budget for his or her area of responsibility. Occasional one-on-one meetings may be needed to clarify or revise specific items. Departmental directors will consolidate and pass budget requests on up the line. Probably the only formal meeting needed in the budgeting process is one by upper management to reconcile gaps.

GETTING RESULTS:
IMPLEMENTATION AND EXECUTION

This is a book about developing business strategy, but strategy is useless without implementation and results. The book ends, in Chapter 10, with observations on the importance of two powerful drivers of strategy: (1) programs for continuous improvement of customer satisfaction, and (2) management's visible day-by-day commitment to and implementation of the strategy.

Whether your continuous improvement program is called Total Quality Management, Quick Response, Just In Time, Customer Satisfaction, or something else, it ultimately focuses on the customer. The best of these programs reduce functional barriers, empower employees at all levels, enhance teamwork, and reduce costs—as well as help you meet customer wants better than your competitors.

The other driver of strategy is the day-by-day expression of management's commitment. It's the job of the CEO and senior managers to keep the strategy, expressed in the mission statement, alive by constantly referring to it in speeches and publications. Senior management should routinely make it the foundation for their business decisions. Failure to "work your plan" creates cynicism. Everyone starts to ignore it and the organization becomes reactive.

CONCLUSION

The goal-oriented Four-Cycle Strategy Planning Process makes sense for senior management. It gives the CEO control and helps him or her to lead and manage the business. It allows the CEO and senior management to anticipate and respond to external change, on the one hand, and to implement and control internal change, on the other.

Cycle 1 produces a superior strategy since it focuses on customers and competitors and reflects industry and company realities. Three-cycle annual planning keeps the long-term strategy fresh and action oriented and leads to superior implementation. Above all, it gets results.

The key to business success is the development of superior strategies—strategies that beat competitors in meeting customer wants.

3

KNOW THYSELF
The Business Definition

If the beginning of wisdom is the dictum, "Know thyself," then the beginning of strategy is the question, "What business am I in?" You've already seen how General Motors' slight change in the definition of the automobile business in the early 1920s produced a winning strategy. Ford offered basic transportation in one model for everyone. GM offered basic transportation plus style and a separate model for every price segment. GM's market share climbed from 20 percent in 1923 to 41 percent a decade later, while Ford's declined from 46 percent to 21 percent. That's the power of business definition.

Developing a good business definition provides a solid foundation for your Cycle 1 strategy. It is a creative decision which can significantly affect success. This chapter covers four topics that will help you develop a winning definition for your business:

1. The nature and importance of business definition.
2. The four dimensions of business definition.
3. Key considerations in defining the business.
4. Adapting the definition to new circumstances.

Examples of effective business definitions are discussed throughout this chapter. Some of the examples show how the right business definition led to developing a strategy that provided sustainable competitive advantage (SCA). Some are examples of ineffective business definitions. These examples support the observation that "Business strategy pivots on defining the business in a way that leads to competitive superiority in the customer's eyes."[1]

NATURE AND IMPORTANCE
OF BUSINESS DEFINITION

In his influential essay on marketing myopia, Theodore Levitt made the case, summarized in Exhibit 3.1, for the importance of a proper business definition.[2] If America's railroad executives had not had such a short-sighted product orientation, they might have seen that their customers needed transportation, not railroads. The rail companies then could have become the main-line winners in the transportation revolution of the 20th century instead of side-tracked losers.

Levitt also found poor vision in Hollywood. When faced with the new technology of television, the moguls who owned and ran the great movie companies reacted with the same competitive contempt so often exhibited by other Goliaths just before they are brought down by the Davids of the business world. Defining their business strictly as *movies*, they scorned TV and treated it as a threat, which in fact it was, given their definition. However, if they had defined their business as *entertainment*, they could have seen TV as an opportunity. Today, after the failure and restructuring of the old movie industry, the infusion of new blood from the now-larger TV industry, and the belated redefinition of the business as entertainment, movies and television have formed a profitable relationship.

Definition Basis	Railroads	Hollywood
Product	Railroads	Movies (excludes TV)
Customer wants	Passenger and freight transportation	Entertainment

Exhibit 3.1   Business definitions based on "product" vs. "wants."

Both the railroad and movie executives were fixated on product and production, when their business success required a focus on the market. According to Levitt, the key consideration in a proper business definition is *customer need*, not just the product used at any one time to satisfy that need.

FOUR DIMENSIONS OF
BUSINESS DEFINITION

Levitt's 1960 essay and the growing interest in strategy during the 1970s and 1980s opened the eyes of many to the importance of business definition. Few today would challenge Levitt's assessment of the business community's too-frequent instances of myopia, then and even now. There's also agreement that customer wants are at the core of a successful business definition.

Today, the concept of business definition usually includes four dimensions:

1. *Customer. Who* are you serving?

2. *Wants. What wants* of the customer are you meeting?

3. *Mechanism. How* do you satisfy those wants?

4. *Vertical integration.* To what extent do you integrate forward or backward to meet customer wants?

Together, dimensions 1 and 2 form the "served market," the demand side of the business definition. Dimensions 2 and 3 combined form the "product description," or the supply side of the business definition. Dimension 4, vertical integration, is qualitatively different from the other three, but in many situations it can be a critical consideration in meeting customer wants.

Not all of these dimensions will necessarily have the same weights in your business definition. For instance, most small businesses will have little reason to consider vertical integration. A high-tech business in an emerging market may focus on the "product description" (wants and mechanism), while a consumer products company should probably emphasize the "served market" (customer and wants). But in both instances, the second dimension, wants, is central to the definition.

The four dimensions are clearly interdependent, and changing one dimension often requires changing another. Ford's successful redefinition of the automobile business with his Model T was driven primarily by a change in the customer dimension—"the multitude"—but that change also entailed changes in the customer want—basic transportation—and in the mechanism—mass production.

Customer

Ford's redefinition of the automobile business dramatically expanded the market. Almost as dramatic was Honda's redefinition of the American motorcycle business in the 1960s, a case perhaps even more relevant to most businesses because it was a "mature" industry. By changing the definition of one dimension, the customer, Honda sparked a 2,000 percent growth of the American motorcycle market during the next decade.

Up to the 1950s, the American firm Harley Davidson had dominated the U.S. motorcycle market, with smaller shares held by Great Britain's Norton and Triumph and Germany's BMW. Harley Davidson's business definition is shown in Exhibit 3.2.

After the Great Depression and World War II, big, powerful motorcycles had come to be popular with two groups of customers. The primary customers were bands of roving, black-leather-jacketed hoodlums—at least, that was the way most "respectable" Americans viewed the motorcycle market. Motorcycle gangs like the Hell's

	Harley Davidson	Honda
Customer	Cops and "robbers"	Middle-class youth
Wants	"Macho" image, transportation	Inexpensive basic transportation
Mechanism	Big motorcycles (750 cc engine)	Small motorcycles (50 and 90 cc engines)
Vertical integration	Low	High

Exhibit 3.2   Business definitions of Harley Davidson and Honda.

Angels and movies like *The Wild One* did a great job of reinforcing that image. The other customers for the big machines were the gangs' arch-enemies, the police.

Honda, however, targeted a different and much larger customer segment, the post–World War II generation, the "Baby Boomers," now reaching the 18- to 24-year age range. The wants of these young middle-class Americans were for cheap, uncomplicated, and fun transportation. So, Honda introduced small, inexpensive but high-quality motorcycles. Their wants also included respectability. So, Honda advertised to them with the slogan, "You meet the nicest people on a Honda." The extraordinary fuel efficiency of the Honda bikes also appealed to the growing environmental consciousness of Americans; right in the front ranks of this movement marched these young, college-enrolled Baby Boomers.

Honda's success paved the way for other Japanese motorcycle makers. Harley Davidson's market share began a steep decline from about 70 percent in 1959, when Honda came to America, to less than 6 percent in 1977.[3] By then, Japanese makers had captured 90 percent of the market, with Honda controlling half of that amount. The *number* of bikes sold by Harley had not declined, only the *share*. Thus, a change in the customer dimension of business definition greatly expanded the motorcycle market and revitalized a stagnant "mature" industry.

Wants

Wants, of course, are inseparable from the customer dimension. Redefining the customer leads to redefining wants. Honda's new customers certainly wanted motorbikes that were very different from those big, burly Harley "Hogs" which the Hell's Angels wanted.

However, a redefinition of wants doesn't always mean a change in the customer dimension, since the wants of the same customers can and often do change over time. That's what happened to food retailing in the United States during the 1930s, as shown in Exhibit 3.3.

The typical food shopper traditionally had to make daily trips to several neighborhood shops—the grocer, the butcher, the baker, the

	Corner Grocer	**Supermarket**
Customer	Everyone	Everyone
Wants	• Groceries (excluding meat) • Credit, delivery	• Groceries, meat, produce, dairy • Low prices
Mechanism	Full-service, labor-intensive, limited variety	Variety, self-service, "cash & carry," larger stores
Strategy	Low volume, high prices	High volume, low prices
Sustainable competitive advantage	Within walking distance (lost importance with advent of cars)	• Economies of scale • High value, low prices
Comments	Doomed by advent of cars and refrigerators	Price sensitivity from the Depression caused timing

Exhibit 3.3   Business definitions of corner grocers and supermarkets in 1930s.

dairy, etc. — to make small-volume purchases. But by the 1930s, several social and economic forces were at work to change this pattern:

- The economic depression made consumers much more price sensitive.

- The growing number of automobiles made shoppers less dependent on walking-distance stores, and it also permitted large purchases that could be hauled home by car instead of carried home by hand.

- Similarly, the growing number of home refrigerators made frequent small-volume buying trips unnecessary, since fresh goods could now be bought in quantity and stored safely for several days or even weeks.

These changes led to the demise of the high-cost and limited-variety corner grocer. A new definition of the food store took hold: a self-service, low-price, departmentalized, one-stop food store for less frequent but larger purchases — the supermarket.

Mechanism

The third dimension of business definition is the mechanism used to meet customer wants. For those new supermarkets of the 1930s, it was a cluster of things: much larger stores, an increase in the number and types of products carried, and the introduction of self-service. Often, the mechanism is the product or technology. In Levitt's example, Penn Central defined its business by its existing technology—"We are a railroad"—and failed to respond to new technologies, the truck and airplane. This is shown in Exhibit 3.4.

Exhibit 3.4 also shows that it's never too late to redefine a business. Union Pacific's current definition of the business includes all major forms of transportation, some acquired through strategic alliances, and all of it pulled together through a computerized network to provide customers with a seamless movement of goods across shipping modes and geographic boundaries. At last, the railroads are in the transportation business.

The dimension of mechanism is frequently central to the business definitions of new industries, especially high-tech ones like computers or biotechnology. The customers and their wants both depend largely on what is technologically feasible and available at any time. This is shown by the evolution of the computer industry, Exhibit 3.5.

Initially, IBM's mainframe computers defined the computer industry. At a cost of millions of dollars each, mainframes obviously did not appeal to small users and individual consumers. Mainframe customers were large organizations and their staffs of specialists in information systems.

But as technology evolved, Digital Equipment saw an opportunity to sell smaller minicomputers to a new customer segment—technically trained scientists and engineers. The next advances in computer technology put desk-top computers within the reach and capabilities of nontechnical people, first in offices and then in homes. Apple Computer took advantage of this to pioneer the market for personal computers (PCs).

Vertical Integration

The fourth dimension, vertical integration, differs qualitatively from the other three and contributes less frequently to business defini-

	Old Definition	Levitt's Definition	Union Pacific Currently
Customer			High-volume, bulky products shipped over 300 miles
Wants		Transportation	Transportation
Mechanism	Railroads		Railroads and trucks
Vertical integration	None	None	Strategic alliances with other railroads, ships, truckers
Strategy	Focus (shifting to low cost as they lost their near monopoly)	Differentiation (offering mode that makes most sense)	Low cost (but with good-quality service)
Sustainable competitive advantage	Near monopoly on long-distance transport before interstate highways	Would have allowed railroad companies to maintain growth by expanding into trucking and airlines	Provides customers with seamless movement of product across shipping modes and geographical boundaries
Comments	Disastrous failure to change business definition in response to changing climate	Focusing on needs is not always superior: High-tech companies focus on mechanism to stay on leading edge	Considering all four dimensions in their business definition leads to a pragmatic strategy for Union Pacific

Exhibit 3.4   Business definitions of railroads.

	IBM: Mainframes	Digital Equipment: Minicomputers	Apple: Personal Computers
Customer	Computer professionals	Technically trained scientists and engineers	Nontechnical
Wants	Develop "big systems" that take months or years. Long learning curve and not "friendly" to nonprofessionals.	• Individual projects that take weeks • Need technical background to learn programming	• Individual projects often completed in less than a day • Easy learning curve for application software
Mechanism	Batch processing; slow turnaround	Interactive; instant turnaround	Interactive; instant turnaround
Strategy	Differentiation (broad computer market through mid-1980s)	Focus (on wants of technical professionals)	Differentiation, but evolving into low cost
Sustainable competitive advantage	Lack of under-standing by senior managers and risk aversion led to major entry barriers.	"Hands on" and interactive features made minis superior to mainframes.	"User friendly" nature led to huge market and use by managers and secretaries.
Comments	The winning formula since the introduction of "open systems" has been high performance, low cost, and ease of use. IBM's efforts to differentiate and maintain high margins in PCs were disastrous.		

Exhibit 3.5 Business definitions of computer manufacturers.

tion, especially for smaller businesses. However, it can be an important dimension that helps drive strategy.

Depending on your circumstances, vertical integration can be good or bad. Among potential benefits are the following:

- Backward integration generally can be important if you are following a low-cost strategy, such as Ford with his Model T. If your suppliers charge excessive prices, backward integration can encourage them to come into line.

- Forward integration can improve your understanding of final consumers, but there's a risk here. You may alienate your wholesalers or retailers, because forward integration would put you in competition with some of them.

- If you are using independent distributors, who are likely to have higher markups than you would charge, forward integration can lower consumer prices and increase volume.

- Vertical integration can reduce response time and cost when transaction costs are high. For example, Coke and Pepsi both acquired about half their independent bottlers during the 1980s. First, they modernized and consolidated inefficient operations and increased volumes. Second, they used the greater purchasing power to get lower prices on cans.

However, not being vertically integrated can also provide benefits:

- Less vertical integration means lower capital intensity, which is closely associated with a higher return on investment.

- A low level of integration allows greater flexibility, since changing outside suppliers is easier than redirecting and retooling internal business units. Frequent model changes make flexibility important, and that is the reason GM avoided vertical integration in the 1920s.

- External suppliers will usually be better at innovation, since they deal with customers of varying wants and usually have greater depth of expertise in their industry.

- Suppliers can often provide goods at a lower cost than you can internally, since they usually have greater economies of scale than you in their area of expertise.

- Forward integration usually results in serious conflict with distributors or retailers. Hence, this search for higher margins and incremental volume can undercut current sales.

One way of having the best of both worlds is to follow Union Pacific's example. Through strategic alliances with other carriers, Union Pacific in effect integrated forward to carry out its strategy of providing seamless transportation of its customers' goods. They got the benefits without the drawbacks of vertical integration.

KEY CONSIDERATIONS IN DEFINING THE BUSINESS

These four dimensions—customer, wants, mechanism, and vertical integration—largely determine which served market you target, either the broad market or a specific niche, and which strategy makes most sense in that market. The following concepts help ensure that your business definition is right for your market:

- *Strategic business units.* If your organization is large and complex, divide it into coherent and manageable units and develop a business definition for each unit.

- *Key success factors.* Ensure that your definition is consistent with the essentials of your industry for high market share and profits.

- *Competitive and climate forces.* Determine the forces that have the greatest impact on your business and account for them in your definition.

Strategic Business Units

If you have a small or single-product company, you can probably manage it as a whole. Large organizations with multiple product lines, however, cannot be intelligently managed as a single unit. Nor are they likely to be adequately entrepreneurial and customer-driven. It's important, then, to subdivide the company into manageable smaller units commonly called strategic business units, or SBUs. GE, for example, has 350 product lines, which it has organized into 13 SBUs.

Typically, each SBU is managed independently with

- Its own resources, costs, and profits.
- Its distinct and identifiable customers, competitors, and products.
- Its own financial goals and business objectives.

Note that SBUs should be defined by *external* criteria. SBUs may share production facilities and staff services such as legal and human resources, but each SBU will have its own business definition and long-term strategy. However, the collection of SBUs must form a coherent whole to allow effective strategic corporate management. Don't repeat the failed strategy of conglomeration that was the vogue of the 1960s. Even with a diversity of products and business units, the corporation itself needs an identity, which requires a corporate business definition and long-term strategy.

Conglomerates tend to reduce the value of their SBUs in two ways. First, their overhead costs drain cash. Second, the extra layer of management increases bureaucracy and slows response time. A corporation should be structured so that the benefits of synergies among SBUs and corporate management expertise exceed the costs of corporate overhead.

Key Success Factors

It is important to identify your industry's key success factors, or KSFs. Every industry has its own unique set of KSFs; yet there are some variables common to the success of all businesses. You must consider both sets in your business definition.

Factors Common to All Businesses

A major research project begun in the 1970s has established correlations among hundreds of business variables and the relative weight of each in predicting the ROI of any business. Called PIMS (Profit

Impact of Market Strategy), this ongoing program uses a massive data base compiled from the actual business experience of around 3,000 SBUs operated by 450 American and European companies.[4] Chapter 4 covers the PIMS project in greater detail.

The PIMS project has collected empirical data on the following:

- Business position of SBUs, such as market share, relative quality, and degree of vertical integration.
- Industry attractiveness, such as rates of market growth, inflation, and distribution channels.
- Performance measures of each SBU, such as return on investment and market share.

Analysis of the PIMS data has revealed that the most important factors for the success of any business are high quality, high market share, and low capital intensity. While there are many other critical correlations that have come from the PIMS analyses, these three should weigh heavily in developing your business definition.

Factors Unique to Your Business

In addition to the broad success factors identified by PIMS that apply to all businesses, every industry has its own unique set of success factors. These will influence one or more of the four dimensions in your business definition, so you should take the two or three most critical of these into account.

For example, the KSFs for computer software are *efficient distribution channels* and *after-sales support*. The implications for business definition are that the mechanism dimension (software and its distribution) is critical, that the customer dimension should include both your retailers and the end-users, and that the wants dimension includes not only great product but also continuous improvement and personal service. The KSFs for management consultants are communicating with executive decision makers (customer dimension) and fully meeting the client's expectations (wants dimension).[5]

If you own a convenience store, your KSFs are location, product selection, pricing, and operating efficiency. For brewers, they are quality, distribution, and marketing. For apparel manufacturing, fashion design and manufacturing efficiency are key.[6] The list goes on and on, with KSFs varying from industry to industry. No single listing of industry-specific KSFs similar to the PIMS list exists for all businesses. You will need to do a thorough analysis of your industry to uncover those critical to your success.

Competitive and Climate Forces

Much of that industry analysis will emerge from a look at the competitive and climate forces affecting your business. A study of external forces should reveal much about where your industry is going and about what you must do in order to create a sustainable competitive advantage.

Michael Porter has developed a useful schema for conducting this analysis.[7] Exhibit 3.6 is based on Porter's five competitive forces and the interactions among them.

A careful consideration of the five competitive forces and the five climate forces will reveal both current and longer-term opportunities and threats and suggest how you should respond to them. This analysis is essential not just in each Cycle 1 process but also in each annual Cycle 2 review and revision of your long-term strategy.

The importance of these forces for your business definition and strategy is clear in the case of today's supermarket industry. Exhibit 3.7 lists some climate forces affecting supermarkets. This list certainly is not intended to be exhaustive, just illustrative.

Two of the demographic forces—two-earner households and single-person households—have reduced the amount of food that is prepared at home. Thus, there's a greater demand for take-home prepared foods. The baby bust means that the young, low-wage labor pool that supermarkets depend on is shrinking, and this has put pressure on supermarkets to pay higher starting wages.

Probably the greatest governmental forces supermarkets face are employment-related laws and regulations. Supermarkets have avoided the unemployment taxes and fringe benefits they would have to provide for full-time employees by hiring mostly part-time employees.

During all recessions, there is a tendency of shoppers to "trade down." Supermarkets have responded to the early 1990s recession with a greater range of their own lower-price store brands, a move

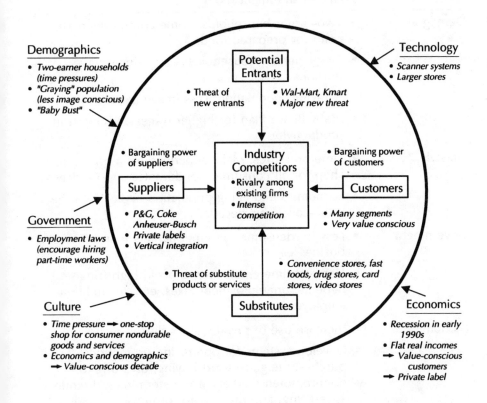

Exhibit 3.6 Porter's five competitive forces embedded in the five climate forces (with supermarket forces in italics).

that is likely to endure because they've learned to use store brands as leverage against their suppliers. Customers are also more price-conscious because the real income of most households did not increase from 1980 to 1993.

Recent technology has changed the way supermarkets do business. The computerized bar-code scanners now in widespread use have made checkouts faster and more accurate. This same technology is also being used to respond to competitive forces, which are shown in Exhibit 3.8.

Generally, the most successful supermarkets have responded to these competitive forces in a couple of ways. First, the scanner

Force	Examples and Implications
Demographics	• Two-earner households: "Time crunch" increases need for prepared foods. • Single-person households: Carry single-serve portions. • "Graying" population: Less image conscious. • "Baby Bust": Plan for higher wages and invest in productivity.
Lifestyle	• Time pressures: Make supermarkets a one-stop shop for all consumer nondurables and services. • Economics and aging population make 1990s the value-conscious decade.
Government	• Less burdensome for supermarkets than other businesses. • Use part-time employees to avoid high fringe benefits, unemployment taxes, etc., for full-time employees.
Economics	• Increase use of private labels during recessions. • Develop systems for optimizing promotion purchases (e.g., forward buying, diverting to nonpromoted markets, and determining discounts, advertising, and displays for promos).
Technology	• Scanner-based systems for reducing costs and managing. • Larger stores to offer all one-stop services.

Exhibit 3.7 Climate forces impacting supermarkets.

systems have become a powerful tool the supermarkets use to manage the supplier-customer axis. The data gathered by these scanners have given them unprecedented knowledge of their customers' buying patterns, which has allowed them to meet their customers' wants better.

This knowledge has also given them control over suppliers. Supermarkets now know exactly how much shelf space to give to each product, on a store-by-store basis. They have also developed sophisticated systems for advertising, price promotions, and dis-

Force	Examples and Implications
Customers	Use scanner-based systems to customize each store to meet customer wants (e.g., products to carry, shelf space allocation).
Suppliers	Scanner-based systems have led to fact-based category management and shifted power from suppliers to retailers.
Substitutes	• Convenience stores are losing sales to lower-cost supermarkets. • Fast-food restaurants: Counter with prepared foods. • Drug stores: Offer pharmacies and health and beauty aids. • Video stores, florist, card stores, photo development: Upgrade these services (e.g., photo development while shopping). • Include noncompetitive stores in your strip mall (e.g., real estate and white tablecloth restaurant instead of a card store).
Industry competitors	• Build new stores in all attractive locations. • Maintain clear positioning (e.g., everyday low prices *or* aggressive promotions; low price or differentiation). • Superior execution via continuous improvement program.
Potential entrants	• New supermarkets: Avoid need through continuous improvement. • Membership warehouse stores: Offer large sizes at low prices. A major threat that must be countered more effectively.

Exhibit 3.8 Porter's five forces impacting supermarkets.

plays. Previously, suppliers had much more influence on shelf-space allocation and promotions.

Second, they have learned to manage the threats from the potential entrant-substitute axis. By offering a broader range of products and services, they have taken over many market segments that potential entrants and substitutes might otherwise have occupied.

	Old Definition	New Definition
Customer	Everyone	Everyone
Wants	Food for preparation at home	One-stop shop for frequently purchased nondurables and services. (Mall business definition is similar, but for durables.)
Mechanism	30,000–50,000-square-foot stores. One shelf-set for all stores	75,000-square-foot stores. Scanner-based systems allow customizing shelf-set for each store (as well as sophisticated buying and promotion).
Vertical integration	Private labels to improve margins	Private labels to improve margins and leverage with suppliers.
Strategy	Differentiation (with good prices and convenience)	Differentiation (with good prices and convenience). No change.
Sustainable competitive advantage	Better cost, variety, and quality than convenience stores and corner grocers	• Prepared foods and delis help compete with fast-food operators. Compete with other retailers via video rentals, photo finishing, florist department, and cards. • Scanner-based systems for continuous improvement.
Comments on supermarkets	Changes in the external environment have forced supermarkets to significantly change their business definition in order to execute the same strategy: • They increased product variety to compete with "substitute retailers" such as fast foods, warehouse clubs, and gas station convenience stores. • Scanner-based systems allow sophistication in purchasing and meeting customer wants.	

Exhibit 3.9   Business definition of supermarkets.

In doing so, the supermarkets have themselves become a substitute for fast-food outlets, drug stores, card shops, florists, and many others. Customers on their way home from work now have little incentive to make multiple stops at, say, the Blockbuster Video store, the Walgreens pharmacy, and the Kentucky Fried Chicken outlet when they can get it all with one stop at the neighborhood supermarket.

Supermarkets have done a good job of adjusting their business definitions to account for virtually all these forces. Exhibit 3.9 shows how supermarkets have accounted for these forces in their business definition. Becoming a one-stop shop for all frequently purchased consumer nondurables and services has provided the foundation for an effective strategy and sustainable competitive advantage.

ADAPTING THE DEFINITION TO NEW CIRCUMSTANCES

A business definition that's a winner in one era is often a loser in the next. No business definition is forever. That lesson is critical for long-term success, but it's a hard one for many successful businesses to accept and apply. The key is knowing when changed circumstances require a new direction. The Four-Cycle Planning Process is designed to deal with that problem.

The importance of adapting to new conditions can be seen in the history of retailing from the 1850s to the 1970s, which is summarized in Exhibit 3.10. The industry has periodically been redefined to cope with new climate and competitive forces. A look at specific companies, however, shows that the leader in redefining the industry in one era does not always make a successful transition to a new definition in a subsequent era.

It's interesting to note that while the business definition changed, retailing followed the same basic strategy from the first department stores through the triumph of Wal-Mart—a strategy of lower prices, convenience, variety, and consistent if not high quality. Sam Walton's family has become the richest in America by wonderful execution of that 140-year-old low-cost strategy. Walton simply changed the dimensions of customer and mechanism to take discount department stores to small-town and rural Americans.

Retailing redefinitions reflected mostly changes in climate forces—new technologies, such as streetcars and railroads; demographics,

Era	Retailers	Benefits	Key
Department stores	Wanamaker's; Macy's (1852–1910)	Low, known price, convenience, variety, good quality	Concentrated markets in metro areas; trolleys
Chains	A&P (1859); Woolworth (1879)	Low, known price due to mass buying, consistency due to operating procedures	Brought good strategy to neighborhoods
Mail-order houses	Ward (1872); Sears (1876)	Brought benefits of volume and standardization to people on farms and in West	Rapid expansion in West; railroads; literacy
Rural general merchandisers	J. C. Penney (1902)	Convenience of not waiting vis-à-vis Sears	Brought low prices to rural America
Supermarkets	King Kullen (1930)	Lower prices due to self-service and operating economies of volume	Depression created appeal
Discount department stores	E. J. Korvette (1948); Kmart (1961)	Lower prices	Beat "fair trade" laws
Rural discount department stores	Wal-Mart (1962)	Brought discount department stores to rural America	Brought good strategy to rural areas

Exhibit 3.10   Industry evolution of retailing: 1850–1970.

such as the settlement of the West; or economics, such as the Great Depression of the 1930s. One constant, however, in the evolution of retailing was the customer "want" for low prices. Comparatively lower prices was a major appeal of the first department stores and chains. Ironically, the traditional department stores have today found themselves left behind by the latest "revolution" in retailing— the discount department store movement led by E. J. Korvette and Kmart and carried to new heights by Wal-Mart.

Retailing strategies have become more complex since the 1960s. In Chapter 5, you'll see how retailers have successfully implemented differentiation, focus, sales, and guerrilla strategies. However, empirical evidence indicates that the low-cost strategy continues to be extremely powerful in retailing. A study of retailer profitability using the PIMS data base showed that discounters have the edge when it comes to profitability, as shown in Exhibit 3.11.

	Average Pretax ROI	Profit Percent of Sales	Conclusions
Sales/sq. ft.:			
Below average	4.6%	4.2%	Traffic is the key to profitability. Americans love to get products they want at a bargain.
Average	12.3%	5.8%	
Above average	41.3%	9.0%	
Market share:			
<8%	8.4%	7.2%	Traffic leads to high market share, and high share leads to high ROI.
8–14%	20.1%	5.9%	
14+%	28.7%	5.8%	
Relative price:			
Discount	24.9%	6.7%	Discount retailers have significantly higher ROI due to lower capital intensity and more inventory turns per year.
Average	18.9%	6.9%	
Premium	13.4%	5.0%	

Source: Private communication from the Strategic Planning Institute using the PIMS data base.

Exhibit 3.11   Keys to retailer profitability.

Type of Retailer	Percent Return on Net Worth	Price-to-Earnings Ratio	Stock Price/ Book Value
Department stores	10.0%	13.1	1.38
Special lines	11.5%	16.4	2.12
Discount/ warehouse stores	12.5%	17.9	2.64

Source: Value Line, November 29, 1991.

Exhibit 3.12   Median financials for retailers.

The same story is told by Exhibit 3.12, giving median financials for retailers.

Discount and warehouse stores have higher returns on net worth and higher growth rates, which is why Wall Street would rather put its money there than in full-price department stores. In May 1994, the shares of Home Depot, the country's leading chain of building supply/home improvement superstores, sold at 40 times earnings. That compares to the industry median of 24.

CONCLUSION: WINNING AND LOSING DEFINITIONS

Throughout this chapter, there have been winners and losers. Most of the losers lost because they failed to adapt their business definitions to changing times. In the 1990s the dominant characteristic of most consumer markets will be "value"—quality products at a low price. Hence, the business definition of high-price stores like Neiman Marcus is poor compared to that of Wal-Mart.

You should look for the continued growth of "category killers" in several markets, the rise of discount malls, and the continued creeping encroachment of factory outlets on their current retailers' markets. Stores like Home Depot, Office Depot, and Toys 'R' Us offer discount prices and great depth of variety in their narrow product category. They are called category killers since they cause smaller retailers, with less variety and higher prices, to go out of business. Traditional department stores will have a tough time, especially those who get "caught in the middle." That's what nearly killed Sears. Sears' management has finally begun the process of redefining and repositioning the company, part of which was killing its historic catalog business. Sears is redefining itself as the low-price mall anchor and is targeting middle-income households. Time will tell whether Sears has successfully adapted to new circumstances, but at least it now has a clear business definition.

Many companies won't adapt, even previously highly successful companies, and they will falter because their business definitions are inadequate to their markets. Losing business definitions generally result from two management failings:

1. Static minds in changing times.
2. Losing sight of the customer.

Two final examples illustrate these shortcomings. First, static minds in changing times is illustrated in Exhibit 3.13, giving two definitions of the credit card business. The American Express definition reflects a past era when the customer was a small group—the wealthy five percent. The American Express cachet of elitism fed the longing of a growing number of high-income earners for exclusivity and prestige up through the 1980s.

The market is very different today, but American Express is still trying to compete with the old definition. Today's customer is everybody, prestige has become irrelevant or even a stigma, and the real want is often the financing of goods, not just charging. The American Express definition may have been right for another era. Visa and MasterCard are defined right for the 1990s.

Second, losing sight of customers and becoming internally focused is illustrated in Exhibit 3.14. Guided by founder Akio Morita, Sony once showed the world how a strong customer orientation could take a small Japanese electronics company onward to spectacular global success. But Sony today is showing signs of repeating the mistake successful enterprises often make after a time—they take the customer for granted and focus on their internal needs.

	Visa and MasterCard	American Express
Customer	Middle- and upper-class worldwide (Visa name changed from Bank-AmeriCard to allow global strength)	Affluent Americans (name prevents global strength)
Wants	Charging and financing goods and services; value; access to ATMs	Charging goods and services; prestige
Technology	Credit cards; electronic transfer	Credit cards; copies of receipts sent to AmEx and cardholder
Strategy	Differentiation (good value)	Sales strategy
Sustainable competitive advantage	Meets primary wants of customers: low annual cost, financing, universal acceptance (value)	At a disadvantage to Visa on most desired benefits. Doesn't offer financing. Prestige worked in 1980s but not in value-oriented 1990s.
Comments	• Visa also provides superior value to a second important customer, retailers, with a lower percentage fee and quicker payment. • American Express has tried to turn around its declining market share and profits with aggressive advertising and selling efforts, but marketing cannot overcome an inferior business definition.	

Exhibit 3.13 Business definition of the credit card business.

Sony's current business definition and strategy seem to be driven more by Sony pride than by customer wants. Sony was a pioneer in the videotape industry with its BetaMax technology. However, customers rejected BetaMax in favor of Matsushita's VHS system. Today, virtually all videotapes are in the VHS mode.

Using incomprehensible marketplace logic, Sony seems to have convinced itself that BetaMax failed not because customers rejected it but because not enough movies were videotaped in that format.

	Old Definition	New Definition
Customer	Global mass market	Global mass market
Wants	Entertainment	Entertainment
Mechanism	Hardware	Hardware and software
Strategy	Differentiation to achieve high share, economies of scale, and high profits	Belief that BetaMax failed because not enough movies in the format. Have enough software to support hardware.
Sustainable competitive advantage	Speed to market, innovation, quality, and wide product line	Maintain position in hardware. Purchased Columbia Pictures and CBS Records to supply software for hardware.
Comments	The latest *Value Line* report says Sony has yet to make hardware and software work together. Sony should have assured adequate software through strategic alliances, not by spending nearly $7 billion on poorly related acquisitions.	

Exhibit 3.14   Business definition of Sony.

Sony's response: Change its business definition to add entertainment software to the first-rate entertainment hardware it is famous for making. That way, when it pioneers another technology in the future, it will be able to package the movies or music to fit the technology. It won't have to rely on others to supply software for its hardware.

Guided by this new definition, Sony forked out $7 billion to purchase Columbia Pictures and CBS Records. This was a strategic mistake. Sony has always been brilliant at technological creativity (hardware), but artistic creativity (software) is a fundamentally different business. That fact was recognized by Wall Street, which disliked Sony's diversification into Hollywood, and share prices began a three-year decline.

Even if Sony's new definition had been sound, Sony could more successfully have assured a supply of software through strategic alliances instead of poorly related acquisitions. But its new definition is a loser. Sony does not have a strategic competitive advantage in movies and music. Moreover, management's efforts to make a winner out of this loser will distract them from the hardware side of the business, and that too will suffer. A 1994 *Value Line* report says Sony has yet to make hardware and software work together.

Business definition often is the difference between success and failure. And even the big companies—perhaps in particular the big companies—are capable of coming up with losing definitions, as times change or as their comfortable perch atop the heap puts them too far away from the customer and too close to themselves. Business definition makes a difference. A winning one leads directly to a strategy that beats competitors in meeting customer wants.

4

DETERMINE YOUR ROLE
The Three- to Ten-Year
Strategic Objective

When Soichiro Honda's first puny little motorbike rolled off the boat onto the Pacific shore, America's motorcycle industry slumbered in a stolid state of apparently impermeable equilibrium. Norton, Triumph, and BMW held small stable shares of a market virtually monopolized by Harley Davidson. Had no one wanted Honda's laughable little machines, there'd be no story to tell here. But within five years, Honda's redefinition of the motorcycle business in America[1] had placed the market in profound disequilibrium.

Instead of responding to the threat with a new strategic objective that would have made it more competitive, Harley Davidson continued to behave as if the old equilibrium still held. Thus, Harley lost out on the most profound explosion in the motorcycle market since an internal combustion engine was first mounted on two wheels.

Business definition leads directly to the strategic objective or role of a business. It in turn leads to a goal-oriented strategy that beats competitors in meeting customer wants.

The "evergreen" strategic objective of every business is to make its owners wealthier—to maximize shareholder value. The essence of business is to take one dollar in assets and create significantly more than one dollar in value. People who can do that consistently are very well rewarded.

But what does maximizing shareholder value mean, for strategy and execution? With regard to execution, "maximizing shareholder value" doesn't motivate many people below senior management. That objective needs to be restated in more inspiring terms.[2]

As for strategy, "maximizing shareholder value" per se gives little guidance on how to reach that objective. Hence, it needs to be taken to a lower level of abstraction and translated into objectives that are *actionable*. Strategically, you can take action on either *sales* or *profitability* (ROI), or both, to increase shareholder value.

Strategic objective or role, however, is not the same as quantitative annual sales and profit goals, which are set in Cycle 2. Instead, the strategic role is the single *qualitative* objective that will guide decisions over the next three to ten years. It has a meaning more closely related to "purpose" than to "target."[3]

A strategic role might be, for instance, "profits today" as opposed to "profits tomorrow." "Profits today," which focuses on immediate profitability and cash flow, is often appropriate for businesses in weak positions or in unattractive industries. These businesses can increase shareholder value by achieving high free cash flows in the short term through such means as reducing costs, minimizing investments, and raising prices. "Profits tomorrow," which emphasizes sales growth, is appropriate for stronger businesses in highly attractive and growing industries. While short-term free cash flows are lower, the higher expected growth creates shareholder value. Also, risk is lower, since greater consumer value makes competitive challenges less likely.

As long as the role is appropriate to the business, stock price will reflect increased value. To select the appropriate role for your business, you will need to consider the characteristics of your industry and your strategic position within it.

That's what this chapter is about—how to determine the strategic role that will maximize shareholder value in your business. It covers the following:

- Factors affecting profitability.
- Determining equilibrium and disequilibrium.
- Developing a strategic objective or role.

FACTORS AFFECTING PROFITABILITY

In the late 1960s and 1970s, planners and strategists moved beyond forecasting-based predict-and-prepare planning and began to take greater notice of marketplace variables and business position in the market. This led to what became known as "formula" planning, since strategy consultants devised various formulas that told just what role each business unit should pursue. Formula planning was particularly attractive in this era of conglomerates, offering strategic guidance to CEOs with a large number of businesses to manage.

Formula Planning

The best-known and most influential proponent of formula planning was the Boston Consulting Group (BCG) with its Growth/ Share matrix, shown in Exhibit 4.1. BCG assumed that the two most important determinants of profitability were size of market share and rate of industry growth. Your position in these two dimensions located you in a two-by-two matrix, and the appropriate strategic role for your business depended on which quadrant your business landed in.

A "star" is the share leader in a fast-growing industry. It should have a high ROI, but high growth causes its free cash flow to be small or negative. A "cash cow" has leading market share in a mature industry; it should generate lots of cash. A "question mark" is, well, questionable; you have to decide whether it's a potential "star" or an inevitable "dog" as the industry matures. A "dog" is a cash trap, at least in the BCG view of the world. You should dump it since your weak position in a low-growth industry will supposedly generate a poor ROI.

The problem with the BCG matrix is that it oversimplifies reality. There's a lot more to an attractive business environment than industry growth and market share. Sensitive to this fact, General Electric worked with management consultants McKinsey & Co. to develop a more realistic three-level matrix, shown in Exhibit 4.2, that plotted businesses along more comprehensive dimensions—"industry attractiveness" and "business position."[4]

		Market Share (Business Position)	
		High	**Low**
Industry Growth (Industry Attractiveness)	**High**	*Stars* Increase share (maintain good margins)	*Question Marks* Double share or divest
	Low	*Cash Cows* Supply cash to other subs (maintain share)	*Dogs* Supply cash, harvest, or divest (depends on strength)

Exhibit 4.1 Roles of businesses according to BCG's Growth/Share matrix.

		Business Position		
		High	**Medium**	**Low**
Industry Attractiveness	**High**	Grow aggressively	Grow	Double or divest
	Medium	Grow	Maintain	Harvest
	Low	Generate cash	Harvest	Divest

Exhibit 4.2 Roles of businesses according to the GE/McKinsey Industry Attractiveness/Business Position matrix.

In this process, senior executives weighted and ranked a series of variables, such as market size, rate of growth, and market concentration, to determine "industry attractiveness." Likewise, they determined "business position" by considering such variables as their current technology, marketing expertise, market share, and manufacturing efficiency. Based on their rankings in these variables, a business unit would fall into one of nine boxes, each of which called for a specific strategic role.

PIMS—Profit Impact of Market Strategy

The question is, how do you determine which variables to include in "industry attractiveness" and "business position"? How should you weight them? Planners at GE, scholars at Harvard Business School, and others struggled with those questions, and their research ultimately led to a much better approach than BCG's arbitrary selection of industry growth and market share as the primary variables. The result was PIMS—Profit Impact of Market Strategy. This is a unique research program that provides quantitative guidance on what variables are important in determining the attractiveness of your industry and the strength of your position in the industry.[5]

PIMS is by far the most comprehensive and sophisticated empirical study ever of the correlation between ROI and those variables that relate to strategy, structure, and business position. The PIMS data base uses the experience of 3,000 business units in more than 450 companies. Drawing upon that mass of data, PIMS uses a regression model to show how 65 variables correlate with ROI and to calculate a "par" or expected ROI for any business unit.

The PIMS correlations indicate that the specifics of an industry and company are less important than certain variables common to all industries, whether industrial products, consumer durables, or consumer nondurables. For instance, a market share leader with high quality and low capital intensity will likely have a high ROI regardless of whether the industry is computers, steel, or financial services. Similarly, a company with low quality, low share, and high capital intensity will likely have a low ROI regardless of size, geographical location, or industry.

While the PIMS results establish correlations and do not prove causation, the fundamental PIMS findings demonstrate that *business position* variables (e.g., market share, relative quality) and *industry attractiveness* variables explain two-thirds of the variation in ROI. Your business definition should make sure these variables are as beneficial as possible. Still, the large residual variance of ROI indicates the importance of strategy in performance: Strategy + Business Position + Industry Attractiveness = Performance.

Business Position Variables

Relative market share, relative quality, and capital intensity (whether in the form of fixed capital or working capital) are critical influences on the pretax ROI of all businesses. In fact, these are the three most important business position variables in their impact on ROI, as shown in Exhibits 4.3 and 4.4, based on the pretax ROI of the 3,000 businesses in the PIMS data base.

Exhibit 4.3 shows the combined relationship of relative quality and market share to ROI. For example, a business with a market share less than 13 percent but with very high perceived quality

		Relative Quality		
		Bottom Third	**Middle Third**	**Top Third**
Market Share	**Bottom Third** <13%	10%	16%	18%
	Middle Third 14–27%	18%	20%	26%
	Top Third 28+%	26%	29%	37%

Source: Adapted and reprinted with the permission of The Free Press, an imprint of Simon & Schuster from THE PIMS PRINCIPLES: Linking Strategy to Performance by Robert D. Buzzell and Bradley T. Gale. Copyright © 1987 by The Free Press.

Exhibit 4.3   The effect of relative quality and market share on pretax ROI.

		Working Capital/Sales		
		<20%	**20–30%**	**30+%**
Fixed Capital/ Sales	**<25%**	41%	28%	18%
	25–50%	29%	23%	13%
	50+%	18%	14%	7%

Source: Adapted and reprinted with the permission of The Free Press, an imprint of Simon & Schuster from THE PIMS PRINCIPLES: Linking Strategy to Performance by Robert D. Buzzell and Bradley T. Gale. Copyright © 1987 by The Free Press.

Exhibit 4.4   The effect of capital intensity on pretax ROI.

——————— Reducing Capital Intensity ———————

Even in capital intensive industries, individual firms have a lot of control over levels of investment. Here are some suggestions:

- Use recycled materials and avoid the investment in mining and primary production. Nucor Steel does this to position itself as a low-capital company in a high-capital industry. Nucor's 1994 market value was 136 percent above that of U.S. Steel.

- Buy bargains in plant and equipment during the "down" side of the business cycle. Jefferson Smurfit in paper making won't buy capacity at prices above 50 percent of replacement cost.

- Lease plant and equipment on favorable terms. Marriott sells its investment-intensive hotel buildings but retains the highly profitable management contracts.

- Smooth the business cycle. Increase capacity utilization rather than build capacity for peak demand. In the mid-1980s Ford ran its plants over capacity and cut back price promotions. Even if this reduced sales, it increased profits, ROI, and shareholder value.

- Anheuser-Busch went from 75 percent to 95 percent capacity utilization by building up wholesaler beer inventories in refrigerated warehouses during off-peak winter months and then selling them down in peak summer months. The result was an investment savings in capacity of over $2 billion.

- Think like Wal-Mart. Reduce working capital by reducing inventories, increasing turnover, accelerating accounts receivable, and slowing accounts payable.

relative to competitors should have an expected, or par, ROI of 18 percent. Market share and relative quality combined can account for up to a 27-point spread in ROI (top third/top third 37 percent minus bottom third/bottom third 10 percent). Clearly, market share has a strong relationship to profitability, although using it as the sole indicator of business position greatly oversimplifies reality.

Capital intensity also has a strong impact on ROI, as you can see in Exhibit 4.4. Often, capital intensity is assumed to be a fixed industry characteristic, more or less beyond the control of an individual business. Certainly mining or steelmaking demands heavy investment, but there is a lot of room for individual businesses to control their capital intensity relative to competitors. Some thoughts on this subject are presented on page 81.

Reducing your capital intensity, both fixed capital and working capital, can have a dramatic impact on your ROI. As Exhibit 4.4 shows, the difference between the average ROI of a business with high capital intensity and the average ROI of one with low capital intensity is an incredible 34 points.

Industry Attractiveness Variables

PIMS also looks at industry- and market-related variables that determine industry attractiveness. Exhibit 4.5 lists the key industry attractiveness variables in the order of their impact on ROI. This exhibit compares ROIs of those businesses in the most attractive quintile for each variable with those in the least attractive quintile.

If your products are big-ticket items (individual orders over $10,000) and they constitute a significant percentage of your customers' total purchases (more than 5 percent), then your customers will shop around for the best deal and they will negotiate hard from a position of strength. The result is that your expected ROI is going to be lower by 14.0 points (9.2 + 4.8) than it would be in an industry where purchase sizes are small and relatively less important to your customers.

The degree of unionization in your industry affects profitability. An industry that is more than 75 percent unionized is less profitable than a nonunionized industry by an average of 5.3 percentage points. Which causes which? Perhaps unions make industries less

	Percentile		Impact on Pretax ROI		
Variable	**20th**	**80th**	**20th**	**80th**	**Spread**
Purchase amount	$10K+	<$1K	−4.0%	5.2%	**9.2%**
Percent unionization	75%	0%	−2.4%	2.9%	**5.3%**
Purchase importance	5+%	<1%	−3.0%	1.8%	**4.8%**
Industry growth	−4%	+11%	−1.2%	1.1%	**2.3%**
Inflation	4%	8%	−1.0%	1.0%	**2.0%**
Other			21.4%	23.9%	**2.5%**
Expected ROI			9.8%	35.9%	**26.1%**

Source: Adapted and reprinted with the permission of The Free Press, an imprint of Simon & Schuster from THE PIMS PRINCIPLES: Linking Strategy to Performance by Robert D. Buzzell and Bradley T. Gale. Copyright © 1987 by The Free Press.

Exhibit 4.5   The effect of industry attractiveness variables on ROI.

profitable. Or perhaps they're low profit to begin with, and workers feel they have to organize to get their fair share of the meager profits. As with all PIMS correlations, causality is a matter of judgment.

Inflation is also a factor. High inflation seems to allow price increases that also increase profitability. Industry growth is the fourth most important of the industry attractiveness variables and certainly not the strongest indicator of industry attractiveness, which was the assumption in the BCG Growth/Share matrix.

Not one, not two, but all of these company and industry variables together determine the attractiveness of a market and the position of specific businesses within it. Hence, the strategic role of your business depends on where you are in relation to these variables.

EQUILIBRIUM AND DISEQUILIBRIUM

A critical question for you to resolve is whether your business is in *equilibrium* or *disequilibrium* with regard to both ROI and market share. Are its actual ROI and market share roughly equivalent to its expected, or par, positions? The answer to this question helps determine what role your business should have for the next three to ten years.

ROI Equilibrium/Disequilibrium

If actual ROI is close to par ROI, your business is in equilibrium. If actual ROI differs significantly from par, it's in disequilibrium. There are a couple of ways you can determine if your company is in ROI equilibrium or disequilibrium. One way is to pay $30,000 annually to become a subscriber to the PIMS program. Benefits of membership include a precise calculation of your par ROI and strategy advice on how to increase ROI. The other way to get an idea of your par ROI is to use your own knowledge of your company and industry, the collective wisdom of your management team, and the information in Exhibits 4.3, 4.4, and 4.5. Here are some guidelines:

Above-par ROI disequilibrium exists if either:

- Your actual ROI is at least a few points over your cost of capital (see page 86) and you're in a weak position (Exhibits 4.3 and 4.4) in an unattractive industry (Exhibit 4.5); or

- Your actual ROI is very high and your business position and industry attractiveness are just average.

Below-par ROI disequilibrium exists if either:

- Your actual ROI is less than or equal to your cost of capital and your business position and industry attractiveness are about average; or

- Your actual ROI is only a few points above your cost of capital and you are in a strong business position in an attractive industry.

Market Share Equilibrium/Disequilibrium

As shown in Exhibit 4.6, you can also be in equilibrium or disequilibrium in market share. The concept is similar, in that certain market and company characteristics make it possible to predict an expected, or par, longer-term market share.

		Actual ROI		
		< Par	= Par	> Par
Market Share	< Par	Home Depot	Anheuser-Busch in 1960–1990; McDonald's in 1960–1980; Wal-Mart since 1970	Compaq before 1992
	= Par	Ralston Purina in 1980	Equilibrium	Pharmaceuticals until 1993
	> Par	Eastman Kodak, Sears, Tenneco in 1980s	Xerox in 1980; IBM in 1986–1990; Procter & Gamble in 1980s	U.S. Steel through 1962; Ralston Purina in 1990s

Exhibit 4.6   Examples of companies with disequilibrium market share or ROI.

Market share equilibrium exists if your expected market share in five or ten years will about equal your current market share, assuming that you and your competitors maintain current policies and that current trends in the external climate continue. Equilibrium is most likely in commodity markets, other mature markets, and consolidated industries where market shares change slowly. Today's American beer market is a good example. The industry consolidated steadily from the repeal of Prohibition in 1933 up through 1990. Economies of scale and premium brands gave the national brewers major advantages. From a combined share of about 13 percent in 1960, the three largest brewers today control about 75 percent. Shares are now stabilizing as more value-conscious consumers consider less expensive brands from smaller brewers.

Market share disequilibrium exists when the external climate or market forces indicate that your current market share is far above or below what it will be in five or ten years, assuming that competitors maintain current strategies and fundamental market and climate forces remain constant.

Below-par share disequilibrium typically exists in highly fragmented markets where a "new rules" competitor starts to consoli-

———————————— **Cost of Capital** ————————————

Cost of capital is simply the weighted average cost of the two major sources of capital—debt and equity. Here's how to estimate cost of capital, using "Baby Bell" NYNEX Corporation on November 29, 1993, as an example:

Cost of Debt

Cost of debt is the after-tax *interest rate* a company would pay on new debt financing. NYNEX's long bonds yield 7.4% to maturity. Assuming a 37% total tax rate, NYNEX's *cost of debt is 4.7%.*

$$\text{Cost of Debt} = \text{Bond Yield} - \text{Taxes}$$
$$= 7.4\% - (7.4\% \times 37\%)$$
$$= 4.7\%$$

Cost of Equity

Cost of equity represents the *return* that stockholders expect. Over the last half century, the average annual return of the Standard & Poors 500 was 10.3% and the yield of 20-year government bonds was 4.5%, a difference of 5.8%. If long government bonds today yield 6.25% and NYNEX stock has a beta coefficient of 0.80 (from *Value Line*), then the *cost of equity is 10.9%.*

$$\text{Cost of Equity} = \text{Risk-free Rate} + (\text{Beta Coefficient} \times$$
$$\text{Average Risk Premium of Stocks})$$
$$= 6.25\% + (.80 \times 5.8\%)$$
$$= 10.9\%$$

Cost of Capital

Debt and equity costs should be weighted by the company's capital structure, using market prices (also from *Value Line*), not book value. NYNEX's capital is 33% debt ($8.7 billion) and 67% equity ($17.7 billion: 413M shares × $42.875 per share).

Cost of Capital = (33% × Cost of Debt) + (67% × Cost
               of Equity)
             = (33% × 4.7%) + (67% × 10.9%)
             = 8.9%

Remember that the PIMS ROI is pretax and should be multiplied by approximately 63% to make it comparable to your cost of capital.

---

date the industry. "Category killers" like Office Depot in office products and Home Depot in home improvement currently have market shares significantly below what they are predicted to be when their shares peak. Wall Street has recognized this position for each by awarding an astounding price-to-earnings multiple (P/E) of 47 for Office Depot and 40 for Home Depot. Wal-Mart has been consolidating the "Main Street" retail industry for more than two decades, but it still has a below-par market share, if its P/E of 24 is any indicator.[6]

Above-par market share disequilibrium is usual for a startup business with a monopoly on a new product or technology, perhaps protected for some time by patents. If the business is successful and the market grows, eventually competitors will come in and take market share. Well-known examples are Xerox with photocopiers in the 1960s and IBM with personal computers in the early 1980s.

Another type of above-par market share company is the industry leader who provides poor value and steadily loses market share because of it. Sears in the 1980s and U.S. Steel since its establishment in 1901 are classic examples.

The U.S. auto industry in the 1970s and 1980s presents a good illustration of disequilibrium states—and of strategic failures in responding to them. In the early 1970s, Detroit's Big Three automakers were roughly in an equilibrium state, even though Japanese automakers were rapidly establishing strong positions in new low-end market segments that Detroit had disdained anyway.

But the 1973 oil shock, and the consequent fuel shortages and soaring prices, made the smaller, fuel-efficient Japanese cars much more attractive to American consumers. More and more of Detroit's traditional customers moved over to these imports, never to return to their previous loyalties. Soon, it began to become clear that the American makers faced a disequilibrium state of above-par market share as their shares continued to erode.

The American companies should have worked on improving par market share by bringing out new products and improving marketing to make them more competitive. Instead, they responded with business as usual, as if they were still in equilibrium. By the 1980s, this strategic mistake had also destroyed ROIs for the Big Three and had done nothing to reverse their declining market shares.

In 1981, they responded—not with customer- and competitor-driven strategies but by seeking government protection. They lobbied the federal government to impose "voluntary" import quotas on Japanese autos. This supposedly temporary measure gave them an opportunity to get in a more competitive situation by strengthening actual ROI *and* improving par market share. Their response, however, was to take big price increases, which quickly moved their ROIs far above par. To be competitive in the future, they now needed to aggressively increase par market share by improving product quality and downsizing their cars.

Ford and Chrysler did turn some attention to market share. Ford especially began a decade-long campaign of quality improvement and new product development. But General Motors again lapsed into a strategically disastrous business-as-usual equilibrium role, which produced record losses and further share erosion by the 1990s.

Potential Disequilibrium

Equilibrium and disequilibrium, either ROI or market share, depend on known or predictable company and market variables. Sometimes, however, potential destabilizing threats are only distant and vague. In those cases, we can talk about *potential disequilibrium.*

American healthcare organizations are in a state of disequilibrium today, as the federal government is on the verge of forcing massive reforms of the system. They were in a state of potential disequilibrium long before. The healthcare crisis in America has been building for years if not decades, with soaring costs, declining benefits for the insured, and growing numbers of uninsured.

Perhaps the potential disequilibrium was becoming obvious with the November 1991 special election upset victory by Harris Wofford, who ran for U.S. senator from Pennsylvania on a platform calling for a national health system. Certainly with the July 1992 presidential election of Bill Clinton, the crisis was coming to a head, and the disequilibrium was moving from potential to actual.

The important point about potential disequilibrium is that it tells you enough to develop contingency plans. Some, such as the new health maintenance organizations, adopted roles and strategies apparently consistent with the potential disequilibrium. With below-par market share, they stand to benefit from healthcare reform. Preparation on the part of most insurance companies, hospitals, and doctors' organizations, who now stand to lose, has been inadequate. Those who continue to deny or resist the current disequilibrium will be eliminated in the "managed" competition of the late 1990s.

DEVELOPING STRATEGIC OBJECTIVES
AND ROLES

Businesses in equilibrium have different strategic needs from those in disequilibrium. Hence, they face different analytical problems in determining three- to ten-year roles.

Equilibrium Roles

Companies in equilibrium in both ROI and market share can use a "Business Position/Industry Attractiveness" map, such as the BCG and GE/McKinsey matrices, which appear here in Exhibits 4.1 and 4.2.

Once you've located your business on one of these matrices, you will need to consider a market share role—increase share, maintain share, or divest, as shown in Exhibit 4.7, along with the implications for ROI, investment required, and cash generated.

Business Category	Market Share	ROI vs. Cost of Capital	Investment Required	Free Cash Flow
"Star"	Hold/increase	Highly positive	High	Around zero or slightly negative
"Cash cow"	Hold	Positive	Low	Highly positive
"Question mark"	Double share	If negative	Very high	Highly negative
	Divest	If very negative	Disinvest	Positive
"Dog"	Maintain	If positive	Very low	Positive
	Harvest/divest	If negative	Very low	Positive

Exhibit 4.7   Roles from the growth/share matrix.

If your business is a "star," your role is to grow. It should have a high ROI but it also demands a lot of investment to grow. Therefore, its free cash flow may be negative.

A "cash cow" is put to pasture to generate large quantities of cash, little of which is reinvested. Some of it goes to fund the rising "stars" and the promising "question marks." Some also goes for dividends or stock repurchase.

A "question mark" requires additional analysis. Rapid industry growth provides opportunity, but its low market share means it's way behind the pack. If heavy investment can dramatically increase its market share and move its ROI from below to above your cost of capital, then its strategic role might be to double its market share. If that's impossible, divest it.

A "dog" is not necessarily a loser, in spite of the name and the role—divest—originally assigned to all "dogs" by BCG. If its ROI is below your cost of capital, BCG was right—harvest it for all the cash possible or divest it. However, some "dogs" are "hot dogs" with good ROIs. In fact, many businesses fall into this category. They should be maintained rather than harvested or divested.

Selecting the wrong role can be a fatal blunder, as illustrated in

Exhibit 4.8. To continue with the BCG analysis, the proper role of a "cash cow" is to provide the investment funds to turn today's "star" into tomorrow's "cow" and today's promising "question mark" into tomorrow's "star." That is the ideal sequence—"question mark" to "star" to "cash cow."

Catastrophe lurks in selecting the wrong sequence. Stuffing a "cash cow" produces waste, but starving it produces a "dog." Likewise, starving a "star" turns tomorrow's "cash cow" into a "question mark," which will become a "dog" as industry growth slows.

Disequilibrium Roles

Some disequilibrium roles are similar to the equilibrium roles, but they differ particularly in the need to improve actual values or to increase par values.

Cost of Capital vs. Par ROI

If you are in disequilibrium, your first concern has to be whether or not your par ROI is above or below your cost of capital. If it's below,

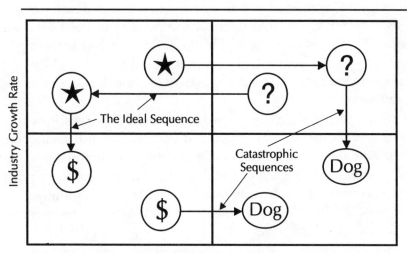

Relative Market Share

Source: Adapted from Arnoldo C. Hax and Nicolas C. Majluf, *Strategic Management* (Englewood Cliffs, N.J.: Prentice Hall, 1984) p. 136.

Exhibit 4.8 Selecting the wrong role is often a fatal strategy blunder.

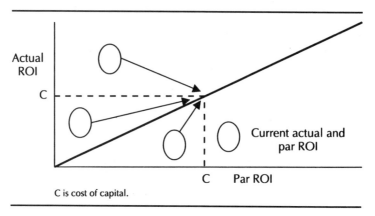

Exhibit 4.9   Role: Restructure and divest.

you have only two strategic choices—get par ROI above your cost of capital, which requires restructuring, or divest the business. Selecting any other role squanders shareholder value. The need to get your par ROI above your cost of capital is shown in Exhibit 4.9.

Restructuring—aggressive steps such as exiting products, massively reducing manpower, and closing capacity—is appropriate if the business has long-term value to you. This is often the situation when marginal companies are hit by a major event or development, such as U.S. Steel with international competition in the 1970s and McDonnell-Douglas with the end of the Cold War. Restructuring is only a three- to five-year role. Don't stay with it too long. Once you get the company back on its feet, move on to a market-driven, more competitive role.

If restructuring won't do enough, or if the business is worth more to someone else than to you, divest it. Defense contractor General Dynamics successfully adopted this role for many of its businesses with the decline of the defense industry. Its stock price increased from under $20 in 1990 to over $100 in 1992. Many personal computer (PC) clone manufacturers may also have to merge in order to obtain critical mass.

Market Share and ROI Roles

If your par ROI is above your cost of capital, then your position in Exhibit 4.10 determines which of the following roles is appropriate:

- Increase market share.
- Increase ROI.
- Improve par market share.
- Improve par ROI.

Keep in mind that these are general guidelines and should be considered in the context of the specific external and competitive forces, your position in the product life cycle, and your long-term strategy. For example, Home Depot is below par in both ROI and market share as it aggressively consolidates the home improvement industry. Its recommended role, in Cell 1 of Exhibit 4.10, would be to increase market share. If Home Depot increased profits too much now, it would give breathing room to competitors and slow its market share growth. Increasing market share has priority since the resulting economies of scale will increase par ROI, and actual ROI should increase with par ROI. Companies in the enviable position of

		Actual ROI		
		< Par*	= Par	> Par
Market Share	< Par	1 Increase share (and thereby improve par ROI)	4 Increase share	7 Increase share (and move toward par ROI)
	= Par	2 Improve ROI	5 Equilibrium (see Exhibits 4.2 and 4.7)	8 Improve par ROI
	> Par	3 Improve ROI; improve par share	6 Improve par share	9 Improve par share (aggressively)

*ROI below par but above the cost of capital. (Restructuring is the appropriate role if ROI is below the cost of capital.)

Exhibit 4.10 Roles for companies with disequilibrium market share or ROI.

Home Depot should often balance share growth and profits by pricing to generate a ROI above their cost of capital but below par ROI.

Role: Improve ROI

As illustrated in Exhibit 4.11, improving ROI is a natural role when a new CEO takes over an "opportunity," that is, a business with actual ROI significantly below par (Cell 2 in Exhibit 4.10). It may be a business with unsuccessful diversifications that need divesting, one with excess capacity requiring plant closings, or one with low productivity or excessive bureaucracy. William Stiritz, for example, did an outstanding job with an "improve ROI" role at Ralston Purina during his first few years as CEO. He divested "dogs" such as mushrooms, tuna, and animal feed. He acquired industry-leading Continental Baking and Eveready Batteries. And he cut costs and increased earnings per share by repurchasing stock.

However, keep in mind that improving ROI is a near-term strategic objective—three to five years. If carried on too long, it turns into a "milking" role, and milking inevitably turns into "harvesting." Stiritz stayed with the "improve ROI" role too long. Focusing on costs rather than increasing value lowered the company's par ROI. He milked the Ralston cow dry and moved it to Cell 9. The stock in 1994 was at its 1987 level. It had lost significant share in baking, batteries, and baby food.

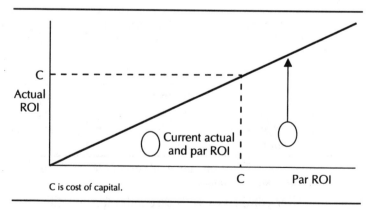

Exhibit 4.11   Role: Increase ROI and control costs.

Financially driven strategies may be necessary to get a company into financial shape to be competitive, but then it's time to focus on the word "competitive." ROI doesn't motivate employees to give 100 percent and doesn't give customers superior value. Without a customer- and competitor-driven role and strategy, you eventually give the advantage to competitors.

Sears and Tenneco in the 1980s are good examples of "turnarounds"—companies that are above par in market share and below par in ROI, Cell 3. This combination is typical of once-powerful companies that have gotten fat and no longer meet customer wants. They lose market share to competitors who provide superior value. These companies have below par ROIs because of high costs. They need to do two things simultaneously: (1) cut costs to improve ROI and (2) increase customer value to bolster par market share. Both companies have moved in that direction since 1990. Tenneco brought in Mike Walsh in 1991 and Sears brought in Arthur Martinez in 1992, each with a mandate to turn his company around.

Role: Increase Market Share

Increasing market share is the natural role when you have a superior strategy and have the opportunity to consolidate an industry (Cells 1, 4, and 7). As shown in Exhibit 4.12, accepting a slightly-below-par ROI accelerates the rate at which competitors exit the

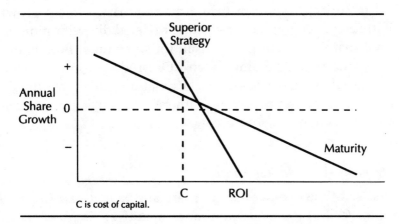

Exhibit 4.12   Role: Increase market share or sales.

industry and produces big market share increases. That's the right role for the "category killers" like Home Depot and Toys 'R' Us, who are consolidating industries.

Using your superiority to increase ROI above par (Cell 7) will slow or halt your share growth. This is usually a serious strategic mistake. Your price umbrella allows inefficient competitors to remain viable and attracts new entrants. It may even allow a competitor to gain share leadership by copying your strategy but with lower prices.

Compaq fell into this strategy error from 1985 to 1990, during which period its after-tax return on equity averaged 26 percent. Its high prices allowed both quality PC competitors such as Dell and dozens of cheap clone makers to enter the market. Similarly, Mercedes Benz and other luxury goods makers basked in the glow of high ROIs and growing shares in the 1980s but shivered in the chill winds of plummeting shares and profits in the 1990s.

Increasing share also is the right role when a strong competitor attacks you. When Miller Brewing attacked Anheuser-Busch in the early 1970s, Anheuser-Busch adopted an "increase share" role. Even though Miller gained share, Anheuser-Busch gained even more share, both of them at the expense of smaller local and regional brewers. Similarly, Gallo adopted an "increase share" role when Coca-Cola entered the wine business in the late 1970s.

Knowing when to change and move on is just as important with "improve market share" as it is with "improve ROI." No role is forever, and this role ends once the industry is consolidated and has reached maturity. If you can turn a mature market into a growth market through geographic expansion or related diversification, the "improve share" role can go on again for some time. But, as indicated in Exhibit 4.12, holding down ROI produces only moderate share gains when your market reaches maturity. It's time to move toward a more appropriate role. Otherwise, you'll unnecessarily sacrifice profits as you "stuff a cow."

Role: Improve Par Market Share

A business with above-par market share and ROI at par (Cell 6) or above par (Cell 9) is increasingly uncompetitive. Competitors are either providing superior value or are catching up in value. In these situations, the appropriate role is to improve par market share.

Xerox in copiers and IBM in PCs in the 1980s are cases of innovators who once had a near monopoly in a product category but then rapidly lost market share. Competitors had begun to provide better value, either through lower prices or by meeting nonprice wants of customers better. In this situation, the response is obvious: Redesign your product line so you provide equal or better value. Xerox reduced costs and increased quality to improve its par market share. As of 1994, IBM had recognized its problems, but had not yet taken effective action.

Procter & Gamble in the 1980s and other leading consumer products companies in the 1990s lost market share because competitors caught up in product quality and consumers stopped paying the price premium that their once-superior quality had allowed. In this situation, the obvious first step is to do what you can to maintain superior quality. At some point, however, the only way to improve par share is to reduce or eliminate the price premium. It is wiser to follow Philip Morris' example of cutting the price of Marlboro cigarettes in April 1993 than to follow the examples of IBM in PCs and Detroit in cars during the 1980s. Their market shares declined while they maintained high prices and inferior value.

Businesses that are above par in both market share and ROI (Cell 9) have followed a "profits today" strategy too long and are no longer competitive. They have priced too high and skimped on product development, marketing, etc. From its founding by J. P. Morgan in 1901 as the steel monopoly, U.S. Steel has steadily lost share by maintaining high prices and underinvesting in research and development (R&D). Ralston Purina in the early 1990s and companies such as TWA that were taken over by raiders in the 1980s also ended up in Cell 9. The solution is to use the profits from above par ROI to improve par ROI: Improve product quality and marketing, and possibly reduce price.

A special case of a Cell 9 business is the company that is being "dressed up" to be sold. Heileman Brewing is a classic example. Heileman CEO Russell Cleary was one of the shrewdest people in the brewing industry. By 1986 he recognized that the Big Three brewers—Anheuser-Busch, Miller, and Coors—would be entering the popular-price beer market and that regional brewers who sold on low price would no longer be viable. Cleary responded by cutting marketing and overhead costs. These cuts hurt par market share and would have been unwise for the long term. But Cleary did not intend to be around for the long term. When the cuts created one last spurt of short-term profit growth, Australian Alan Bond mistook this for accelerating earnings instead of earnings about to collapse. Cleary sold Heileman to Bond for $1.1 billion, an obscene multiple of earnings. Even worse for Bond, the sale went through one month before the 1987 U.S. stock market crash.

Role: Improve Par ROI

You can improve par ROI by increasing market share, improving product quality, and reducing capital intensity—which is a frequent role for businesses in equilibrium, in effect the role of a "star." But, as shown in Exhibit 4.13, this role is also appropriate for companies that have equilibrium market shares but above-par ROIs (Cell 8). This situation usually occurs when a major event causes the par ROI of an entire industry to collapse. Sometimes, industry profits are far above equilibrium, which was the case with U.S. pharmaceutical manufacturers in 1993 with the federal government seeking ways to reduce prices. Beverage can manufacturers in the 1970s created the same situation when they kept can prices so high that brewers began to make their own cans. This situation also frequently involves commodities, as with the collapse of oil prices in the early 1980s. With recent exports of aluminum from Russia, aluminum prices have collapsed.

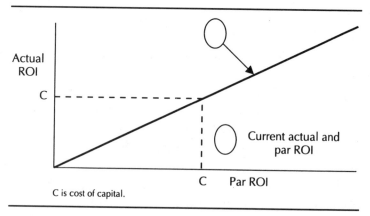

Exhibit 4.13   Role: Improve equilibrium market share or par ROI.

"Improve par ROI" is a difficult role for a company in this situation, since the new par ROI is far below the par ROI that existed before the industry event. The best approach is to avoid getting into the situation in the first place, which is often possible. The pharmaceutical companies left themselves vulnerable because of their huge price increases in the 1980s. The can companies should have recognized the threat of vertical integration by the brewers. With their experience and economies of scale, they could have reduced prices to a level above their cost of capital and still have priced below the brewers' costs. They sealed their own fates by refusing to lower prices aggressively.

Failure to act preemptively or at least in a timely fashion can be disastrous. As you hold prices far above what they should be, your market share and par ROI continue to erode. American Can and Continental Can no longer exist. The traditional high-cost airlines were vulnerable when the U.S. airline industry was deregulated in the late 1970s. Many of them have since gone under. The survivors collectively lost $3 billion in 1991–1992, as the industry leaders have still failed to react to the new industry environment. However, Southwest Airlines, the Wal-Mart of the skies, made money.

"Soufflés" and "Opportunities"

Analysis of the PIMS data base indicates that companies tend to move toward equilibrium ROI over time (see Exhibit 4.14). That means that businesses with below par ROI (Cells 2 and 3) are

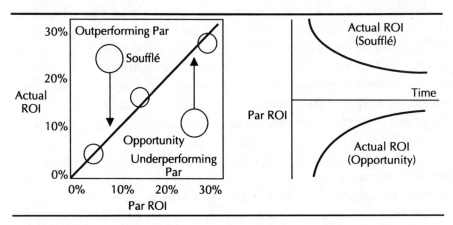

Exhibit 4.14 "Soufflés" and "Opportunities."

"opportunities." Management effort and solid strategy can significantly increase ROI, thus making them attractive acquisition targets. Similarly, businesses with ROI above par (Cells 8 and 9) are called "soufflés." Eventually, their ROIs will collapse toward par. Acquiring a "soufflé" can be devastating to a CEO's career.

CONCLUSION

Choosing the right strategic objective for your company requires a careful analysis of all the variables of your business position and industry that influence profitability. We know from PIMS that the most important variables are relative quality, market share, and capital intensity.

By using these variables, you can determine if you should adopt an equilibrium role or a disequilibrium role. Your business exists either in equilibrium—that is, its current market share and ROI are what you would expect them to be some years down the road if current climate and competitive trends remain the same—or in disequilibrium—which means that either your ROI or market share, or both, are not what you should expect them to be.

These states of equilibrium and disequilibrium largely tell you what your strategic objective should be—increase market share, maintain market share and generate cash, divest, improve ROI, improve par share, or improve par ROI. The variables that affect profitability are the levers you can push and pull to fulfill those roles.

While we now know a great deal about these variables and appropriate strategic roles, many companies, including the market leaders, fail to adopt the right roles. Often the failure is one of timing—not changing roles when needed. An "improve ROI" role is only a three- to five-year role. Carried on too long, this role can harvest a company and drive it into the ground. Don't stay with an "improve market share" role once the market has matured; you'll waste money on unnecessary investment.

Of course, there are exceptions to the rules, none of which are absolute. If you are attacked by a powerful competitor in a mature market, an "improve market share" role may be appropriate, since your competitor will take market share away from you if you don't take it away from the competitor. If you are aggressively consolidating an industry, learn to live with a below-par ROI until the consolidation is complete.

Getting the strategic role right can keep you from turning a "cash cow" into a "dog" or from acquiring a "soufflé" that collapses on you. "Soufflés" . . . "cash cows" . . . "dogs." The main thing is that you use some horse sense to determine the proper role for your business. When you've done that, and then developed the right long-term strategy, you're in a position to beat competitors at meeting customer wants.

5

CREATING A
DEFENDABLE POSITION
Generic Strategies

Strategies vary from industry to industry, company to company, and situation to situation. Like every other business, yours is unique in one way or another—either your products or your customers or your competitors, or perhaps all three. Your final strategy should reflect and reinforce that difference. By the time you finish Cycle 1, you'll have a strategy specific to your company and market circumstances.

However, there is a small number of broad strategic approaches common to many businesses and situations. Michael Porter has identified four of these, which he calls "generic strategies."[1]

A good generic strategy gives you a competitive advantage, while failure to have a clear generic strategy—being "stuck in the middle"—is disastrous. It leads to political infighting and inefficiencies within the company. Worse, it leads to a confused image with customers. Being caught in the middle is a prescription for decline.

In this chapter, the discussion of three general topics will help you select and execute a generic strategy best for your business:

1. Types of generic strategies.
2. Product life cycle and generic strategy.
3. Selecting and implementing a generic strategy.

TYPES OF GENERIC STRATEGIES

A generic strategy is (1) a simply stated approach (2) for achieving financial and other objectives (3) by *creating a defendable position* in an industry. Your generic strategy should fit the stage of your product or industry life cycle. It should also account for the forces affecting your business—the four Cs of Company, Customers, Competitors, and Climate. You have already carefully considered these forces when you developed your business definition in Chapter 3.[2]

What are the generic strategies available to you? Porter identified four by asking two questions:

1. What is your source of strategic advantage, low cost or differentiation (uniqueness)?
2. What is your strategic target, the broad market or a niche?

The answers to these questions yield the four generic strategies shown in Exhibit 5.1.

There are a couple of additional generic approaches businesses sometimes use to gain a strategic competitive advantage. They derive from two other questions:

1. Is the key to success the number and quality of sales calls?
2. Is the key to success the ability to respond quickly to rapidly changing supply or demand curves?

Answers to those questions produce the four additional generic strategies shown in Exhibit 5.2.

The best way to explain these generic strategies is to look at their application to a specific industry. Exhibit 5.3 shows generic strategies in the retail industry.

Large department stores, often anchors in malls, typically follow a *differentiation* strategy. Companies like Dillard's and The May Company try to distinguish themselves through fashion, service, product variety, and store design. They strive for "best price" rather than the "low price" of the discounters.

	Strategic Advantage: Low Cost	Strategic Advantage: Differentiation
Strategic Target: Total Industry (Broad)	*Low-Cost* Comparable product at a lower cost: • Commodities (oil, grain, cans, PCs, memory chips) • Discount retailers (Wal-Mart) • Number 3 or 4 in a differentiation industry • Schlitz and others inappropriately adopted this strategy in the 1970s	*Differentiation* Appeal to customers based on nonprice attributes (e.g., image, quality, service): • "Image products" (beer, soda, cigarettes, clothes) • Real product or service attributes (Hewlett-Packard calculators, Maytag, Caterpillar) • Mass market lifestyle (network TV, movies, pro sports, department stores)
Strategic Target: A Customer Segment or Particular Product (Focus)	*Cost-Focus* Offer a narrow product segment at lowest possible cost. Specialization often leads to customer satisfaction: • Nucor and similar steel companies • Southwest Airlines • "Category killer" retailers (Circuit City, Home Depot, Toys 'R' Us) • Small, low-cost operators (real fringe players)	*Differentiation-Focus* "Real" differences make your product or service significantly better than competitors': • Xerox in 1965, Polaroid, Jeep in 4WD until 1980, pharmaceuticals, small-town drug stores "Targeted" to relatively narrow segment: • Luxury goods and services • Niche leisure/lifestyle (specialty magazines, some cable TV) Mall specialty stores (The Limited)

Exhibit 5.1 Porter's generic strategies.

	Strategic Advantage: Low Cost	Strategic Advantage: Differentiation
Sales Strategy	*Low-Cost—Sales* A.L. Williams term life insurance, used cars	*Differentiation—Sales* Shearson Lehman telemarketing, management seminars, penny stocks
Guerrilla Strategy	*Low-Cost—Guerrilla* "Get rich quick" classified ads in *Inc.* magazine, membership warehouse stores and closeout retailers that only buy on deal (Sam's, Tuesday Morning)	*Differentiation—Guerrilla* Products and promotions linked to movies and TV programs, fads

Exhibit 5.2　Other generic strategies.

	Low-Cost	Differentiation
Broad market	Discounters: Kmart, Target, Wal-Mart	Full-service stores: Bloomingdale's, Dillard's
Focus	Category killers: Toys 'R' Us, Home Depot, factory outlet malls	Specialty mall stores: The Limited, The Gap
Sales strategy	800 number telemarketing: aluminum siding	Some direct mail catalogs, insurance, network marketing (Amway)
Guerrilla strategy	Closeout retailers: Marshall's, T.J. Maxx, C.O.M.B. catalog	Mall Christmas stores, Hong Kong tailors

Exhibit 5.3　Examples of retailers' strategies.

Followers of a *low-cost* generic strategy include discount department stores such as Wal-Mart, Dayton Hudson's Target Stores, and Kmart. These stores also carry a wide variety of products, but they appeal to customers through low prices.

In the niche or focus category, mall shops tend to follow a *differentiation-focus* strategy. Each store carries a particular product category, such as women's clothing at The Limited and books at Brentano's. Most of these stores rely on convenience, variety, fashion, quality, and "good" value rather than low price.

A relatively new type of retailer is the "category killer," which relentlessly follows a *cost-focus* strategy. Leading examples of this type of retailer include Toys 'R' Us in toys, Home Depot in home improvement, Office Depot in office products, and Circuit City in consumer electronics. They are called "category killers" because small independent retailers and even local chains in a category tend to close up after one of these "killers" comes to town. They meet customer wants so well and have such favorable economies of scale at both the corporate and outlet level that direct competition is usually suicide.

The *sales* generic strategy is appropriate when success depends on the quantity and quality of sales calls. Often, the products sold through this strategy are those that do not provide instant gratification, such as pre-need funeral arrangements, a service you can hardly beat for delayed gratification. Many other products that one "ought" to have rather than "want" fit this category—life insurance, stock market investments, or credit card protection plans.

The sales strategy can be either differentiation or low-cost. Cold-calling stockbrokers use differentiation, pitching their offerings as having superior returns and growth probabilities. While some insurance companies rely on a differentiation-sales strategy, the A.L. Williams Company follows a low-cost sales strategy to sell term life insurance on price.

The generic *guerrilla* strategy, which can also be either low-cost or differentiation, is based on opportunism, flexibility, and timing. It often capitalizes on the shifting fashions and fads of popular culture. For example, any number of products were named after the highly popular movie cartoon characters, the Teenage Mutant Ninja Turtles.

Guerrilla strategy can be seasonal—tree lots and mall holiday shops and stands at Christmas time, for example. It can be itinerant, that of the nomadic "snake oil" salesmen and tin pan peddlers of the American frontier. Today's Hong Kong tailor who makes an occasional tour of American and European cities is in the same mold.

Guerrilla operators in decades past used questionable tactics to scam customers. Today, however, you can find real value in a growing number of retailers like Marshall's and the C.O.M.B. catalog, which carry only closeout merchandise or products bought on deal. Moreover, promotional products for hit movies may have only a short life but are a multibillion dollar business.

Generic strategies should not be followed simplistically. A business following a differentiation strategy must offer reasonable prices. It may also strive to be the lowest-cost producer, thereby increasing margins and ensuring maximum strategic advantage in case of a price war. Similarly, a discount retailer such as Wal-Mart benefits from the friendliness of its associates (employees) and quality name brands. The trick is to offer "best value" for your strategy without becoming "stuck in the middle."

Sears was stuck in the middle in the 1980s. It wasn't low cost so it couldn't compete with discounters such as Wal-Mart and Kmart. Except for hardware, it wasn't high quality. Sears seemed to develop a new strategy every few years. The result of an unclear strategy at headquarters was mediocrity in the stores. Customers left Sears and went to Wal-Mart for low prices and to mall stores for fashion.

PRODUCT LIFE CYCLE
AND GENERIC STRATEGY

The product (or industry) life cycle is an important factor you must consider in selecting a generic strategy. The product life cycle (PLC) concept postulates that products and industries all follow a similar, if not identical, course from birth to death, as illustrated in Exhibit 5.4.

Early proponents of PLC even treated this course as somehow preordained, as if marketers had little control over the life of a product. Clearly, this deterministic view is oversimplified, and the concept has been severely criticized.[3] Yet, the concept endures, and for good reason: So long as you appreciate its limitations, it can be a useful tool for understanding and explaining markets.

The idealized PLC version in Exhibit 5.4 has only a limited application. It sometimes accurately describes the life cycles of products, but when it is extended to product categories (personal com-

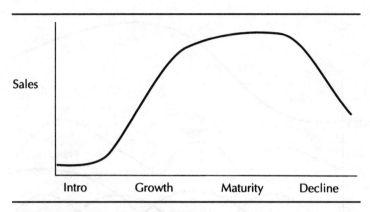

Sales

Intro   Growth   Maturity   Decline

Exhibit 5.4   The idealized product life cycle.

puters), to companies (Apple Computers), and particularly to whole industries (the computer industry), the symmetrical growth-and-decline curve is less applicable.

As you move further from the specific product out to the entire industry, the life cycle curve will tend to show longer and slower growth stages, often successive periods of growth, perhaps extended maturity, slow decline, and in many cases no decline. Exhibit 5.5 illustrates the relationship between industry, company, and brand life cycles.[4]

Companies and industries characterized by inactive or reactive managements who let events control them sometimes actually do follow the idealized curve. However, life cycles often take different forms for leaders who attempt to control their destinies. The shape of the life cycle depends not only on uncontrollable market forces—an aging population, for example—but also on your actions and those of your competitors. The future is controllable to a significant extent. That fundamental belief underlies the Four-Cycle Strategy Planning Process.

Product Life Cycle Models

Even if the real world isn't always like the original idealized PLC concept—with its inevitable and invariable sequence of introduction, growth, maturity, and decline—products, companies, and industries do experience one or more of those stages in varying

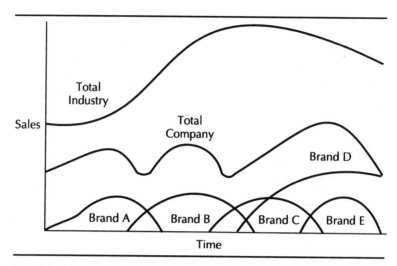

Exhibit 5.5 PLCs for an industry, a company, and its individual brands.

patterns and sequences. Hence, the concept should be broadened to include a variety of PLC models.

Exhibit 5.6 illustrates three additional versions of the PLC. Some industries follow a "scalloped" curve of repeated cycles of growth-maturity-growth. An industry will grow to maturity, but before decline sets in, new products, marketing innovations, or technological advances ignite a new growth phase. Companies often follow a scalloped growth curve through new product development. As one product matures and begins to decline, another new, improved, or upgraded version creates renewed sales growth for the company. Television enjoyed renewed growth in the 1960s when color replaced black and white. A second wave of growth will occur in the later 1990s with "high-definition" television.

Other products and businesses go through a "cycle-recycle" life, characterized by introduction, growth, maturity, early decline, and then renewed growth. Like the scalloped cycle, this may result from technological breakthroughs, new uses, creative marketing, or the introduction of new products. For example, beer volume in the United States declined from 88 million barrels in 1948 to 85 million barrels in 1958 as people switched from beer to hard liquor as their incomes increased. The beer industry reversed this decline through

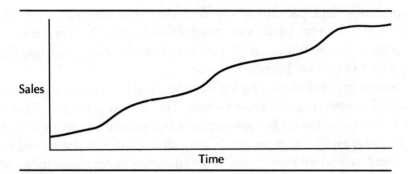

Exhibit 5.6a   A "scalloped" PLC.

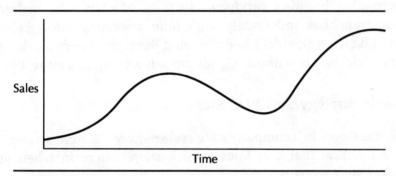

Exhibit 5.6b   A "cycle-recycle" PLC.

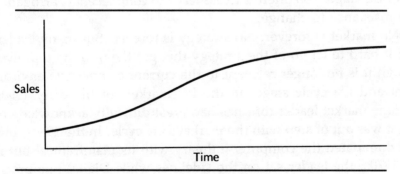

Exhibit 5.6c   An "extended maturity" PLC.

more convenient packaging. By replacing inconvenient returnable bottles with metal cans and nonrefillable glass bottles, brewers encouraged more home, or off-premise, beer drinking. Volume then grew to 181 million barrels by 1980.

Similarly, after declining for decades, the U.S. railroad industry has had a resurgence in recent years. The reason is simple: The rail lines had always been the low-cost transportation mode for hauling large volumes of bulky products long distances, but the sales turn-around came when they focused on customer service and increased reliability.

In "extended maturity," products and companies may grow to maturity and then remain flat for decades. Many commodities and supermarket branded products, such as Morton salt, maintain strong franchises indefinitely with little marketing effort behind them. Likewise, Speidel has dominated the replacement market for better watchbands without significant advertising since the 1950s.

Generic Strategy and PLC Stage

Different stages in a company's life cycle require different strategies, and it's critical that you know which stage you're in when you develop your strategy.

Industry leaders generally have the greatest freedom to select a generic strategy. Ironically, they are often the slowest to adjust to a new PLC stage. Too often, success leads to complacency, arrogance, and resistance to change.

No market is forever. No strategy is forever. But many leaders find it hard to let go of the strategy that got them to the top, even though it is no longer relevant to the current competitive environment and life cycle stage. In the PC markets of the early 1990s, onetime market leader IBM has had great difficulty acknowledging that it was out of step with the market's life cycle. In the 1960s, IBM had dominated the computer industry with its mainframes. But in the 1970s, the leader sat on the sidelines while Digital Equipment created and dominated the minicomputer segment of the industry.

That wasn't to happen again. When Apple Computer pioneered the personal computer category, IBM responded with a product that was eventually to become the industry standard. Apple relied on its own proprietary technology, but IBM used "open architecture," that is, it used parts and technology made by outside suppliers. Intel supplied the microprocessors and Microsoft provided the operating system. Open architecture allowed imitators, or "clones," to come to the market quickly, since they could get the same components. However, IBM was then clearly ahead of the clones in quality and performance. That, and the company's strong reputation in mainframes, gave it dominance.

As the PC market matured, however, IBM faltered. Compaq routinely provided the latest technology before IBM. Other clones moved to parity with IBM in features but at dramatically lower prices. IBM was increasingly "caught in the middle"—and continuously lost market share.

Ironically, it was IBM's initial use of open architecture that had set the industry on the course IBM now found so hard to follow. The differentiation strategy served IBM well in mainframes and the early stages of the personal computer PLC. But the differentiation strategy was simply inconsistent with the competitive reality that the market for PCs had matured. The PC had become a commodity product.

Competitive and market forces had created the need for a low-cost generic strategy for PCs—a fact IBM fully recognized only when it suffered an all-time record loss of $5 billion in 1992. IBM responded with massive cost cutting, price slashing, and bloodletting, including that of its CEO. Time will tell whether the company has successfully moved to the low-cost generic strategy, which is appropriate for a mature commodity.

Knowing where you are on the PLC curve helps you know which strategy is appropriate for you. Exhibit 5.7 shows how certain generic strategies are more appropriate for the leader during certain life cycle stages than during others.

Introduction

During a product's introduction and its early growth, differentiation-focus usually is the appropriate strategy. The product probably has no significant competitors at this stage, and customers are more interested in benefits than price. Overall costs are high since pro-

	Introduction	Growth	Maturity	Decline
Strategy	Differentia-tion–focus	Differentia-tion	Low cost or dif-ferentiation	Cost-focus or low cost
Role	Growth	Growth	Generate cash	Harvest
Profits	Negative	Strong	Weaken	Low
Costs	Very high	Declining	Low	Very low
Product line	Narrow	Growing	Prolifera-tion	Prune
Prices	High	High but declining	Price war "shake out" in early maturity	Low
Promotion	Very high for awareness	High to create brand equity	Shift toward price promotion	Very low advertising
Distribution	Selective	Broaden	Intensive; heavy "push" incentives	Selective; pare un-profitable channels

Exhibit 5.7   Strategy and tactics for the industry leader by PLC Stage.

duction experience is limited, production runs small, and distribution is selective. Moreover, advertising and promotion costs are high because of the need to increase awareness. Classic examples are Polaroid, Xerox, the IBM PC, pharmaceuticals, and the Lotus 1-2-3 spreadsheet.

If the segment is small and will not support more than one competitor (e.g., a barber in a small town) or prestige is more important than low price (e.g., luxury goods such as Rolex watches), differentiation-focus is a stable strategy that can last indefinitely.

Growth

During the growth phase, as a broad market emerges, the strategy should move to differentiation throughout the potential market. High margins have begun to attract competitors, and the greatest concern of the leader becomes that of maintaining market share against the growing competition. In order to preempt competitors, the leader introduces product variations for most if not all niches in the broad market. Growing competition limits price increases. Still, margins remain high or even grow, since the market continues to expand while the experience curve and economies of scale reduce costs.

Maturity

With maturity, leaders in some industries (e.g., beer, soda, cigarettes, clothing) may continue with a differentiation strategy. Leaders in commodity industries, however, will be forced into a low-cost strategy. The market has ceased to expand. Any gains in sales must now come at the expense of someone else, and competition intensifies. Smaller competitors use lower prices to nibble away at the leader's market share, and the leader retaliates. Relying on a superior cost position due to greater economies of scale and production experience, the leader instigates a price war to "shake out" weaker competitors and to encourage the survivors to coexist in a "better state of peace." Prices may rebound a little when that "peace" is established. Still, competition remains price and cost driven. Even for "image" products, product differences become smaller, and price promotions increase at the expense of advertising.

Decline

During the decline phase, the leader's interest is to consolidate the industry and avoid excessive competitive warfare. The company now begins to "harvest" the business. It moves from "profits tomorrow" to "profits today," even if this means lower sales. It controls costs tightly. The company prunes the product line to get rid of marginal products and focus only on those niches where it is dominant. A "low-cost" strategy is appropriate if the industry has major economies of scale. A "cost/focus" strategy of exiting unprofitable segments is appropriate if economies of scale are small.

"False Decline" and "False Maturity"

Determining the right generic strategy is critical for each stage of the PLC. That can sometimes be difficult. Two common errors are "false decline" and "false maturity."

"False decline" occurs when economic conditions, competitive activity, or mediocre marketing causes sales to stagnate. Management misinterprets this temporary sales decline as permanent and turns it into a self-fulfilling prophecy by cutting R&D and promotion expenses to harvest cash flow. Brand equity suffers, and long-term sales and profits continue to fall. There are certain clues that can help you determine if you've encountered a "false decline":

- If several markets in different stages of the PLC begin weakening at the same time, you're probably looking at a softening economy.

- If your sales decline but your competitors' don't, then the decline is due to competitive activity or problems with your marketing. The appropriate response is to improve your marketing mix.

"False maturity" occurs if management fails to recognize the actual decline of a market and tries to turn sales around with new product variations and promotions. Aggressive spending on R&D and advertising in an effort to reignite sales would not only waste money but also cause you to miss the opportunity to increase cash flow through cost controls. When objective analysis of market trends, or of your competitors' strengths and your weaknesses, shows that a profitable sales turnaround is not feasible, you should manage that business for cash and shift the bulk of your time and attention to your potential winners. Classic examples are the corner grocer who tried to compete head-on against supermarkets and the "Main Street" retailer who went on with business as usual after Wal-Mart came to town.

Objective analysis of the PLC can prevent major strategic mistakes. Make sure your role and generic strategy are right for your stage in the PLC.

"Evolution" vs. Product Life Cycle

In many ways, the metaphor of biological evolution better explains the lives of products and industries than does the life cycle metaphor. The PLC was originally conceived of as analogous to an individual organism's life from birth through maturity to death— with clear limits on each stage. Many industries, however, can go on forever. A carefully nurtured brand can also live indefinitely, as illustrated by Budweiser and Coca-Cola dominating their markets for over 100 years.

The original PLC concept is mechanistic and deterministic, whereas the evolution analogy is dynamic and adaptive. As with biological species, businesses and industries that adapt to environmental changes (climate forces) and other species (competitors) can avoid extinction.

Today, biologists are divided into two schools of thought on evolution. The "gradualism" school follows Charles Darwin's classic theory, arguing that evolution works continuously and gradually through the mechanisms of accidental variation and natural selection. A species variation survives and multiplies if it is better adapted to the environment than are competing species.

The other school maintains that evolution occurs through "punctuated equilibrium." They cite the geological and fossil record as revealing long periods of little change in species, alternating with short periods of sudden and momentous change. Dinosaurs, for example, simply disappeared "overnight," if you're on geologic time. These short-lived periods of destruction and creation of species result from natural catastrophes, such as large meteorites smashing into the earth, or from the sudden release of steadily accumulated stresses.

Whatever the biological "truth," both are apt metaphors for business. Gradualism is at work every day in a free market. Businesses continuously improve their products, and "natural selection" occurs as customers switch to brands that provide superior value.

Punctuated equilibrium is also at work. "Sudden" marketplace upheavals, such as the emergence of Japan as a powerful global competitor, can lead to the destruction of many businesses unable to adapt to the new competitive environment. Breakthroughs in technology can suddenly replace one product with another or create a whole new market—electronic calculators, for example, quickly displaced slide rules. Marketing innovations, government actions, or new entrants all can result in marketplace cataclysms and sudden spurts of destruction and creation, reminiscent of Joseph Schumpeter's theory of "creative destruction."

The evolution analogy has a couple of important implications for strategy. One is "strategic windows"[5]—those occasional periods of fit between market requirements and company strengths, which change more slowly than the marketplace environment. A company alert to external change and able to adjust its strategy quickly can exploit these opportunities as they occur. In the 1980s, one such strategic window opened for bottled water producers. Trends toward greater affluence, an aging population, and health awareness created a market of upscale adults who could afford bottled water, who didn't want the sweet taste of soft drinks, and who wanted a sophisticated alternative to alcohol. Savvy bottled water producers took advantage of this strategic window and repositioned their product from being an alternative to polluted tap water to being a substitute for soft drinks and even the fabled luncheon martini or three.

Another implication for strategy is that looking outside your own company and your own industry will make you more "fit" and therefore more likely to flourish. You will be alert to developments or changes in technology, consumer trends, or even marketing that you can adopt to give you an advantage. If your product is sold through supermarkets, for example, you should "benchmark" it against Frito-Lay or other "best of store" vendors and not just against competitors in your category.

The evolution model should not be applied literally, of course. Biological evolution is mostly passive, while successful companies actively initiate and control change. Winning organizations monitor the horizon for threats and windows of opportunity and aggressively implement change. Don't wait for "natural selection" to weed you out of the marketplace.

SELECTING AND IMPLEMENTING
A GENERIC STRATEGY

You are now ready to select and implement the generic strategy that will give your business a defendable position in the market. Your generic strategy depends upon your industry life cycle and your position in the industry, and the strategy must be consistent with competitive and climate forces. For reasons of competitive strategy, which are discussed in detail in Chapter 7, followers should rarely adopt a strategy similar to the leader's. That creates a head-on confrontation, and the follower will lose. Only a large number two competitor can sometimes mimic the strategy of the leader and get away with it.

Selecting a Generic Strategy

If you are the leader, you are free from some of the competitive constraints on the followers. You may focus on meeting *customer* wants, while smaller competitors must pay more heed to the *competitive* situation. That does not mean the leader can indulge in competitive complacency. Instead, it means that the leader's strongest competitive weapon is continual improvement of customer satisfaction, and the leader gets first choice of strategies most likely to do that. Exhibit 5.8 lists the factors that determine which strategy is most appropriate for the industry leader and the "key" to sales success for each generic strategy.

If you are a follower, you must take into account the leader's strategy as well as customer wants. Competitive considerations are more important for followers.

In the American beer industry examples listed in Exhibit 5.9, leader Anheuser-Busch has adopted a differentiation strategy. Number two Miller has adopted a similar strategy, as has the third-place competitor, Coors. Anheuser-Busch and Miller have continually made gains at Coors' expense, and Coors eventually may have to move to a low-cost strategy.

Stroh, Heileman, and Pabst all follow a low-cost, low-price strategy. Imports and "micro-breweries," following a focus-differentiation strategy, have found a niche where small volumes and very high prices prevail. This niche, however, accounts for less than five percent of the American beer market.

Sometimes competitive and climate realities make one of the generic strategies unattractive or impossible. In the case of the beer industry, that's the cost-focus strategy which no one is following.

Generic Strategy		Appropriate for industry leader when . . .	Key to sales success
Broad Market	**Low-Cost**	• Commodities (i.e., segment differences are small; price elasticity is high) • Major economies of scale or experience curve • Strategy is to consolidate the industry	Low price
	Differentiation	• Lots of competitors • Many dimensions to the product • Price not overriding variable	Product features or image
Focus	**Low-Cost**	Consumers focused on both price and meeting their needs	Effectiveness (meets consumer wants qualitatively better than other products)
	Differentiation	Consumers focused on meeting their needs more than price	
Sales		• "Delayed gratification" products. ("Should buy" rather than "want to buy" products.) • Products that need explanation	Number and quality of sales calls

Exhibit 5.8   Generic strategy for the industry leader.

Implementing Generic Strategies

Implementing each generic strategy requires a significantly different marketing strategy. Exhibit 5.10 provides guidance on the relative importance of each marketing variable for each generic strategy. Exhibit 5.11 summarizes the skill, resource, and organizational requirements for each generic strategy. The likelihood of

	Low Cost	**Differentiation**
Broad Product Range	*Low-Cost* Stroh, Bond, and Pabst (Nos. 4, 5, and 6) without premium image	*Differentiation* Anheuser-Busch, Miller, and Coors (The Big 3)
Narrow Product Range	*Cost-Focus* Economics unattractive; no viable businesses	*Differentiation-Focus* Imports, micro-brewers, and brew pubs (total share < 5%)

Exhibit 5.9 Examples of generic strategies for industry followers.

success increases as you match the profile for your selected strategy. For example, disaster is likely if you use the tight controls appro-priate for a low-cost strategy in implementing a differentiation strategy.

Differentiation-Focus Strategy

Differentiation-focus basically seeks a monopoly in an exclusive product niche—either a new product for which there are no competitors or an existing product or service that is so different that the targeted customer is not price sensitive. The latter could be luxury goods, such as high-end jewelry or luxury automobiles. It could also be small-ticket pleasures, such as highly focused magazines, movies, and records.

Appropriate for truly superior, unusual, or proprietary products and services, this strategy requires a profound understanding and anticipation of customer wants. Your R&D and marketing people should be constantly and eagerly interacting with end-users. Internally, there must be a close linkage of the R&D, engineering, and marketing functions in the product development process. You should consider using task-oriented project teams with participants from each of these functions.

Be aware that big successes with this strategy attract competition. Your task, then, is to anticipate and lead the industry in the evolving competitive environment, so that you are alert to competitive realities and avoid such failures as IBM's loss of dominance in

Generic Strategy		Costs	Promotion	Prices	Packaging	Distribution
Broad Market	**Low-Cost**	Critically important	Minimal	Critically important	Relatively unimportant	Minimize logistics costs
	Differentiation	Somewhat important	Critically important; build brand equity	Low price can hurt image	Critically important	Must reinforce differentiation
Focus	**Low-Cost**	Important	Very clear positioning in people's minds . . . so don't need to do a lot of advertising	Important	Relatively unimportant	Minimze logistics costs
	Differentiation	Relatively unimportant		Relatively unimportant	Critically important	Strategy sometimes increases logistics cost
Sales		Somewhat important	Highly targeted; expensive per call	Not too price sensitive	Critically important	Critically important

Exhibit 5.10 Marketing profiles for generic strategies.

Generic Strategy	Skill and Resource Requirements	Organizational Requirements
Focus-differentiation	• Strong R&D and product engineering • Understanding underlying consumer wants	• Strong coordination among R&D, engineering, marketing, operations • Subjective measurement and incentives
Differentiation	• Strong marketing and creativity • Reputation for quality • Strong distribution channel	• Able to attract strong marketing people • Able to anticipate market changes • Intense commitment to core values
Low-cost	• Low-cost production and distribution • Sustained capital investment • Process engineering skills • Intense labor supervision	• Tight cost controls and control reports • Structured organization and responsibilities • Incentives based on meeting quantitative targets
Cost-focus	Same as "low-cost" but directed to the specific target market	Same as "low-cost" but directed to the specific target market
Sales	Strong sales and distribution channels	Training and incentive systems

Source: Adapted and reprinted with the permission of The Free Press, an imprint of Simon & Schuster from COMPETITIVE STRATEGY: Techniques for Analyzing Industries and Competitors by Michael E. Porter. Copyright © 1980 by The Free Press.

Exhibit 5.11 Skill, resource and organizational requirements for generic strategies.

the PC market. Clearly, you should protect yourself from competitors through patent protection to the extent you can, but do not come to rely on a protected position. As illustrated by Canon's successful attack on Xerox copiers, it won't last long. Besides, the strongest "protected" position is that of being number one in your market with a thorough commitment to serving customer wants.

Sellers of luxury goods often use a differentiation-focus strategy, but they face their own special problems. One is that luxury products tend to be highly fashion driven—and fashions change frequently. The other is that demographic changes, cultural changes, and other broad social and economic trends can fundamentally change long-term buying patterns. For example, Mercedes Benz initially followed a broad-market differentiation strategy in the United States, using quality and style to differentiate its cars. But Mercedes lost control of costs and moved up to the luxury niche of the auto market. Now, with a major consumer shift away from prestige and toward "value," Mercedes is hurting.

Differentiation Strategy

The differentiation strategy is most appropriate when (1) customer wants are diverse (i.e., there are many ways of meeting their needs) and (2) product attributes, performance, or prestige are more important to buyers than price. Your objective with this strategy is to position your product or service in the broad market as unique. When you do it right, customers are willing to pay a premium that exceeds your costs in providing the uniqueness. This strategy puts you in a more defendable position than does a low-cost strategy; someone can always figure out how to sell something cheaper.

Differentiating your product can be done along several dimensions. *Quality* is an obvious differentiator. Budweiser beer and Coca-Cola, for example, have cultivated an image as high quality. Hewlett-Packard created a unique market position for its calculators not only through quality manufacturing but also through special features. Maytag has built unusual reliability into its appliances, and it has wisely made this the primary message in its advertising for many years. The personal computer wars have been driven partly by the desire for ease of use; Apple leaped ahead of Microsoft DOS-based systems through this aspect of quality, but Microsoft successfully countered with Windows.

Great *customer service* is often the basis of a competitive advantage. Businesses like the Nordstrom department stores and the L.L. Bean mail-order operation have become legendary for their follow-up with customers and other attention to customer service. The Lexus automobile has earned a reputation for service. When Lexus had to recall a certain model for a minor defect, not only did the dealers pick up the cars at the owners' homes and repair them, but they also returned them freshly washed and topped off with gasoline.

Price is a differentiator. Many high-end buyers are willing to pay a premium for the image conferred by a high price. Ralph Lauren's Polo clothes, for example, command premium prices. However, it is important to avoid an excessive price premium. Just ask a Porsche dealer.

Price also contributes to the brand equity of many more ordinary products. If you lower the price of an established brand too much, you can erode image and brand loyalty by creating an impression of cheapness. The growing number of price promotions in the early 1990s has severely undercut loyalty for many brands.

Peripheral services that rely on computer systems have provided huge competitive advantages by differentiating companies from their competitors. American Hospital Supply, now part of Baxter International, obtained dominant or even 100 percent share of supplies at many hospitals. Its computerized supplies-ordering system was easy for hospital employees to use and allowed administrators to reduce working capital by lowering inventories dramatically.

Walgreen pharmacies track drug purchases to alert customers to possible undesired interactions of two or more drugs. American Airlines under Robert Crandall has had two mega-successes using peripheral services: the SABRE reservation system and the frequent-flier program.

Most products are differentiated along several dimensions. Both Lexus and Caterpillar are good examples of this. Lexus, now known for its attention to customer service, also appeals because of quality and prestige. Caterpillar not only has dealers everywhere but also provides extraordinary service—spare parts are available within 24 hours.

Successful implementation of a differentiation strategy requires an intense commitment to core values and superb execution throughout the organization, from manufacturing to marketing. The perception of superiority must be based on reality. A great product can fail due to poor marketing, but it's rare that a truly shabby product can be made a success through great marketing.

An important part of differentiation strategy since the 1970s has been *product proliferation*. This is especially important as a market approaches saturation or as patent protection is about to expire. By moving into niches on your flanks through several highly targeted marketing strategies, you reduce the chances for competitors to establish strong positions.

Low-Cost Strategy

Whether you pursue the broad market or a niche, implementing a low-cost strategy is basically the same for each. A company that adopts this strategy is usually one of two types—very weak or really strong. Companies too weak to compete on product quality are forced to minimize all costs and sell on price alone. Their role is to "harvest" and give up share. Sometimes this can be a very profitable near-term strategy. When Paul Kalmanowitz acquired Falstaff and Lucky Lager beers, sales continued to fall, but he created solid margins by eliminating virtually all administrative and marketing overhead.

A low-cost strategy can also be the best for an industry leader, depending on the industry life cycle and competitive environment. Leaders should consider a low-cost strategy in four cases:

1. When product differences are so small that a differentiation strategy is not possible. This is the case with commodity industries.

2. When a price war will shake out weak competitors, consolidate the industry, and perhaps expand the market at the same time.

3. For high-tech industries in which costs often decline by 15 to 30 percent each time cumulative volume doubles. Hence, market share leaders in new industries with high growth (such as PCs

and semiconductors) often have significantly lower costs than competitors.

4. When economies of scale are large. Unit costs for capital-intensive manufacturing firms typically decrease 20 or 30 percent as annual volume doubles. Similarly, a local supermarket chain's costs decline with volume since the costs of advertising, purchasing, managers, and stores are fixed and become spread over the higher volume.

The low-cost strategy in the last two cases allows you to hold prices down, which increases sales and leads to still lower costs. This feedback system leads to a significant competitive advantage.

McDonald's and other fast-food restaurants have followed a low-cost strategy since the 1950s, replacing local "Ma and Pa" restaurants. Wal-Mart has used this strategy for 25 years against "Main Street" retailers to consolidate the market.

If you are the market leader who moves to a low-cost strategy to shake out marginal competitors, be sure the timing is right. Do it only in early maturity. By late maturity, most competitors will have developed the financial strength to survive an attempted shakeout. A price war then would only cause everyone to suffer, including you.

Be careful that your low-cost strategy does not turn into a "low-quality" strategy. That way, you would be differentiating yourself from your competitors on their higher quality, thus giving them an opportunity to take market share from you. Companies like Wal-Mart show that low cost does not imply cheap, shoddy products or services. But a low-cost strategy does imply a company-wide obsession with continuous cost reduction and Total Quality Management.

CONCLUSION

The proper generic strategy gives you a defendable position and competitive advantage. Getting it right requires two things: First, the strategy must be consistent with the external environment—the climate and competitive forces—and with the product or industry life cycle. Second, be alert to change. No strategy is forever—and you must be able to anticipate change and adapt your strategy as necessary. The Four-Cycle Strategy Planning Process gives that control. Through a new Cycle 1 every three to ten years, you can respond to major shifts in forces or to a new PLC stage. In addition, Cycle 2 annual planning allows gradual adaptation to smaller external changes. It also allows you to seize "strategic window" opportunities when they present themselves.

Finally, don't be "stuck in the middle." Make sure that everyone in your company understands your generic strategy and acts consistently with the strategy. The right generic strategy for the times helps give you the power to beat competitors in meeting customer wants.

6

MEETING CUSTOMER WANTS
Customer-Driven Strategy

Consider the Mustang. Introduced in April 1964, it quickly became Ford Motor Company's most successful car since the Model A. That was no accident. The Mustang was the product of a superb customer-driven strategy.

Appointed Ford Division general manager in 1960, Lee Iacocca and his hand-picked group of "bright and creative young guys" saw that "the car market would be stood on its ear in the next few years." His instincts and market research convinced Iacocca that there was a new market emerging, one based on the growing "economic power of the younger generation."[1]

What Iacocca and his team saw coming was the front end of the post–World War II "Baby Boom" that would dramatically change so many facets of American life. Demographic data confirmed that the following would happen during the 1960s:

- The 20–24-year-old age group would increase by 50 percent.

- Young adults (18–34) would account for at least half the increase in auto sales.

- The number of college students, who wanted fun but inexpensive transportation, would double.

Additional research confirmed the existence of a trend toward a youthful market for cars. Consumers had been moving away from larger, more functional cars toward smaller, sportier models. There was an enormous growth in two-car families, whose second car tended to be more "youthful" and less utilitarian than the first. Women and singles, who also preferred sportier cars, were growing as a proportion of the car-buying public.

This and other information led Iacocca and his "bright young guys" to envision a very special car, one designed to meet the wants of this emerging market. As Iacocca saw it: "Any car that would appeal to these young customers had to have three main features: great styling, strong performance, and a low price."[2] The Mustang team considered the wants of their customers during every step of development, and they researched the market right up to the launch of the car. As a final preintroduction test, they invited 52 Detroit-area couples into their styling showroom to get their impressions. This test confirmed that the Mustang was a winner, and 418,812 Mustangs were sold during the first year—more than any Ford car in an introductory year since the Model A.

But success didn't last. Sales grew to 550,000 in 1966, and then plummeted to 150,000 in 1970. "Our customers had abandoned us because we had abandoned their car," Iacocca says. "The Mustang was no longer a sleek horse. It was more of a fat pig."[3] By 1970, the small, sporty, youthful Mustang had been redesigned into a different vehicle—twice as powerful, eight inches longer, six inches wider, 25 percent heavier, and 40 percent more expensive. The Ford people had stopped listening to the customer. They had lapsed into the traditional Detroit mentality, which had an unwritten rule that an established car could only be made bigger—never smaller.

Do you know your customers' wants? Do you have products that satisfy those wants? Do you continuously strive to increase your customers' level of satisfaction?

The answers to those questions are at the heart of customer-driven strategy. You first have to know who your customers are and what they want. Next, you have to develop products and a marketing program that precisely meet those wants. And then you have to keep doing the first two steps better and better so that you continuously improve customer satisfaction. Iacocca was brilliant in executing the first two. He admits Ford failed on the third.

Successful customer-driven strategy allows you to do all three well. That's the focus of this chapter, which covers the following subjects:

- Fragmentation of the mass market.
- Segmentation—knowing your customers and their wants.
- Positioning—finding the precise way of satisfying those wants.
- Continuous improvement of customer satisfaction.

EMERGENCE OF THE MODERN MARKETING SYSTEM

Segmentation and positioning are standard and universal marketing procedures today, but the concepts are only 40 and 20 years old, respectively. They are natural responses to a fundamental transformation of the market at midcentury.

The industrial, transportation, and communications revolutions of the nineteenth century had created a *mass market* that dominated the first half of the twentieth century. Industrial advances made possible mass-produced standardized products that could meet large-scale human needs. The same forces also fueled urbanization and the growth of a large middle class with buying power. The transportation revolution and the rise of mass media broke down local and regional boundaries and even brought the "hinterlands" into the new mass market. Witness the Sears and Roebuck catalog, which in 1896 began to bring to farm families the same products available to their city cousins.[4]

Mass production for a mass market permitted great reductions in manufacturing costs and increases in efficiency. This led to lower prices, which brought even more people into the market and continued to raise the general standard of living. World War II and its aftermath accelerated this process. The release of a huge pent-up demand at the end of the war brought the mass market to its fullest development. As fast as companies could produce, customers bought. The concept of the mass market guided business, and ever more efficient manufacturing drove it.

Marketing as it is thought of today was little known and largely unneeded. Most CEOs devised strategy by applying experience and judgment to a basic analysis of sales and profit performance. Or they simply copied the competition. The typical marketing system, such as it was, looked something like that illustrated in Exhibit 6.1. It was adequate to the needs of a business leader like Henry Ford. Along with most of his fellow CEOs, Ford devoted his time and energies to financial considerations and to improvements in the production process.

Around 1970, the mass market began to fragment. Markets had grown to a size where little was left to be gained from economies of scale. New production techniques made it possible to produce a greater diversity of products at low cost, thus lowering prices and increasing the demand for custom products. Higher education levels and increased affluence created choosier customers who demanded greater variety. Finally, the walls of once-stable national or regional markets were breached by global competitors willing and able to offer consumers virtually any product they desired at high quality and a low price. The mass market was dead.

Businesses responded with a much more complex and demanding marketing system, as shown in Exhibit 6.2. Marketers now offered a range of differentiated products to targeted homogeneous segments. The orientation of top management shifted away from

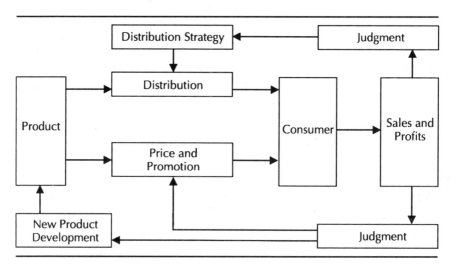

Exhibit 6.1 The marketing system based on judgment.

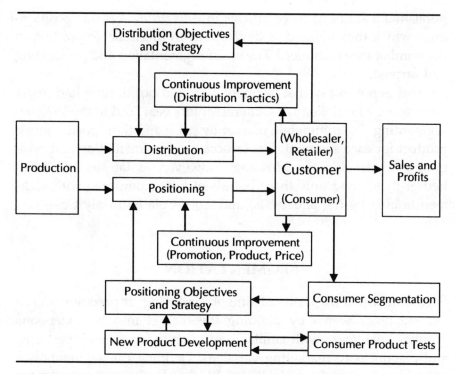

Exhibit 6.2 The marketing system based on segmentation and positioning.

production and finance to the marketplace—to satisfying the wants of customers.

Individual judgment was no longer adequate. Marketing strategy and tactics now required sophisticated analysis of large quantities of data—not only sales data but consumer surveys, demographic data, product tests, advertising experiments, and more. To gather and analyze these data, companies hired large staffs expert in sophisticated analytical techniques. Hence, the proliferation of MBAs and consulting firms.

The modern marketing system is based on *segmentation* and *positioning*. By the late 1950s, "segmentation" had emerged as a marketing concept that helped businesses divide the market into groups of customers with similar wants so that they could more effectively target their customers. In 1972, Al Ries and Jack Trout published a series of three articles in *Advertising Age* on "positioning," which they defined as developing an unassailable position in the mind of the consumer.[5] The era of segmentation and positioning had arrived.

This is not to say that segmentation and positioning had never been done. Alfred Sloan of General Motors beat Ford in the 1920s by segmenting the automobile market by price and then positioning a product for each segment. Lee Iacocca used segmentation and positioning to develop the Mustang. However, as late as 1976, Anheuser-Busch had only three brands of beer (compared with eighteen brands by the late 1980s) and Coca-Cola had only Coke and Tab.

SEGMENTATION

Segmentation is the demand side of marketing. It precisely identifies customer wants by dividing the market into homogeneous groups—customers with similar wants, attitudes, buying patterns, and responses to marketing variables. Defining the segments is a critical process, and a difficult one. It's the classic problem of taxonomy—classifying "like" with "like." If you group all two-legged animals together, ostriches, apes, and corporate executives all belong in the same category. For most purposes, that classification will have somewhat limited usefulness. It's not hard to find a classification in which everyone is alike in some respects. The trick is to find a classification that is useful. Poorly done market segmentation in effect creates random classifications. You're worse off than you were before you started.

Requirements of Good Segments

To be useful, a segment must meet certain requirements, shown in Exhibit 6.3. First, customers that make up the segment must be *identifiable*. That was one of the problems with earlier attempts to segment by personality types.

Second, a segment must be *accessible*. If the customers are dispersed geographically, they'll be harder to reach than those that live close together. Their media habits will have a lot to do with how

Requirements	Explanation
Identifiable	Able to be classified into segments (difficult with some personality theories)
Accessible	Able to be reached efficiently using media or sales people
Substantial	Offer adequate sales and profit potential
Homogeneous	Similar in wants, behavior, and responses to marketing stimuli (the four Ps)
Distinctive	Differ in wants from other segments

Exhibit 6.3 Requirements of good segments.

accessible they are. For instance, if you are trying to reach cardiologists, you'll pay less to reach more of them if they have a specialized journal, compared with an effort to reach them through a general publication that goes to all physicians.

A segment must be *substantial.* Don't define your target market so narrowly that you will need a 500 percent market share to break even.

A segment must be *homogeneous.* Consumers in each segment should be similar in wants, behavior, and responses to marketing stimuli—the four Ps of Product, Price, Place (distribution), and Promotion (advertising). If the segment is not homogeneous, you will have to make compromises in developing the four Ps, which will increase costs and lower the effectiveness of your marketing efforts.

Finally, a segment must be *distinctive.* It must be different enough from other groups to require meaningful differences in strategy.

Customer Characteristics for Segmentation

Marketers have used a variety of categories to identify customer segments, ranging from readily available industry classifications and demographic characteristics to personality types. A time-honored approach is copying the competition, based on the assumption that your competitor's customers are also your customers. This is not a good approach. It inevitably makes you a follower. It's appropriate only for a low-market-share competitor with a low-price strategy.

Another traditional basis of segmentation is price, which General Motors used successfully against Ford in the 1920s. The Edsel, however, became a classic flop by segmenting only on price. There were already seven other competitors in the same midprice category, and Edsel had nothing to differentiate it. Mustang, as you have seen, avoided this trap. American beers segmented only on price for years, until Miller Brewing introduced a different type of beer, Miller Lite, in the early 1970s.

Other, more useful analytical classifications are shown in Exhibit 6.4. This exhibit also makes a critical distinction between *identifiers* and *behaviors*. Marketers frequently use identifiers, such as gender/

Identifiers	Behaviors
Industrial Markets:	• Benefits sought or derived from the product
• Industry (SIC code)	
• Size (sales volume, number of employees)	• Product application or use occasions
• Profitability, growth, industry position	• Purchase behavior and loyalty: – Channel used – Volume and frequency of purchase – Switching among brands – Readiness to buy
• Geography (country)	
Consumer Markets:	
• Demographics (age, sex, race, religion, family size)	
• Socioeconomic factors (income, occupation, education)	
• Psychographics (lifestyles, interests)	
• Media habits	
• Geography (country; urban, rural)	

Source: Adapted and reprinted with the permission of The Free Press, an imprint of Simon & Schuster from MARKET DRIVEN STRATEGY by George S. Day. Copyright © 1990 by The Free Press.

Exhibit 6.4 Customer characteristics for segmentation.

age groups (e.g., males 18–34 years old), partly because their use has become conventional and partly because the data are readily available. However, their use can actually make targeting more difficult. For instance, segmenting an industrial product on four SIC codes, three customer sizes, and five geographic locations does not create a homogeneous segment but instead 60 segments that are not substantial, homogeneous, or distinctive. Identifiers are extremely useful for reaching customers once you have targeted them, but they should not drive your classifications.

Far better are the behavior classifications. After all, it's behavior you're after. Customers purchase not because they happen to be male or 21 years old, but because they seek specific benefits. You want to identify the target group and then match your products to their wants so they will buy your products. Once you've identified those that will buy, then for accessibility it is valuable that they also fit into a demographic, socioeconomic, or some other identifier group.

A *use-occasion* classification is defined by the manner in which a product or service is used. For instance, within the larger category of shippers of parcels, letters, and documents is a subcategory of those who want rapid delivery. Thus, Federal Express targeted this segment and positioned its service to meet their key need: "If it absolutely, positively has to be there overnight. . . ."

Among beer drinkers there is a segment of more affluent drinkers who tend to buy beer for special occasions such as social entertaining. Anheuser-Busch successfully targeted this segment for its super-premium beer Michelob: "Weekends were made for Michelob." When it tried also to go after the masses of regular beer drinkers through more convenient cans, price promotions, and the slogan "Put a little weekend in your week," sales declined, even among its original consumers. The new campaign made its positioning fuzzy in everyone's mind.

Purchase behavior segmentation is based on such variables as the distribution channel used, frequency of purchase, brand loyalty, and readiness to buy. ABB Electric had great success with a customer-driven strategy, the core of which was segmentation based on two of the purchase behaviors—about to make major purchases and not loyal to any one manufacturer. By focusing its transformer sales efforts here, and not on those who were already loyal to ABB Electric or to some other manufacturer, it greatly increased sales success. Even as a new competitor going against giants like GE, Westinghouse, and McGraw-Edison, ABB Electric raised market share from 6 percent to 40 percent over a 14-year period.[6]

Purchase behavior has become increasingly easy to track with modern techniques and technologies, such as bar-code scanners. Retailers and consumer products companies increasingly rely on these for segmentation and marketing strategies.

Another way to use purchase behavior to identify and reach customers is to use a "geodemographic" system. The PRIZM system, for instance, has used large quantities of demographic data, primarily from census data, to identify 40 "lifestyles" clusters, which have been given such vivid names as "Pools and Patios," "Gray Power," "Blue-Collar Nursery," and "Shotguns and Pickups."[7]

Each of the 250,000 "census block groups" in the United States has been classified into one or another of these lifestyle segments. Because census block groups are subdivisions of postal ZIP codes, you can also determine the lifestyle composition of each ZIP code. This knowledge of ZIP code lifestyles allows selective and targeted advertising and direct mail campaigns. For instance, national magazines like *Newsweek* and *Time* ship different editions with different advertisements to different ZIP codes. Editions with luxury car advertisements go to "Blue Blood Estates" but not to "Norma Rae-Ville."

You can identify purchase-behavior segments and their locations by doing a small-scale test-market mailing to all 40 lifestyle clusters. Then, by analyzing the sales response, you can determine the five or ten PRIZM segments for future mailings.

Of the behavior classifications, *benefits-sought* works particularly well. "For strategic relevance," writes George Day, "there is no other variable that is as revealing as the benefits the customers are seeking from the product or service."[8] All other variables, both identifiers and behaviors, are retrospective and inferential. They are retrospective in that membership in a class depends on previously defined categories or previously observed behaviors. They are inferential in that you must assume from their membership in a demographic class, for example, that they want your product.

With a benefits-sought group, you *directly* ask the consumers what their current and future wants are. There's no guesswork based on group membership or past behavior. This strength of a benefits-sought group, however, is also its major drawback. Getting the special data you need costs considerably more than the readily available industry data you can use for other variables.

Benefits-sought is usually inappropriate for segmenting image products such as soda and cigarettes. Consumers are often unable or unwilling to discuss their wants for such products accurately.

Targeting Segments

Once you've defined segments that are identifiable, accessible, substantial, homogeneous, and distinctive, you need to rank them in order of their attractiveness and your competitive position in them.

To be attractive, a segment must offer adequate sales and profit potential to make targeting it worth your while. You need to look at each segment for its size, rate of growth, and the profit margins you can command. It must also be accessible through a reasonable mix of the four marketing Ps.

You should go after only segments where you can compete. Don't target an otherwise attractive segment that is firmly dominated by a strong competitor. As discussed in the next chapter, assaulting an industry leader head on is generally disastrous. Before you target a new segment, take a look at the current level of customer satisfaction with existing products. If satisfaction is low, you have an opportunity. If high, someone else probably already "owns" that segment, and you will have a difficult time becoming competitive.

Obviously, you do not want to go after segments where you won't make money. Target those where you will make the greatest return on your marketing investment. The number of segments you target also depends on your industry position. If you are the industry leader, you will want to cover nearly all segments in order to defend your leadership position and discourage potential competitors from gaining a foothold on your flanks. If you are a follower, you should move into only those attractive and accessible segments not now occupied or well defended by a competitor.

POSITIONING

Positioning is the supply side of marketing. A fundamental belief of marketing is that you will achieve a dominant market share if you meet customer wants better than competitors. Segmentation divides the total market into large groups with similar wants. Positioning allows you to precisely meet the wants of each segment by using the four Ps of marketing.

Perceptual Maps

An extraordinarily powerful positioning tool is the perceptual map, which was discussed briefly in Chapter 2. Perceptual maps can tell you what the market looks like *as your customers perceive it*. Hence, you can locate yourself and your competitors in the current market, and you can detect opportunities for positioning yourself to meet unfulfilled customer wants.

Research-Based Perceptual Maps

To understand the explanatory power of a perceptual map, let's look at Exhibit 6.5. This is a *research-based* perceptual map. It was developed by asking a group of consumers to grade their city's seven hospitals according to how well each performed on a list of 16

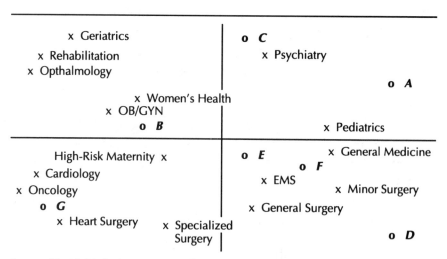

Source: *Health Marketing News,* Market Opinion Research, Detroit, Mich., Fall 1988.

Exhibit 6.5 A perceptual map of 7 hospitals and 16 hospital services.

healthcare services. The statistical sorting and correlation behind such a map can be complicated; you'll probably want to farm that process out to professional market researchers and statisticians.[9] But the result—the perceptual map—is a marvelously clear and revealing picture of how customers view the market. This one shows the following:

1. Certain niches are dominated. Hospital C controls the psychiatric segment, B the women's health segment, and G the specialized, higher risk surgery segment. These hospitals should focus on serving these segments so well that potential competitors detect little opportunity.

2. Hospitals E and F are "community hospitals." If they are geographically close and thus competing for the same customers, they might consider merging. That way, they can maximize economies of scale and eliminate duplication.

3. Hospitals A and D are weak and have no unique strengths. If they cannot find new segments where they have something special to offer, they remain vulnerable and a source of market share for the others.

4. In the areas of geriatrics, rehabilitation, and ophthalmology, no one has a strong position. These are "opportunity" segments. Hospitals A and D should consider targeting one of these segments.

Typically, a perceptual map "locates" customer wants and products, services, or suppliers on a two-dimensional space. Unless you have predefined the axes in your customer survey, the statistical analysis does not tell you what the x-axis or the y-axis means. The identification of these dimensions is left to you, based on the information gathered in the study and your own knowledge of the market. In the example in Exhibit 6.5, the x-axis appears to run from "specialties" to "general medicine" and the y-axis from "surgical/physical care" to "mental/psychological care."

Judgment-Based Perceptual Maps

This hospital example is just one kind of perceptual map, one based on hard research data. Another is the *judgment-based* perceptual map. A judgmental map is simply one that is based on your own extensive knowledge and understanding of your market. Quite obviously, you cannot have the same degree of confidence in a judgmental map that you can in a research-based map. But judgmental perceptual maps can be a powerful tool for a variety of positioning issues.

The experience of Office Pavilion, a Herman Miller office furniture dealer in St. Louis, shows the value of a judgmental perceptual map. Herman Miller had a unique capability in highly flexible modular work stations. Modular flexibility was its strength, providing the greatest value, distinguishing it from the competition, and returning the greatest unit profits.

Previously, Office Pavilion had followed a product-driven strategy, perceiving its customers to be on a one-dimensional continuum that precisely paralleled its product strength, as shown in Exhibit 6.6.

With this view of the market, it seemed logical that its strategy should be to convert customers over time from being lowest-cost commodity buyers (Category 3) into buyers willing to pay for style and quality (Category 2), and to convert those in turn into buyers willing to pay for flexibility in addition to style and quality (Category 1). This segmentation and positioning scheme simply did not produce the results envisioned. Office Pavilion had been trying without much success to move middle- and senior-management consumers in Category 2 (quality and style) to Category 1 (quality and style *plus* flexibility). They developed a perceptual map, shown in Exhibit 6.7, which helped them see that their old segmentation scheme did not reflect actual benefits sought. Modular flexibility is valuable for

	Description
Category 1	Customers willing to pay for both style and quality and flexibility
Category 2	Customers willing to pay for style and quality but not for flexibility
Category 3	Commodity buyers who are unwilling to pay for either style and quality or flexibility

Exhibit 6.6   Segmentation scheme for office furniture dealer before perceptual map.

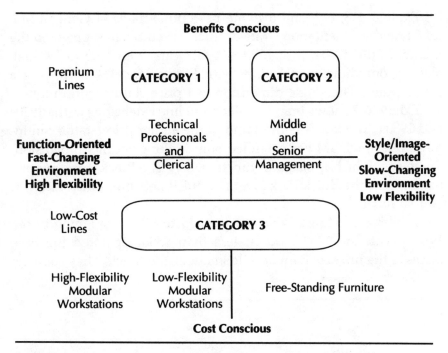

Exhibit 6.7   A perceptual map for office furniture dealer.

technical professionals but not for management. Office Pavilion has now redefined customer segments and refocused efforts and resources where they are most effective. They no longer try to move Category 2 customers up to Category 1.

Perceptual Maps and Line Extensions

Judgmental perceptual maps are also useful for resolving the thorny issue of line extensions. Some people argue that you should never resort to line extensions. They believe a line extension almost always erodes the parent brand's market position.[10] But the fact is, many companies have had success with line extensions—Coke and Diet Coke, for example, or Budweiser and Bud Light. The most successful automobile makers have long used line extensions.

When using perceptual maps to position brands and line extensions, you should locate brand families along the most important customer dimension, the x-axis. Line extensions within each brand family should then be positioned along the secondary dimension, the y-axis.

Exhibits 6.8, 6.9, and 6.10 are perceptual maps of General Motors' brand segmentation strategy since Alfred Sloan segmented the market in the 1920s. In Exhibit 6.8, GM cars from 1923 to 1973 fall along a one-dimensional map, with Ford's Model T occupying a single point. The single dimension is a price/status continuum.

Exhibit 6.9 shows brand families and line extensions in the 1970s and 1980s. The x-axis is the same as the earlier price/status continuum. But now, GM has extended brands along another dimension, the y-axis, which is size and functionality. The Buick, for example, has become the Buick Park Avenue, Buick LeSabre, Buick Skylark, and so forth.[11]

Exhibit 6.10 shows what's happened to GM positioning in the 1990s. With the 1993 models, less than $500 separated the base prices of the full-size Pontiac, Oldsmobile, and Buick. They compete

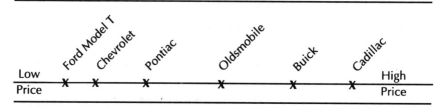

Exhibit 6.8   Original price segmentation of GM.

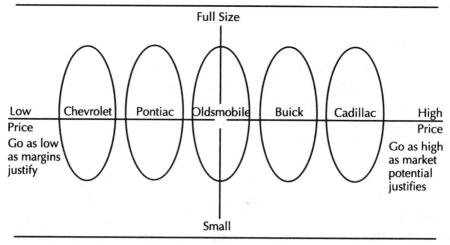

Exhibit 6.9   Brand family segmentation of GM.

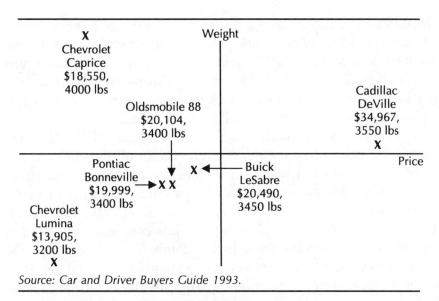

Source: *Car and Driver Buyers Guide 1993.*

Exhibit 6.10 Base price of 1993 full-size General Motors cars.

against each other and leave a huge hole in the market wide open for competitors. They incur all of the production and marketing costs for different car lines without the benefits of effective segmentation and positioning.

A similar judgmental perceptual map showing brand-family positioning strategy can be developed for other industries. In the beer industry, for example, Anheuser-Busch has positioned the Natural, Busch, Budweiser, and Michelob brand families along the x-axis (price and status) and, for example, Budweiser, Bud Dry, and Bud Light along the y-axis (taste and body). The beer industry is also in danger of copying GM's positioning mistake of targeting all brands to the same segment. Nearly all beer advertising appears to target 20-something males.

CONTINUOUS IMPROVEMENT OF CUSTOMER SATISFACTION

Customer-driven strategy doesn't stop with segmentation and positioning. In fact, they're just the beginning. The end is customer satisfaction. That's what delivers results. A winning customer-driven strategy depends on a devotion to continuous improvement of customer satisfaction. Thus, you need some sort of program for tracking customer satisfaction and buying behavior. Without it, you won't know if your strategy is working. Moreover, the customer-driven strategy you developed several years ago may have become as irrelevant today as it was brilliant back then.

You have to start with what customers really want. Use customer research to find the relative importance of their 10 to 50 key wants. Then track how well you are meeting those wants compared with your leading competitors. It's important that you use quantitative measurements so that you minimize subjectivity. Every company believes it is the high-quality, low-cost supplier—until it quantitatively compares itself to the competition. Make sure the customer satisfaction system leads to constant incremental improvement. Involve your entire organization. Provide performance feedback to everyone. Assign responsibility. Work with your managers to reach agreement on customer satisfaction objectives. Give them authority. Have them develop action programs that will achieve these objectives. Finally, reward performance. Tie pay, promotion, recognition, and noncash awards to attainment of objectives.

One of the best systems for driving continuous improvement of customer satisfaction is the Maritz "Performance Improvement Planner,"[12] developed by Maritz Inc. of St. Louis.

With this system, you first compile a list of all the attributes that influence customer satisfaction, such as price, after-sale service, courtesy of the sales force, and convenience of locations. Next, you derive the following information from customers about each attribute: (1) How *important* is this attribute to you? and (2) How *satisfied* are you with our performance on this attribute? The results are plotted on a matrix shown in Exhibit 6.11.

The objective is to increase satisfaction with your company's performance on those attributes customers consider important. If an attribute is high in importance and your customers are highly satisfied (Quadrant B), then it's a critical strength you must maintain. You may not need to invest more in it, but be sure to support it at its current level. If, however, customers are dissatisfied with your performance on an important attribute (Quadrant A), you are vulnerable to a competitor who does this better than you. The attribute is an "opportunity" that needs urgent attention.

High ↑ Importance Rating ↓ Low	A **Opportunity/Problem Area** (high importance; low satisfaction)	**Current Strengths** B (high importance; high satisfaction)
	D **Nonpositioning Factors** (low importance; low satisfaction)	**Unnecessary Strengths** C (low importance; high satisfaction)
	Low ◄———————— **Satisfaction** ————————► High	

Exhibit 6.11 The Maritz Importance/Satisfaction grid.

If an attribute is not important to customers, you should use few resources supporting it. Since customers don't really care about it, a low level of satisfaction (Quadrant D) shouldn't be important to you. If customers are highly satisfied with an unimportant attribute (Quadrant C), you could safely move some of the resources you expend here to help improve performance on attributes in Quadrant A. But, be careful. Sometimes customers elevate the importance of an attribute in their own minds if they see too much or too quick an erosion of performance. Moreover, they might see slippage on that attribute as a reflection of a general decline in performance that affects other attributes they consider more important. Seek "excellence" on the key measures and "acceptable" on the unimportant measures.

With this analysis in hand, the Maritz customer satisfaction program proceeds as follows:

Step 1. Determine the relative importance of key customer wants.

Step 2. Track your performance on each key want compared with your competitors' performance. This quantitative measure is critical to objectivity.

Step 3. Assign responsibility for improving each dimension. If no one is accountable, no one will make it happen.

Step 4. Develop quantitative goals, a timetable for achievement, action plans, and a budget. This creates top-down and bottom-up commitment and agreement on a plan for improvement.

Step 5. Track performance versus plan and reward accordingly.

Steps 3, 4, and 5 are discussed in more detail in Chapter 9.

The key to the satisfaction of final consumers often lies in superior performance by your distributors, store managers, sales people, and other employees. Maritz has also developed the Excellence® System for continuous improvement of the performance of these key groups.

The Excellence® process has both strong similarities to and important differences from the Performance Improvement Planner. The difference is that the Excellence® criteria are designed by your 15 or 20 most outstanding store managers (or sales people or distributors). They first identify the 25 to 50 "Keys to Excellence" ("Best Practices") and then determine the relative importance of each by allocating 1,000 possible total points. The most important element, for instance, may have a maximum of 75 points, the next most important 60 points, the next 50 points, and so on. Then, within its maximum number of points, each element is rated by level of performance. The most important element, with its maximum of 75 points, may have 75 for excellent, 50 for good, and only 25 for adequate performance.

In a traditional sales contest, participants compete against each other and only a limited number can win, say, a trip to the Caribbean, for example. With the Excellence® program, the participants compete only against themselves according to a set of objective standards. For example, they may receive bronze, silver, or gold awards if they receive over 500, 650, or 800 points. They can still earn awards, such as the Caribbean vacation, but now everybody is a potential winner. And if they win, you win.

Continuous improvement of customer satisfaction is the final step in effective customer-driven strategy. Quantitatively measured and verified, a continuous improvement program keeps customer-driven strategy fresh and relevant.

CONCLUSION

The mass market fragmented and new forces such as global competition emerged in the 1970s and 1980s. Many American and European businesses found themselves unable to compete effectively in this strange new world. CEOs scrambled to put their companies into competitive shape, relying on business definition and financial strategies as the keys to success. Business definition helped liberate them from the conglomerate bondage of the 1960s and allowed them to focus instead on attractive SBUs with strong positions in their industries. Financial strategies revitalized many reactive companies and killed off others that wouldn't or couldn't become competitive.

The era of redefinition and financial restructuring is largely over. In the 1990s, the key to business success is customer- and competitor-driven strategy—strategy that allows you to beat competitors in meeting customer wants.

Meeting customer wants is ultimately the only reason businesses exist. Doing it successfully requires at least the following:

- Profound knowledge of your customers.

- Accurate segmentation of your market and proper positioning of your products and company in the market.

- An effective marketing mix to create value for your customers.

- A continuous improvement process to track and increase customer satisfaction.

Meeting customer wants better than competitors is the reason for a customer-driven strategy and is critical for winning in the competitive world of the 1990s. Once you get your customer-driven strategy right, you should then worry about your competitors. It's not enough for you to have great products. Customers must also believe your products provide greater value than competitive products. So if you are not worrying about your competitors, you had better start now. That's the subject of the next chapter.

7

WAR AND PEACE
Competitor-Driven Strategy

In the 1990s, a customer-driven strategy is necessary. But that's no longer enough. You also have to do a better job than your competitors of satisfying your customers. It's necessary to be both customer driven *and* competitor driven. Your business strategy must also take into account the market positions and strategies of your competitors.

GE, RCA, and Xerox learned this the hard way, at a cost of hundreds of millions of dollars each, when they took on IBM in the mainframe computer market in the late 1960s.[1]

Each of these companies developed excellent mainframe computers that did exactly what potential customers wanted them to do. But customers didn't buy them. The problem wasn't with the products. It was with these upstarts' insensitivity to the strategic advantage IBM had with its undisputed leadership position in the mainframe marketplace. Customers simply refused to take a risk with a "me-too" product made by someone else.

These challengers to IBM needed a competitor-driven strategy. In fact, they had one—a frontal attack—but they came upon it by default. If they had gone through a careful competitive strategy development process, they would have realized the futility of a frontal assault on IBM's position. They would have found another way to enter the computer market.

Which is just what Digital Equipment, Apple Computer, and Sun Microsystems did. Each of them broke into the computer market successfully, but not by going head-on against giant IBM. They respected IBM's unassailable position in mainframes, so they adopted flank-attack strategies to create new market segments— Digital in minicomputers, Apple in personal computers, and Sun in work stations.

Your strategy, then, must take your competitors into account. This chapter presents strategy options you can use for different competitive situations:

- Strategies for current business "wars."
- Long-term strategies to gain industry leadership.
- Win-win strategies for a mature industry.

THE BASICS OF BUSINESS WARFARE

During the last decade or so, business or marketing "warfare" has become a familiar concept. A string of pundits has applied military principles, strategies, and tactics developed by the great generals and military strategists of the past 3,000 years to business competition.[2]

Obviously, the battlefield, the enemy, and the weapons of military conflict differ from those of business competition, but it's remarkable the degree to which similar strategies lead to similar outcomes—victory or defeat.

The concept of business warfare provides a framework for determining how every competitive business or organization can obtain competitive advantage. But be careful not to carry the warfare metaphor too far. Competition among businesses, like competition among nations, does not always mean a state of war. There is peace maintained by diplomacy; there are "cold" wars and "hot" wars.

War and Peace

Success in business competition springs less from a theory of war than it does from a theory of war *and* peace. War in the short term is less profitable than peace and should not be an end in itself. The most successful military strategists have long said the same thing. More than 2,500 years ago, the Chinese general and strategist Sun Tzu said: "To win without fighting is best."

In this century, Sir Basil Liddell Hart put it this way: "The object in war is to achieve a better state of peace." In business, the "better state of peace" is increased long-term profitability, and that, not the defeat of your competitor, is the object of business warfare.

Thus, you should undertake war only for longer-term strategic reasons, with peace as your objective and peaceful competition the expected norm.

The Principles of War

Over the centuries, professional military strategists have developed universal and essential principles of warfare.[3]

1. *The objective.* The objective must be a clear, conclusive, and obtainable result. Otherwise, there is no basis for going to war. Likewise for a company, the objective must be big enough and profitable enough to risk the struggle. Your company's mission statement must articulate the objective so powerfully that everyone works together to achieve it.

2. *The offense.* Victory requires offensive action. Defensive operations only prevent defeat.

   To reverse a cliché, the best defense is a good offense. Seize the initiative and attack a market segment not well defended by your competitor. If you are a small company, this means dominating a small niche.

3. *Unity of command.* Forces must be under one commander with full authority and responsibility. Napoleon said: "It is better to have one incompetent general than two good ones."

   Clear responsibilities allow everyone to focus on meeting customer wants better than your competitor. The alternative is an internal focus that leads to political infighting.

4. *Mass.* Victory goes to the army with superior forces at the point of contact.

   Focus your attack as narrowly as possible, so you have

superiority at the decisive time and place. Highly targeted competitors have proven the value of this at the expense of mass-market magazines, broadcasters, and retailers.

5. *Economy of force.* Allocate only the essential minimum of forces to areas of secondary importance.

   For business, this means keeping costs at a minimum while allocating resources where they will be most effective. Otherwise, "lean and mean" competitors will exploit your high costs and correspondingly high prices.

6. *Maneuver.* Forces must be deployed so they come together in the right place at the right time.

   In business, this means integrating the four Ps of marketing and all other tactics so they work together smoothly.

7. *Surprise.* If you strike your enemy at a time or place or in a way it does not expect, you can often win your objective before the enemy even reacts.

   Speed to market and quick response systems are key sources of competitive advantage for many companies today.

8. *Security.* Surprise cannot exist without security. During war, an army must safeguard its own intentions and plans from the enemy.

   In business, security for the market leader means providing superior customer value and aggressively countering all competitive challenges. For the small company, it means keeping your intentions quiet lest they stir the leaders to action.

   Security through strength is also important in preserving peace. Countries seldom attack a strong foe. Similarly, companies seldom enter markets in which a strong competitor is doing an excellent job of meeting customer wants.

9. *Simplicity.* Objectives, strategies, plans, and orders should be clear, concise, and simple. Simplicity keeps forces motivated, focused, and unified.

   Complex business strategies and objectives don't motivate people, and the likelihood of good execution declines with complexity.

10. *Maintenance of morale.* Superior morale compensates for many weaknesses in other areas. All else equal, the force with the higher morale will win the war.

    Employees who are well led and who understand the company's objectives and strategies are the most effective.

11. *Administration.* An army must be efficiently supplied and administered so total attention and resources are focused on the battle at hand.

    In business, this means maximum efficiency with minimum structure, for a preoccupation with administration can lead to excessive bureaucracy and "paralysis by analysis."

Taken together, these principles of war can be stated this way: Hit the other guy as quickly as you can, as hard as you can, where it hurts him the most, when he isn't looking.

Defensive and Offensive Strategies

The principles of warfare form the foundation for a variety of strategies, in both military and business warfare.[4] They can be divided into defensive and offensive strategies.

Defensive Strategies

Strategies for the industry leader are defensive. Presented in Exhibits 7.1 and 7.2, defensive strategies are designed to reinforce your market position or to fight off an attacker trying to move in on that position. Keep in mind, however, that "defensive" does not necessarily mean "passive." In the dynamic, volatile, and intensely competitive markets of the 1990s, a leader can't afford to adopt a passive and reactive strategy. At a minimum, the leader should always react quickly and powerfully to major competitive challenges.

Position Defense. This is the "default" defense strategy of those who haven't thought about strategy. It's a passive defense con-

—————— **Twelve Guidelines for Business War** ——————

The 11 principles of war are fundamental. Combining them leads to 12 pragmatic guidelines for waging your competitive battles.

The importance of force. Big fish eat little fish, and big companies eat little companies. As Napoleon said: "God is on the side of big battalions." Economies of scale give the market leader advantages in every dimension. However, making sure that the organization stays focused externally is a challenge that grows with size.

12. *The superiority of the defense.* Both the army behind strong walls and the dominant product have strong advantages. A 1923 survey* identified 25 dominant brands, and only 5 of these brands lost their leadership position in the following 60 years. To be successful, the attacking force should have a superiority of at least three to one at the point of attack. Losing a dominant position indicates poor management.

13. *Frontal assaults seldom work.* This rule, the first law of the offense, follows from the first two. The leading firm has the advantages of the defensive position and usually has more resources in the contested area. Avoid frontal assaults!

14. *The position defense never works—no strategy is forever.* This is the first law of the defense. A competitor can eventually meet consumer wants better than an unchanging leader. The classic business example is Henry Ford staying with his Model T's low-cost strategy too long instead of adopting GM's differentiation strategy.

15. *Launch the attack on a narrow and weakly defended front.* Concentrate your resources where the competitor's

*George H. Hotchkiss and Richard B. Franken, *The Leadership of Advertised Brands* (Garden City, N.Y.: Doubleday, Page & Co, 1923).

(continued)

forces are limited. Have superiority at the point of attack. Make sure that your four Ps meet target segment desires better than do the competitor's. Assign minimal forces to secondary positions. Two-front wars are usually disastrous. An organization's strategy should be focused on one critical objective (Motorola's "Six sigma quality" or Honda's "We will crush, squash, slaughter Yamaha").

6. *Attack a weakness inherent in the leader's strength.* Coca-Cola simply could not respond to 7–Up's "Uncola" campaign and Hertz couldn't respond to Avis's "We're #2 so we try harder" attack.* Leaders can usually respond quickly to lower prices, new products, or new marketing campaigns unless the innovation requires the leader to significantly reduce margins or write off investments in plant, brand equity, or distribution or service systems.

7. *Strategy directs tactics.* Direction and vision must come from the top. All functional strategies and action plans should support and reinforce the overall strategy of the organization.

8. *Strategy follows tactics.* The point of strategy is to achieve success by having tactical superiority at the point of combat.[3] The key tactical weapon in World War II was the tank, and strategy was concerned with having more tanks than the enemy at the point of attack. The key marketing weapon in the 1960s and 1970s was television, but the key weapon today is sales and distribution. A good strategy must come from a deep understanding of what is happening on the battlefield. The senior management team must really know its industry and be close to its customers.

9. *Good strategy can succeed with run-of-the-mill tactics.* If a strategy identifies a valuable target that is weakly de-

*Al Ries and Jack Trout, *Marketing Warfare* (New York: McGraw-Hill, 1986).

(*continued*)

fended and assigns enough resources to the battle to have superiority, victory is likely without brilliant tactics. American Express's losing battle with Visa shows that aggressive sales tactics can't compensate for weak strategy in the value-conscious 1990s.

10. *A business general must be flexible.* The most appropriate strategy depends on your current situation. Generals fail when they use the strategy and tactics of the previous war. Anticipate. As the market changes, your strategy must change as well. Honda's initial U.S. success with motorcycles resulted from allowing its strategy to respond to customers.

11. *A business general must act.* Bold implementation of a good strategy wins. In warfare, there is no time for discussions and compromises. As Ulysses S. Grant said: "In war, anything is better than indecision. We must decide."

12. *Exploit your opportunities.* Examples of "stopping too soon" include the Persian Gulf War and Avis and 7–Up moving away from their "We're #2" and "Uncola" campaigns. Ries and Trout's book *Horse Sense*[†] argues that finding a high-potential strategy is so difficult that you need to fully exploit your opportunity once you "find a horse to ride."

[†]Al Ries and Jack Trout, *Horse Sense: How to Pull Ahead on the Business Track* (New York: McGraw-Hill, 1991).

---

ducted from behind a stationary fortification. Don't use it. It works only against a frontal assault, which most attackers quickly learn is folly and then move on to a more effective strategy. When the market leader adopts a fixed position defense, you can bet that a more savvy, even if much smaller, competitor will eventually overtake the leader.

A classic military example of the position defense was the Maginot Line, the string of fortifications the French had erected along their border with Germany in the 1930s. It didn't stop the Germans in 1940. They simply went around it in a classic flanking attack through Belgium. Within six weeks, Germany had conquered France and driven the British back to Britain.

Business examples include "Main Street" retailers, daily newspapers, and labor unions. These organizations have stuck with their business definitions and strategies while the world has changed around them. Fixed strategy in a changing world is a certain formula for failure. No strategy lasts forever.

Preemptive Defense. The preemptive defense starts with the maxim that "the best defense is a good—and relentless—offense." With it, you continually attack your competitors so they can't develop the strength to threaten your leadership. It is the approach IBM should have used with PCs.

The preemptive defense reduces long-term risk by increasing market share and industry domination. You can also use it to consolidate an industry characterized by "mom and pop" competitors. McDonald's in the 1960s and 1970s and Wal-Mart since 1970 are classic cases of companies that have transformed their industries by using the preemptive defense.

This defense typically requires you to provide superior consumer value while accepting somewhat lower short-term profits. Japanese companies do this by making heavy investments in product development. "Category killer" retailers such as Toys 'R' Us and Home Depot apply the preemptive defense through "everyday low prices" and depth of merchandise.

Flank-Positioning Defense. The preemptive defense is often combined with a flank-positioning defense, which uses product proliferation to occupy adjacent territory and erect barriers to entry.

This strategy requires a long-term planning horizon, since you will have to attack yourself before others do. By setting up your own competing brands on your flanks, you will probably cannibalize sales of your mainstream products and modestly hurt short-term profits.

The alternative, however, can be much worse. If you concede flank positions to smaller competitors, you will let them eat into your sales anyway and create a base for more devastating attacks in the future. But with flank positioning, you greatly reduce the likelihood of long-term erosion of your leadership position.

Detroit could have used a flank-positioning defense to make entry into the small-car market difficult, first for Volkswagen and

Strategy	Tactics	Examples	Assessment
Position defense	Find a defendable position and stay there (fortification)	• Ford with the Model T • Coke with the 6½-ounce bottle until 1950s	Doesn't work. No strategy is forever. Competitors will eventually develop a strategy that better meets customer wants.
Preemptive defense	Use offense as a means of defense. Leader puts share growth as first priority.	• Japanese firms in consumer electronics • Wal-Mart	Superior consumer value reduces short-term profits but increases growth and reduces risk
Flank-positioning defense	Protect your main position by occupying adjacent territories with new products or packaging variations (product proliferation)	• Cereal companies used as a barrier to entry. • Detroit should have used to prevent small, imported cars	The "courage to cannibalize yourself" often is difficult but essential to remain the market leader.

Mobile defense	Focus on underlying customer wants, not a specific product. Adjust strategy to meet these shifting wants.	Railroads should have diversified into trucks.	Shows importance of a customer-driven strategy and a corporate culture that is tolerant of change
Counteroffensive defense	Wait until the opponent attacks, determine its weakness, then attack its point of weakness.	• IBM lets others innovate, then responds aggressively. • Gallo's response to Coke entering the wine industry.	Super-aggressive response to challenges discourages future potential challengers
Strategic withdrawal	Consolidate your competitive strength and concentrate mass at pivotal positions (desegmentation).	• Westinghouse has pared product lines from 48 to 30. • RCA exited TVs.	Not appropriate for the market leader

Exhibit 7.1 Defensive strategies.

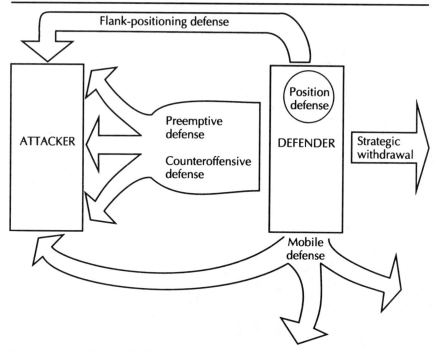

Source: Adapted from Philip Kotler and Ravi Singh, "Marketing Warfare in the 1980s." In Roger A. Kenn and Robert A. Peterson, eds., *Perspectives on Strategic Marekting Management* (Boston: Allyn and Bacon, 1983), p. 77.

Exhibit 7.2 Diagram of defensive strategies.

then for the Japanese auto companies. Detroit didn't—and paid an enormous price.

Most producers of consumer nondurables have taken Detroit's lesson to heart. Soft drinks, cigarettes, beer, and just about every other supermarket category are led by companies that offer package sizes and product variations to meet every need. New entrants find enormous barriers to entry.

Mobile Defense.   This is a moving-target strategy. It requires you to respond to shifting customer wants and market conditions. It sounds just like being customer driven, which it is, but it's more. Think of it as a customer-driven competitor-driven strategy.

The mobile defense is essential if rapid change characterizes the economy and if new substitute products are not only possible but likely. By allowing your business definition to evolve, you avoid sinking with a dying industry.

The "five and dime" chains S.S. Kresge and F.W. Woolworth are good examples of companies that have succeeded with the mobile defense. Kresge transformed itself into the mass marketer Kmart, and Woolworth became the parent company of a series of mall stores such as Foot Locker.

Counteroffensive Defense.   The counteroffensive defense is just what it says—a strategy of fighting back when attacked. Having allowed a competitor to attack, the leader then aggressively counterattacks.

Your counteroffense could be any offensive strategy, but as industry leader, you're in a position to use a mimic defense. Whatever your opponent does, simply copy it. Your superior strength in effect transforms that attack, even a flanking assault, into a frontal assault, the most futile of offensive strategies. However, you must move quickly and with precision; otherwise, you lose the advantage of leadership.

In its glory days, IBM often let others innovate and challenge some of its markets, and then used its dominant strength to counterattack aggressively. You should track competitors' new products and develop counterattack strategies for any that appear viable. That way you can respond as soon as you see the full nature of the attack and have determined the attacker's points of vulnerability. But don't wait too long!

Wine industry leader E. & J. Gallo Winery wasted no time in countering Coca-Cola's frontal assault in the late 1970s.[5] Coke thought it could use its "money, muscle, and marketing" to dominate what it saw as a sleepy, backward, and naive industry. In 1979, Coca-Cola's Taylor California Cellars subsidiary introduced a new line of table wines priced between $2.00 and $5.00. Gallo countered with nine new wines itself, seven of them priced between $2.69 and $3.19.

In early 1983, the wine industry faced a glut of California wines and a flood of cheap imports. When Coca-Cola and others tried price discounting, Gallo undercut them all. Within months, Coca-Cola sold out to Seagram Co. at about its investment cost. Gallo still owns more than a quarter of the American wine market. Coca-Cola has none.

Strategic Withdrawal. Strategic withdrawal is the abandonment of hard-to-defend market segments and then the regrouping of forces at your strongest and most defendable position, usually some core business. Withdrawal by an industry leader indicates management failure since the leader has such strong advantages.

Many companies that diversified broadly in the 1960s and early 1970s found themselves in strategic withdrawal in the late 1970s and 1980s. Still today, many American and European companies continue to reorganize, divest, consolidate, cut payroll, and do any number of other things to become "lean and mean" and to "stick to knitting." This wave of strategic withdrawals in the West was set off by competition from the Far East. In most instances, Japanese competitors attacked the flanks of the Western industry leaders, who often did not respond until it was too late.

Offensive Strategies

Defense is for the leader. Offense is for everyone else. Offensive strategies are shown in Exhibits 7.3 and 7.4. Conventional military wisdom says that an attacking force needs three times the resources of the defender to succeed with a frontal assault;[6] hence, the successful attack concentrates on a weak spot in the leader's defense.

Frontal Assault. This is the "default" offensive strategy of those who haven't thought about strategy. It's instinctively appealing because you are targeting the "big volume" segment. But it's also disastrous. The war will be short and bloody, most of the blood being that of the attacker. Ironically, the industry leader may even emerge stronger, having become energized and more customer driven as a result of the attack.

Miller Brewing's frontal assault on Anheuser-Busch in the mid-1970s woke up that sleeping giant. By 1981 Anheuser-Busch had won its war with Miller, and a reenergized Anheuser-Busch proceeded to increase its market share from under 30 percent in 1981 to 45 percent by 1993.

If the attacker has comparable resources, the war often degenerates into protracted mutual destruction. As in the case of Coca-Cola and Pepsi in the United States market, the war sometimes takes on a life of its own, as if there were no possibility of coexistence. In such a protracted war, consumers instead of shareholders benefit from the lower prices. Indeed, the soft drink wars have trained consumers either to buy only the brand on promotion or to buy enough of their favorite brand on promotion to last to the next promotion.

Flanking Attack.   A flanking attack on uncontested or lightly defended territory may be the most profitable way to fight a business war. The flanking attack can gain you a strong niche position.

The most common flanking attack is to identify and enter a new product category with high-volume potential. That is what Miller did with light beer and Chrysler did with minivans. Another common flanking strategy is to focus on new geographic markets. Wal-Mart, for example, made Sam Walton's family the richest in America by taking discount department stores to small towns.

Encirclement Attack.   You can look at encirclement strategy as a cluster of flanking attacks on several weakly defended market segments at once.

Encirclement is a war of attrition. Your aim is to eat away at the edges of your opponent's market share in each segment to drive down sales and profits, trying to outlast the opponent until it exits the segments, one after the other.

Obviously, you should not embark on an encirclement strategy unless you have far superior financial resources. If you don't have them yourself, you might try to gang up on the opponent—that is, put together joint ventures with competitors, distributors, and others until you have massed superior forces against your opponent.

Bypass.   With a bypass offense, you don't really attack your opponent on any front. Instead, you go around your opponent by diversifying into other products or other geographic markets. You might even take on a superior opponent in the same market segments, but by using a radically different distribution channel, such as direct mail rather than fixed retail outlets.

This is a sound strategy when your opponent is so overwhelmingly strong that any kind of direct attack, even flanking,

Strategy	Tactics	Examples	Assessment
Frontal assault	Mass your forces and go head to head with market leader.	• Pepsi and Coca-Cola • American Motors should have focused on 4-wheel drive instead of competing with Big 3	Nearly always disastrous. Usually short and bloody. Protracted mutual destruction if equally matched.
Flanking attack	Focus all resources on a single, poorly defended position. Create new product segment.	• Digital (minicomputers), Apple (PCs), Sun (workstations) • McDonald's, Wal-Mart, Polaroid when young	Best strategy for moderate-size players without the resources to wage a frontal or encirclement attack. Leads to a strong niche position for the attacker.

Encirclement attack	Attack several weakly defended positions simultaneously to dilute competitor's brand loyalty.	Seiko with 2,300 models.	Can weaken the opponent enough to make a frontal attack possible.
Bypass	Avoid opponent by moving into uncontested geographic area or by creating a new channel, or by creating a new product category.	• Timex watches in the 1950s • Swatch watches in the early 1990s	Difficult to maintain in the long run if the niche becomes significant.
Guerrilla warfare	Make small, intermittent attacks on different positions. Be flexible; move in and out of markets. "New rules" strategy.	MCI in legal challenge to AT&T	Often the only option for smaller companies. Use flexibility and small size to your advantage.

Exhibit 7.3 Offensive strategies.

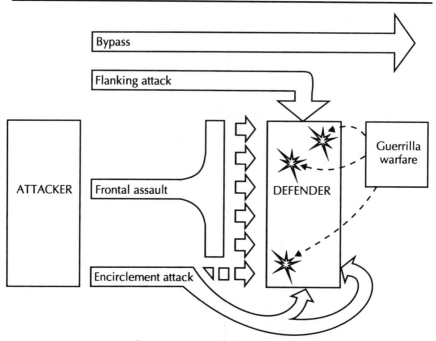

Source: Adapted from Philip Kotler and Ravi Singh, "Marketing Warfare in the 1980s." In Roger A. Kerin and Robert A. Peterson, eds., *Perspectives on Strategic Marketing Management* (Boston: Allyn and Bacon, 1983), p. 77.

Exhibit 7.4 Diagram of offensive strategies.

would be foolhardy. After struggling for years in markets dominated by Procter & Gamble, Colgate adopted a bypass strategy in the 1970s. It moved into a range of sporting goods, textiles, food products, and other product categories where it established leadership, while continuing to compete with P&G in other segments.[7]

Guerrilla Warfare.   Guerrilla warfare is for the very small competitor. It involves short, concentrated surprise attacks on narrowly defined and poorly defended market segments to harass, disrupt, delay, and demoralize your opponent.

Don't try to "defeat" the leader, who will usually ignore you so long as your share of the market remains very small. However, you'd better have a contingency plan in case the leader does counterattack.

The guerrilla offense is a "new rules" strategy. For instance, you might position yourself on the side of an emerging social cause, such as environmentalism or animal rights. You present yourself as the "good" little guy against the "bad" giant. As Wilt Chamberlain has observed, nobody ever roots for Goliath.

Seldom is the guerrilla strategy a long-term strategy. MCI's legal challenge to AT&T's long-distance monopoly was a guerrilla attack. But once MCI won in court, it had to develop another strategy for the marketplace.

USING "STRATEGIC INTENT" TO GAIN INDUSTRY LEADERSHIP

Business war strategies discussed in the previous section are responses to current market and industry conditions. The discussion implicitly assumes that your strategy should have "strategic fit" with those conditions.

However, gaining industry leadership sometimes requires truly long-term vision that transcends today's competitive situation. The dynamic concept of "strategic intent"[8] is more relevant than the static one of "strategic fit" to the small fry who wants to become a big fish—that is, to a small firm whose ambitions greatly exceed its current resources and industry position. Exhibit 7.5 compares the two concepts.

Competitive Strategy Based on Strategic Intent

"Strategic intent," as Gary Hamel and C. K. Prahalad define it, is the single-minded drive of companies "with ambitions out of all proportion to their resources" to become industry leaders over the long run.

Strategic intent focuses on an ultimate goal, and it takes advantage of all marketplace relationships, both warlike and peaceful. Just as most governments rely on diplomacy and economic policy more than on warfare to achieve national advantage, so should it be with a small company pursuing strategic intent. Strategy, then, should focus on developing your potential and avoiding direct confrontation with industry leaders.

Issue	"Strategic Fit"	"Strategic Intent"
Strategic approach	Trim ambitions to match available resources.	Leverage resources to reach seemingly unattainable goals.
How to achieve relative advantage	Search for advantages that are inherently sustainable.	Accelerate organizational learning to outpace competitors in building new advantages.
Competing against larger competitors	Search for niches or simply don't challenge the leader.	Seek new rules to reduce the leader's advantages.
Corporate strategy	Allocate resources to independent SBUs.	Invest in core competencies to produce synergy

Exhibit 7.5 Comparison of "strategic fit" and "strategic intent."

But while it normally shuns direct war, strategic intent is profoundly competitor driven. Hamel and Prahalad state that a company with the long-term goal of overtaking a much larger competitor "must fundamentally change the game in ways that disadvantage incumbents—devising novel approaches to market entry, advantage building, and competitive warfare." For smart competitors, "the goal is not competitive imitation but competitive innovation."

Hamel and Prahalad provide four approaches to competitive innovation:

1. Change the rules of engagement.
2. Attack undefended segments.
3. Compete through collaboration.
4. Build layers of advantage.

Change the Rules

Don't fight the war on the leader's turf or with the leader's rules.

By the 1980s, the name "Xerox" had become virtually synonymous with the word "photocopy" because Xerox so thoroughly dominated that market. Xerox had used its dominance to build huge barriers to entry in high-volume, high-quality copiers for big businesses.

As Hamel and Prahalad put it, Xerox had built high barriers to "imitation." A frontal assault by any competitor would have been disastrous. But by changing the rules, Savin found a lower barrier point of entry into the photocopier market.[9]

Here's how Savin did it. First, Savin analyzed each step in the copier value chain and defined the Xerox advantage. The analysis is summarized in Exhibit 7.6.

	Xerox		Savin	
	Choices	**Attributes**	**Choices**	**Attributes**
Technology	Dry toner	High copy quality	Liquid toner	• Medium quality • Reliability
Product Design	• Features • High speed	• Complex • Frequent service	• Modular • Low speed	• Reliability • Foolproof
Manufacturing	• Custom parts • Integrated	Higher costs/ prices	• Standard parts • Sub-contract	Lower costs/prices
Marketing	Own sales force	Focus on large accounts	Office supply dealers	Coverage of small accounts
Distribution	Lease emphais	High fixed cost	Sales emphasis	• Purchase • Low expense
Service	Own service force	Good service, thin coverage	Dealers	Better for small accounts

Source: Adapted from George L. Farr, "Developing New Game Strategies," a talk at the American Marketing Association's 1983 Strategic Planning Conference, Chicago, April 19, 1983.

Exhibit 7.6 The value chains of Xerox and Savin copiers.

Then Savin used those same steps of the value chain to develop a strategy that would give it a competitive advantage. That turned out to be a cost-focus strategy aimed at low-volume users—low initial cost, medium quality, and high reliability.

Savin had defined a new segment on the periphery of the previously defined photocopier market.

Attack Undefended Segments

Look for not only *undefended* but also previously *undefined* market segments that can provide "an uncontested profit sanctuary" from which to launch later attacks.[10]

These can utilize a flank attack strategy. A key to success with this approach is for you to position yourself close enough to the market leaders to have high-volume potential but sufficiently distant from their "served market" so that the leaders are reluctant to counterattack. In fact, bound as they often are by their conventional wisdom, the leaders sometimes do not even recognize how much of a potential threat you really pose.

In this situation, appearances count. Loudly announcing your strategic intent to the world will only mobilize your competitors into action. Keep them ignorant of the threat you pose. Be like the television detective Columbo. His rumpled appearance and bumbling behavior made the bad guy feel superior to this obviously incompetent cop. The villain invariably let his guard down, and Columbo always won in the end.

The entry of Japanese competitors into the American automobile market was a classic case of attacking an undefended segment. They found a "profit sanctuary" in the low-price segment of the market. Detroit failed to counter them aggressively because doing so would have meant cannibalizing sales of their own high-margin, high-volume cars. Besides, Americans wouldn't buy small economy cars, according to Detroit's conventional wisdom.

From this base, the Japanese companies were able to develop core competencies and add on layers of advantage for a subsequent expanded assault on Detroit.

Compete Through Collaboration

Collaboration is one of the most subtle means of winning without fighting. Joint ventures and original equipment manufacturing

(OEM) arrangements are two forms of collaboration Japanese companies have used to become competitive and eventually achieve superiority in U.S. markets.

In consumer electronics, Japanese companies used their initial low-labor-cost advantage to make televisions for American companies at prices the American companies couldn't begin to match. The Japanese then offered to manufacture "next-generation" products like VCRs, camcorders, and CD players for the Americans.[11]

The Japanese gained long-term competitive advantage this way. The high-volume manufacturing that resulted from these arrangements let them build experience, further reduce costs, and develop quality and reliability. Furthermore, they preempted the U.S. companies in technology development, since they were the ones making the advanced "next-generation" products.

You can also use collaboration to learn the strengths and weaknesses of your competitors. Toyota and GM have a joint venture, as does Mazda with Ford and Mitsubishi with Chrysler. Of course, the Americans have as much of an opportunity to assess the Japanese as the Japanese do the Americans. The advantage goes to the partner more willing to learn, the one less hidebound and more innovative.

Build Layers of Advantage

Initially, a company must exploit whatever competitive advantage it has. Many companies stop there, but one with strategic intent takes a dynamic approach to competitive advantage, building layer upon layer of advantage as it moves from less defendable advantages like low labor costs to more defendable ones like global brands.

Again, take the case of Japanese television manufacturers. Their initial advantage was low labor costs. Competing on price, they became by the late 1960s the largest maker of black-and-white televisions. The resulting economies of scale allowed them to further consolidate their low-cost advantage.

Next, they added new layers of advantage—quality and reliability—by moving into color televisions and becoming manufacturers for private American and European labels. Greater volumes allowed them to invest in new world-scale plants, further strengthening quality manufacturing and lowering costs through process improvements.

Knowing their cost advantage to be vulnerable to rising labor costs in Japan, monetary exchange rates, and international trade policy, the Japanese added an even stronger and more defendable advantage—their own global brands. Finally, they added a broad range of products to their lines.

At that point, it was likely that the Japanese would dominate the U.S. television market. They had global brands with superior price, quality, reliability, and product choice, and they had preempted the technological lead through their manufacturing partnerships with the Americans.

Strategic Intent and Strategic Planning

Overcoming a superior competitor through strategic intent requires "eyes on the future and hands on the present."[12] Winning can take 20 years or more. During that time, however, the business climate, the marketplace, and competitors will probably change several times.

Noting the inability to predict these changes, Hamel and Prahalad say that you can't really plan for global leadership. "As valuable as strategic planning is, global leadership is an objective that lies outside the range of planning."

They are certainly right—but only if strategic planning is thought of as annual "predict-and-prepare" planning, which is what most Western companies have embraced as strategic planning. However, the Four-Cycle Strategy Planning Process is well adapted to the company pursuing a strategic intent. A company bent on establishing global leadership over a 20-year period can plan *strategically* through the following steps:

- First, long-term vision and proper business definition, which embody the strategic intent.

- Second, medium-term objectives achieved through a series of three- to ten-year Cycle 1 strategies.

- Third, short-term action plans focused exclusively on meeting the wants of targeted customers better than competitors do.

The Long Term: Vision and Business Definition

Establishing long-term strategic intent is largely Cycle 1 of the Four-Cycle Process, but instead of a three- to ten-year time horizon, you have a 20-year horizon. The greater uncertainty over how changes in technology, politics, and society will affect industry structure and consumer wants places even greater importance on getting your company's vision and business definition right.

Your business definition especially will guide you in identifying the "core competencies" you will need to fulfill your strategic intent. In packaged consumer goods, for example, marketing and distribution are often the key competencies. Next, you must make sure your company acquires superior expertise in each key competency.

The Japanese firm NEC is a good example of the process of building core competencies in a high-technology field.[13] In the early 1970s, NEC defined its business in terms of what it saw as the inevitable convergence of computing and communications, with semiconductors as the key technological link.

It quickly began to build in-depth expertise in semiconductors. To speed up the process and keep costs down, it used collaboration. By 1987, NEC had established more than 100 strategic alliances in computers, communications, and semiconductors. It also assured that all its subsidiaries' strategies and competencies were linked to this focus so that it would sustain superiority in computing and communications regardless of how the industry evolved.

Compare this focus on strategic intent and core competencies with companies that operate each business as an independent goals-driven strategic business unit (SBU).

The core expertise needed to win a 20-year struggle is often greater than the resources and vision of any one SBU-defined business. In an effort to fix responsibility and accountability, SBUs are usually granted a sacrosanct autonomy and given near-term one- to five-year goals. As a result, SBU managers are unwilling to invest in technologies and expertise likely to pay off only after they are gone.

The Medium Term: Cycle 1 Strategies

Achieving victory in a 20-year struggle requires winning several shorter engagements. The key is a series of three- to ten-year Cycle 1 strategies developed in harmony with your strategic intent.

However, medium- and short-term strategies and tactics must be flexible, adaptable, and easily discarded as conditions change, unlike the stable and durable long-term vision and business definition.

The Short Term: Tactical Actions

Next, three-cycle annual planning translates the three- to ten-year challenges into short-term action plans. With that done, the key becomes aggressive implementation. Your entire organization must be kept focused on exploiting sources of competitive advantage and aggressively satisfying your customers' wants better than your competitors do.

Strategic planning, properly understood, is not incompatible with strategic intent at all. In fact, the Four-Cycle Strategy Planning Process is ideally suited to a company with strategic intent. That process embodies your strategic intent in your company's vision and business definition, which then drive your medium-term strategies and short-term actions.

Avoiding Surrender to Strategic Intent

Time after time over the last three decades, Asian firms have followed strategic intent to penetrate American and European markets and eventually unseat the industry leaders. Those Western industry leaders did not fully appreciate what Chinese strategist Sun Tzu said 2,500 years ago: "All men can see the tactics whereby I conquer, but what none can see is the strategy out of which great victory is evolved."

The lesson for the industry leader is this: You'd better look at each of your competitors as having a 20-year objective to unseat you. Then, you should look at how well prepared you are to meet the challenge. Ask yourself these questions:

- Do I have a 20-year vision, and are we developing the core competencies necessary to realize that vision?
- Do we monitor and anticipate customer wants with greater urgency than our competitors do?

- Do we respond aggressively to every challenge—not just from direct competitors but also from substitute products and potential entrants on the periphery of our market?

- Are we seeing to it that every person in our organization has the skills and motivation to do his or her share in maintaining leadership?

- Do we now have a Four-Cycle Planning Process to give us the advantage in each of the three- to ten-year struggles?

If you answered "yes" to these questions, you are probably prepared to fend off challengers armed with strategic intent.

This exercise should serve as a warning to small companies excited about the concept of strategic intent. Many, but certainly not all, big companies are also well aware of the concept. Some will not only respond to a minor challenge, but also respond out of all proportion to the challenge. The reason is not just that they want you to back off. They also want to send a message to other potential challengers by crushing you: "Attacking us is a prescription for disaster."

HOW THE LEADER CAN DISCOURAGE
WAR AND MAINTAIN PEACE

Blessed are the peacemakers—especially the industry leaders in mature markets. As discussed above, an industry leader should use defensive strategies to wage war. But war is not always desirable, and there's an effective defensive strategy for discouraging war and enforcing peace.

The Product Life Cycle and Warfare

In certain phases of a product's life cycle, competition can be so intense that profits of the industry leader fall below acceptable norms and smaller companies perish. Typically, warfare in these phases is conducted on price. Exhibit 7.7 summarizes the likelihood of business warfare during each stage of the product life cycle.

Stage	Price	Product/Advertising	Potential for War
Introduction	High to recoup costs	Little product variety; high advertising	Very low
Growth	High demand leads to strong margins	Product variety to increase industry sales	Low; compete on product attributes
Early maturity	"Shakeout" leads to low margins	Product proliferation to obtain marginal sales	High likelihood of war, instigated by industry leaders
Late maturity/ decline	Pricing depends on industry strategy and structure	Reduce product line and ads to reduce costs	The degree of warfare—instigated by smaller companies—can be influenced by the industry leader

Exhibit 7.7   Potential for business warfare during the product life cycle.

In the introductory stage, the likelihood of war is low. The company that developed and introduced the product has a near-monopoly. Without direct competition, the company adopts a differentiation-focus generic strategy, selling the product more on benefits than on price at this stage.

Prices start high to cover high costs—development costs that must now be recaptured, high startup production costs, and high introductory marketing costs. As costs decline during this phase, the manufacturer improves margins while reducing price to discourage the entry of competitors and to expand the market.

Margins are high during the growth stage. As the industry expands and cumulative volume grows, economies of scale and the experience curve drive down costs while margins remain high. The high margins now begin to attract competitors, but warfare is unlikely as long as the market grows faster than capacity.

The first wars take place in early maturity, as the industry leader instigates a "shakeout." High margins attract more and more competitors, who often obtain sales through lower price. The leader sees its market share eroding. To maintain leadership and discourage potential industry entrants, the leader then precipitates a short-term price war. Prices plunge below the marginal cost of small inefficient manufacturers, forcing them to exit the industry. Lower prices also increase industry sales, thereby giving the survivors a larger slice of a larger pie.

Late maturity can be peaceful so long as the leader does a good job of meeting customer wants and doesn't price too high. However, the leader too often succumbs to temptation: Economies of scale and barriers to entry tempt the leader to keep prices high and margins growing.

Eventually, margins get so high that a current competitor or a new entrant starts a war with a low-price strategy and goes after the leader's market share. This time, the competitor who starts the war is prepared to hang in there. Since the market is fully penetrated, lower prices do not greatly increase volume. Furthermore, costs don't decline much when the industry is this far out on the experience curve. The result is inevitable: Price wars in late maturity lead directly to lower margins.

As the product evolves toward the commodity or decline phase, the low-price strategy dominates. The degree of war during this phase is influenced by the behaviors learned during late maturity. Industries that have developed a culture of war will continue to have poor margins. Those that have developed less aggressive cultures will do better.

It's critical, then, that leaders learn how to influence the length and depth of wars during late maturity. There is a strategy, based on lessons learned from the "price promoter's dilemma," that the leader can use to discourage war and to enforce peace.

The Price Promoter's Dilemma

Price competition takes many forms—automobile rebates and airline price wars, for example. Also, everyone is familiar with price promotions and coupons from consumer packaged goods companies.

Exhibit 7.8 shows the moves available to competitors in the price promotion game, along with the consequences of those moves. The first number in each cell represents the profit for Company 1 and the second number represents the profit for Company 2; only the relative values of the numbers are important.

Consider the following characteristics of the various price promotion situations:

- When both companies adopt a "cooperative" strategy of low price promotion, each has a good profit of 5 units.

- Either company can increase its profits by 5 units (from +5 to +10) if it defects to a high promotion strategy and if the other stays with the low promotion strategy. Note, however, that this move lowers the competitor's profits by 15 units (from +5 to –10).

- Finally, if one company defects from the low promotion strategy to the high promotion one, the other also has an incentive to adopt a high promotion strategy since it can reduce its losses from –10 to –5.

And that's the dilemma:

- On the one hand, both companies have higher profits in a "low-low" than in a "high-high" promotion environment. Peace is more profitable than war.

- On the other hand, each company has an incentive to go to war by defecting to the high promotion strategy, regardless of the competitor's strategy—since +10 is greater than +5 and –5 is greater than –10.

		Company 2	
		Low Promotion (Cooperate)	High Promotion (Defect)
Company 1	Low Promotion (Cooperate)	+5, +5	–10, +10
	High Promotion (Defect)	+10, –10	–5, –5

Exhibit 7.8 Discouraging war and encouraging peace: the dilemma of price promotion.

Hence, high promotion is the equilibrium, although it produces much lower profits for everyone. Indeed, analysis of scanner data by Information Resources, Inc. shows that only 16 percent of trade promotions are profitable.[14]

How can you break out of this unprofitable high promotion equilibrium? The answer lies in a simple strategy, called "Tit for Tat," a demonstrated means of encouraging competitors to cooperate in a low promotion strategy.

Robert Axelrod[15] coordinated two "promoter's dilemma" competitions. In each round, leading game theorists submitted computer programs for their strategies for playing "promoter's dilemma."

Fourteen people participated in Round 1. Each program played a series of 200 games with every other program. After Axelrod circulated the results of Round 1, 62 participants submitted programs for Round 2. This time, a random number of games, averaging 289, was played between each pair of contestants, for an average of 17,629 games for each program (289 x 61).

In each round, Tit for Tat was the simplest of all the strategies submitted. Tit for Tat has just two rules:

1. Start off cooperating; adopt a low promotion strategy.

2. Do whatever your competitor did on the last move—cooperate if he cooperated; defect if he defected.

Tit for Tat immediately rewards competitors who cooperate and punishes those who defect, thereby encouraging cooperative behavior from your competitors.

In both rounds, the measure of effectiveness was the total payoff over the entire number of games. Tit for Tat was the winning strategy for both rounds. However, Tit for Tat *lost or tied* each series of games. You don't "win" with Tit for Tat, if "winning" means coming out ahead of your competitor in any specific engagement.

Keep in mind that your objective with Tit for Tat, as it should be with all business warfare, is not to "defeat" your competitors; rather it is to maximize your own profits. Tit for Tat wins in the long run by evoking cooperative behavior from competitors.

Tit for Tat is attractive for several other reasons:

- It's simple for the competitor to understand.
- It's "nice." You never defect first.
- It's immediately forgiving. You move back to the "cooperate" position on the very next move after your competitor does.
- There is no need to keep your strategy secret. Tit for Tat is the optimal strategy against Tit for Tat itself.

However, don't apply Tit for Tat mindlessly. A danger with Tit for Tat is that it can spiral out of control. Competitors tend to perceive others' actions as more aggressive than their own—a distortion often made worse by the tendency of sales people to exaggerate threats from the competition. So, if you use Tit for Tat, you should respond with less than a 100 percent "tit" for your competitors' "tats." You should also consider quantitative monitoring of competitors' actions, so that your perceptions are checked against reality.

Tit for Tat is not a strategy for all seasons. It makes most sense during late maturity, when opportunities for increasing margins, best achieved with peace, are greater than those for increasing volume, which can be achieved through war.

Furthermore, intense competition can sometimes be good for you. Even in mature industries, the opportunity for volume gains sometimes exists. In that case, tough competition will lead to lower prices, higher quality, the demise of weak competitors, and the probability of market share gains for you.

Competition can be good for you in another way. Michael Porter[16] has found that extreme domestic competition leads to superior international performance. Companies that do well financially through "gentlemanly" competition at home tend not to be competitive internationally. Since global competition in every industry is more and more the norm, the peace fostered by Tit for Tat may weaken your ability to compete in the long run.

CONCLUSION

Virtually every industry today must compete in a global market. That reality has focused attention on the need to be competitor driven in your strategy development, as well as being customer-driven.

Sometimes, being competitor driven means engaging in short- or medium-term business warfare. The principles and strategies of military warfare can guide you in fighting your business foes. At other times, especially if you are the leader in a mature industry, your best competitor-driven strategy may be to encourage peace through Tit for Tat.

Most of the time in every industry, as many businesses in the United States and Europe have learned the hard way, you need a long-term strategic intent, a vision of where you intend to be 20 years down the road. This applies to both leaders intent on fending off long-term challenges and smaller actors intent on eventually achieving industry leadership.

At all times, the key to business success is the development and execution of superior strategies—strategies that enable you to beat competitors in meeting customer wants.

8

DESIGNING YOUR FUTURE
The Mission Statement

> I have nothing to offer but blood, toil, tears, and sweat. We
> have before us an ordeal of the most grievous kind. . . . It is to
> wage war against a monstrous tyranny, never surpassed in the
> dark, lamentable catalogue of human crime. That is our policy.
> You ask, "What is our aim? I can answer in one word:
> Victory—victory at all costs."

With these words, spoken in the British House of Commons on May
13, 1940, Winston Churchill stated a mission for Great Britain in its
struggle against Hitler and Nazism.

There's nothing new about mission statements. It's hard to think
of any great historic movement or cause that did not rely on a
motivating mission statement in one guise or another. Jesus' Sermon
on the Mount, Martin Luther's Ninety-Five Theses, the American
Revolution's Declaration of Independence, Abraham Lincoln's Get-
tysburg Address—these and many other public expressions of the
purpose, strategy, and underlying values of these grand movements
have moved their followers to great commitment and success.

Great accomplishments flow from powerful visions. In recent
years, more and more CEOs have become sensitive to that fact.
Those who strive to make their companies great have developed
formal mission statements.[1]

Most early attempts were worse than useless. These committee-written documents were designed to make the company sound good to all stakeholders but were taken seriously by none. By glorifying the company as it exists, such mission statements made change more difficult. Why should we change if we are already so great? A mission statement has value only if it is a goal-oriented manifesto for the future.

Still today, too many mission statements simply "don't grab people in the gut and motivate them to work for the common end," in the words of two astute students of mission statements.[2] James Collins and Jerry Porras quote several examples of such banality, cited anonymously to protect the guilty. Here's just one of those that missed the mark:

> We provide our customers with retail banking, real estate, finance, and corporate banking products which will meet their credit, investment, security and liquidity needs.

Every mission statement should possess two characteristics, at least. First, it must be brief. Second, it must inspire. Hence, style is as important as content. Think of the mission statement as the marketing campaign for your strategy. Just as an advertisement should not be a laundry list of your product's benefits or attributes, a mission statement should not be page after page of business babble. An effective ad concentrates a product's attributes into a single, simple, memorable concept that moves people to action. So it is with a good mission statement.

This chapter looks at the process for developing a powerful and goal-oriented mission statement, which is the last step in strategy development and the first step in implementation. Up to this point, the focus has been on "hard" strategy issues related to three of the four Cs—Customers, Competitors, and Climate. With the mission statement, we integrate the "soft" fourth C—Company and its culture—with the strategy. For the mission of a company exists "when strategy and culture are mutually supportive," state Andrew Campbell and Laura Nash. "An organization has a mission when its culture fits with its strategy."[3]

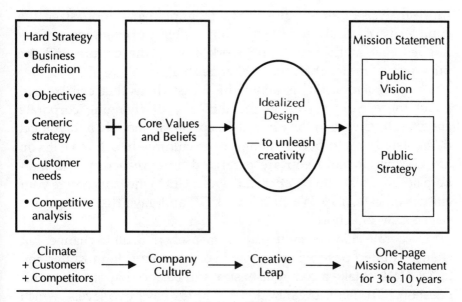

Exhibit 8.1   Developing the mission statement.

The diagram in Exhibit 8.1 illustrates the mission statement process. There are three basic steps, each discussed in separate sections of this chapter:

1. Understanding the fourth C: your company.
2. Using idealized design/redesign.
3. Drafting the one-page mission statement.

UNDERSTANDING THE FOURTH C:
YOUR COMPANY

Understanding your own company is not as easy as you might think. Industry analysis is easy by comparison. Organizations, like individuals, often find it hard to be objective about themselves. Since your idiosyncrasies are yours, they don't seem all that idiosyncratic. It's far easier to see the peculiarities in other people's values and behavior.

Moreover, understanding your company gets you into the murky realm of corporate culture. Early writings on corporate culture—analysis-oriented rather than goal-oriented—emphasized the complexity of culture and the near impossibility of changing it. They implied that managers should work around the culture and the bureaucracy rather than try to change them.

"Overly simplistic" is about the nicest thing that can be said about these early views on the difficulty of changing corporate cultures. If you are in the old Bell Telephone monopoly and you get deregulated, you'd better change your culture—in a hurry. If you are GM or IBM and you are paralyzed by bureaucracy and marketplace myopia, you'd better find a new CEO who can change your culture quickly. Jack Welch did it at GE and gave that company a whole new direction.

Corporate cultures are usually immensely difficult to change. But change is often possible and sometimes necessary. John Kotter and James Heskett take a commonsensical and balanced approach to this question.[4] To them, organizational cultures have two levels, which differ in degree of malleability and visibility. The first level is that of *basic shared values*. These reside at the deeper and less visible level. They resist change and persist even as group membership changes.

The second level is that of *behavior norms and patterns*. Employees tend to conform to these norms, which are reinforced through various rewards and punishments. This level of culture—behavior—is obviously more visible than the first level and, while persistent, far easier to change.

For example, a basic shared value might be the view that individuals are subordinate to the organization. A behavioral norm or pattern, one totally consistent with the shared value, might be that all the men dress in dark suits, so that no one stands out. The second-level behavior could change without violating the basic value, which emphasizes conformity. The CEO might be able to change the dress code to flannel shirts and blue jeans, so long as everyone wore them.

These two levels interact, and changes in one tend to produce changes in the other. Culture at both levels sometimes must change, depending on how fully aligned each is with competitive realities. "Cultures can be very stable over time, but they are never static," Kotter and Heskett argue. "Crises sometimes force a group to re-evaluate some values or set of practices." They also note the impact of personnel turnover, diversification, and geographic expansion as agents of cultural change.[5]

Strong Corporate Cultures and Performance

Another basic assumption of the early writings on corporate culture was that strong cultures and financial performance went together. However, Kotter and Heskett found that the strength of a culture is not as important as the type of culture. They assessed the cultures of 207 companies by talking to more than 600 top corporate executives and then correlated culture strength with return on average investment from 1977 to 1988. In Exhibit 8.2, showing the results of their study, "culture strength" is defined as the simple average of three 5-point scales: (1) extent of "style" in doing things, (2) values stated in a credo and a serious attempt to encourage managers to follow them, and (3) extent that the firm has been managed by long-standing policies.

As you can see, a strong culture does not necessarily lead to a strong performance. Sometimes a strong culture can hurt performance, according to Kotter and Heskett:

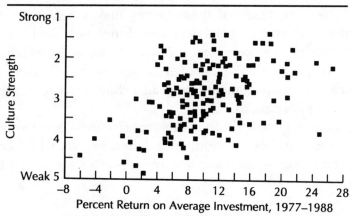

Source: Adapted and reprinted with the permission of The Free Press, an imprint of Simon & Schuster from CORPORATE CULTURE AND PERFORMANCE by John P. Kotter and James L. Heskett. Copyright ©1992 by Kotter & Associates, Inc. and James L. Heskett.

Exhibit 8.2 Culture strength and return on average investment.

In firms with strong corporate cultures, managers tend to march energetically in the same direction in a well-coordinated fashion. . . . Strong cultures with practices that do not fit a company's context can actually lead intelligent people to behave in ways that are destructive—that systematically undermine an organization's ability to survive and prosper.[6]

Of American companies known for strong cultures, IBM most often comes to mind. While its strong culture may have contributed to its admirable performance in earlier decades, its values and behaviors may actually have hurt IBM during the very different competitive environment of the late 1980s.

Healthy and Unhealthy Corporate Cultures

Kotter and Heskett identified certain cultural traits common to companies performing well and certain others common to those performing poorly. These traits are summarized in Exhibit 8.3.

Two fundamental values characterize all healthy, adaptive cultures: (1) a concern for satisfying the needs of *all* key stakeholders—customers, employees, and stockholders—and (2) an acceptance of change. The importance of these values makes sense. Customer wants must be the focus of all businesses. Employees are the mechanism for meeting customer wants. Failure to focus on stockholders can lead to giving all the benefits of success to customers and employees. And management must value change to counter threats and exploit opportunities.

How does a good culture come about? How does a company come to embrace these performance-enhancing values? More intriguing, how does a company lose them? Let's start with this last question first.

The Origins of Unhealthy Corporate Cultures

Kotter and Heskett found a pattern in the evolution of the cultures of those once-premier companies where failure to adapt eventually led to declining performance. Typically, such a company was founded and led to early success by a dynamic and visionary entrepreneur, sometimes aided by a little luck. This leader's unusually suc-

	Healthy Corporate Cultures	Unhealthy Corporate Cultures
Core values	• Managers are goal oriented, focusing on needs of customers, employees, and shareholders. • Recognize importance of leadership and change—to maintain fit between strategy and the four Cs.	• Managers focus on themselves and their immediate work group or product more than customers or shareholders. • Value orderly, risk-reducing management processes more than leadership.

Common behavior	• Strategy and performance drive decision making, reinforcing the goal-oriented, pragmatic culture.
	
	• "Eyes on the future; hands on the present."
	
	  • Creating a desired future drives strategy and action.
	
	  • But achieving annual objectives is a commitment.
	
	• Planning is top-down *and* bottom-up, and action oriented.
		• Political, insular, arrogant, centralized, bureaucratic.
		
		• Subjective decision making reinforces unhealthy culture.
		
		• Strong bias against change stifles initiative.
		
		• Planning is either top-down *or* bottom-up, and process oriented.

Exhibit 8.3   Healthy vs. unhealthy corporate cultures.

cessful business strategy gained an early dominant market position, where the company faced little strong competition.

But its success may have been too much and too easy. Simply to keep control of its rapid growth, the company created a bureaucracy, which required the hiring of managers, not leaders. Over time, these managers were given precedence over leaders; in fact, top management often stifled leadership in the ranks and prevented leaders from becoming senior executives. Preoccupation with managing the rapid growth also caused the company to focus on internal issues. Management gave too little attention to customers and stockholders.

Finally, the company's success led its managers to become arrogant, and senior management did little to counter this attitude. They sometimes even fostered it. Moreover, feeling that their way of doing things was, if not the only way, certainly the best way, the company's executives stuck too long with their previously winning but now losing strategy.

The result was an unhealthy and unadaptive culture. The values and behavioral norms that once helped it reach the heights of success now gave way to a culture of arrogance, insularity, and bureaucratic inertia.

Creating and Preserving
a Healthy Corporate Culture

A failure of leadership, at least in the later phases of its growth, let such a company develop an unhealthy culture. It will take leadership to move it again in the right direction. A performance-enhancing culture requires a leader who can (1) convincingly show the need for change, (2) develop a successful new strategy, and (3) motivate others to help implement the new strategy.[7] In the process, the leader begins to inculcate the two key values – concern for customers, employees, and stockholders, and acceptance of change. The firm's performance begins to improve, and the doubters and resisters in the organization slowly come around to the new way of doing things. Improved performance reinforces the values and behaviors, which then result in improved performance, which then. . . .

Once a performance-enhancing culture is created, senior management's role is to preserve and reinforce it, guarding against tendencies that can undermine it. Top executives continually communicate the core values and behaviors through both words and actions. They do not tolerate forces that can subvert them, quickly eliminating destructive management systems and managers. They guard against arrogance and continually remind their people whom they serve – customers, employees, and stockholders. They encourage leadership at all levels of the organization.

Preserving a performance-enhancing culture also requires that management aggressively implement the current strategy and annual plan while simultaneously adapting to a changing climate. Success requires both hands on the present and eyes on the future.

Core Values and Beliefs:
Analysis of Your Corporate Culture

Your company's culture is a powerful factor that must be considered in developing your long-term strategy. A strategy inconsistent with your culture is certain to fail. The mission statement process creates a fit between culture and strategy. To create this fit, you need to do an explicit analysis of your corporate culture.

Start by making a list of the 10 to 15 most important core values and beliefs of your organization. Here, realism and objectivity are critical.[8] Don't ask yourself, at this stage, what values your company should have. Instead, ask: "What values and beliefs do we actually hold in our gut?" If your listed values are not genuine, they will be seen as hollow rhetoric and produce justifiable cynicism rather than value-driven behavior.

Aside from its value in developing your mission statement, this list of values is always useful to a CEO who strives to reinforce the performance-enhancing values of a healthy culture, just as it's the starting point for changing a culture no longer adequate. A statement of core values can also be a great source of strength in a crisis. Consider the value of Johnson & Johnson's credo during the 1982 Tylenol crisis. That year, several people died from taking Tylenol capsules that had been tampered with and tainted with cyanide. Sustained by their sincere adherence to a clearly stated set of core values (see "Our Credo," Exhibit 8.4), Johnson & Johnson management acted immediately, decisively, and thoroughly to protect consumers from further poisonings. Ultimately, the public rewarded this responsible behavior with renewed trust and confidence.[9]

The moral of the Tylenol tragedy is this: A company that lives by its core values will not die by them. Those values will help it surmount a crisis and survive.

Many companies capture the essence of their core values in a short, simple public expression of their reason for being. Sometimes, it's an incidental statement by the founder or other leader

---

OUR CREDO

We believe our first responsibility is to the doctors, nurses and patients, to the mothers and fathers and all others who use our products and services. In meeting their needs everything we do must be of high quality. We must constantly strive to reduce our costs in order to maintain reasonable prices. Customers' orders must be serviced promptly and accurately. Our suppliers and distributors must have an opportunity to make a fair profit.

We are responsible to our employees, the men and women who work with us throughout the world. Everyone must be considered as an individual. We must respect their dignity and recognize their merit. They must have a sense of security in their jobs. Compensation must be fair and adequate, and working conditions clean, orderly and safe. We must be mindful of ways to help our employees fulfill their family responsibilities. Employees must feel free to make suggestions and complaints. There must be equal opportunity for employment, development and advancement for those qualified. We must provide competent management, and their actions must be just and ethical.

We are responsible to the communities in which we live and work and to the world community as well. We must be good citizens—support good works and charities and bear our fair share of taxes. We must encourage civic improvements and better health and education. We must maintain in good order the property we are privileged to use, protecting the environment and natural resources.

Our final responsibility is to our stockholders. Business must make a sound profit. We must experiment with new ideas. Research must be carried on, innovative programs developed and mistakes paid for. New equipment must be purchased, new facilities provided and new products launched. Reserves must be created to provide for adverse times. When we operate according to these principles, the stockholders should realize a fair return.

Source: Andrew Campbell and Laura L. Nash, *A Sense of Mission* (Reading, Mass.: Addison-Wesley, 1992), p. 141.

Exhibit 8.4 Johnson & Johnson's credo.

that grows into the company's motto. More often, it is a consciously and carefully crafted statement of the company's enduring, almost "eternal,"[10] purpose. Although many companies become known to the public by their credos, the primary purpose of this simple credo is to motivate the entire organization.

An example of an effective credo is that of the pharmaceutical giant Merck & Co.: "We are in the business of preserving and improving human life." The Disney Company's purpose is "to make people happy." Federal Express delivers its credo through the phrase: "If it absolutely, positively has to be there overnight."

You'll notice that each of these credos talks about fundamental, enduring needs. None refers to specific products. "We exist to make computers for knowledge workers" is neither compelling nor flexible enough to last for a 100 years. Far better is Steve Jobs' 1980 statement of Apple Computer's purpose of "making tools for the mind that advance humankind."

This is not to say that a credo should never refer to products or customers, but when it does, it should illustrate the basic wants or needs you serve and your key motivating values. A California mental-health-care company mentions its customers, but the focus is on the basic need served: "Telecare exists to help people with mental impairments realize their full potential."

A small manufacturer of human therapeutics, Celtrix Laboratories, could have said: "We develop, manufacture, and sell human therapeutics." That's exactly what the company does. Instead, Celtrix referred to products to point to the noble end they serve: "Our purpose is to improve the quality of life through innovative human therapeutics."

Stated effectively, your enduring purpose or credo can be highly motivating, and you should develop a credo if you do not now have one. In any case, do a careful analysis of your corporate values and beliefs in order to determine the fit between your strategy and culture.

THE CREATIVE LEAP: IDEALIZED DESIGN/REDESIGN

The next step is to subject your company analysis and your earlier analyses of the other three Cs—Customers, Competitors, and Climate—to a creative process, developed by Russell Ackoff,[11] called "idealized design." It's a way of helping an organization break free from an existing dysfunctional system or strategy and make a creative leap to an ideal alternative. It moves an organization from the constraining thought, "It can't be done," to the liberating and empowering thought, "Yes, we can do that." The outcome will be your final vision and strategy.

The Reference Forecast: Unfreezing the Organization

Inertia is the great enemy of effective new strategies. Thus, before you can design a desired future, you must "unfreeze" your organization from the fetters of the status quo. You can unfreeze an organization by developing a "reference forecast" showing that current strategies will lead to ruin or, at a minimum, performance far below potential.

Ross Perot's 1992 presidential campaign was a reference forecast for the United States. Using his famous televised charts-and-graphs presentations, he persuaded many Americans that the government's economic strategy of a decade or more was leading the country to disaster. Americans must make some sacrifices now, he made the case, if they were to avoid far worse long-term pain.

Unfreezing the organization is easier to do if current results are clearly unacceptable. It was not hard to convince the Chrysler organization in 1980 or the GM organization in 1992 that the need for drastic change was upon them. Severe losses, and imminent bankruptcy in one instance, made the case convincingly. However, it's far wiser, even if much more difficult, to make that convincing demonstration before performance has turned to disaster.

How do you bring an organization to see the need for change? The management of one preeminent R&D organization struck right at the values and pride of its employees. Its researchers thought of themselves as the best of the best—until management proved to them that they had not come up with a real breakthrough in 40 years. They had actually made only incremental improvements in performance, reliability, and costs of existing products. Clearly, the organization was performing far below its perceived potential.

During the 1980s, some perceptive CEOs used the threat of corporate raiders to convince their companies that they needed to change their ways. Some less perceptive CEOs had their ways changed for them—by corporate raiders.

Sometimes, business leaders generate a "quasi-crisis" by amplifying weak signals that point to the need to improve. One way of doing this is to plan for the worst-case scenario. The Japanese heavy equipment manufacturer Komatsu did this when it budgeted on the basis of worst-case exchange rates, using 115 yen to the dollar, for example, when the actual rate at the time was 145 yen to the dollar.

Top management can often use selective measurements of costs and quality compared to those of competitors. Declining customer satisfaction scores, for example, can show that a new strategy is needed—and needed now, since the difficulty in closing the gap between you and your competitors increases exponentially with delay.

Whatever your method, you have to prove the need for change. Only then will you be able to unfreeze the organization and begin the process of moving it to a new strategy.

Designing the Desired Future

The next step in idealized design is to develop a consensus on a challenging but achievable vision of a desired and exciting future. Here's how:

Focus on Ends. At this stage, your sole focus should be on ends. Insist that all discussion of the means needed to achieve the ends be totally off limits for the time being. There's a very practical reason for this. It's far easier to get consensus on a vision than on actions needed to realize the vision. Every proposed action will be countered with a hundred excuses why it won't work.

However, once people agree upon a vision and become excited about it, they will figure out how to achieve it. They'll make short-term sacrifices for greater long-term benefits, and they'll spend less time and effort defending turf and building empires as they work together to achieve the vision.

Design for Today. Visualize where you would like to be today—not five or ten years from now. Focusing on the present forces everyone to really understand and address customer wants. If you focus on the future, the process is likely to degenerate into a forecasting session, which will open the door to all sorts of disagreements and distractions that pull you away from the task of designing a desired future.

Abolish Self-Imposed Constraints. Since idealized design requires breakthrough thinking, you want no limits on creativity. These can be real and imagined policies, organizational systems and structures, investments in plant and equipment, and so forth. These constraints will hold you back from the creative leap needed to move people to extraordinary achievements.

The only acceptable constraints are the laws of physics. So, blow the system up—that is, have everyone assume that the entire system was destroyed and that they have total freedom to design, from scratch, a new system *as it should be.*

Idealized design can produce extraordinary results because it frees individuals and organizations from the constraints that have held them to only incremental improvements at best. There are three specific reasons for this:

1. The resulting vision leads to *quantum leaps in benefits* to customers, employees, and stockholders.
2. The vision excites people and stirs them to give *100 percent effort.*
3. *Teamwork increases* because everyone is focused on the same objective.

Like all other steps in the Cycle 1 process, idealized design depends on the others. For example, if American railroad executives in 1910 had subjected their strategy to idealized design, they would have "blown up" all their existing track and locomotives and rolling stock. They could then have seen their business definition as transportation. That simple modification in business definition would have enabled them to think clearly and creatively about how the newest technology—trucks—fit into their strategy. Later, they would have been receptive to thinking about the place of airplanes in their strategy.

THE MISSION STATEMENT

At this point in the Cycle 1 process, you have arrived at a near-final three- to ten-year vision and strategy for the organization. Most of the analyses and strategy documents, however, are in a confidential form inappropriate for distributing to the public and in an analytic form unsuitable for guiding and motivating your organization.

Hence, you should articulate the essence of the strategy in a succinct, instantly understandable form that stirs the blood of everyone in the organization. That form is the one-page mission statement. In practice, mission statements vary, but the best all strive to convey the organization's mission through two elements:

1. A public vision.
2. A public strategy.

The Public Vision

The vision is a simple and eloquent distillation of the strategy and corporate culture. It can be a simple sentence or even a phrase. Unlike the timeless ("100 years") credo or purpose of the company, the vision states a three- to ten-year mission. It concentrates the formal and abstract statements of business definition, role, strategy, and culture into an energizing goal that impels everyone in the organization to superior execution of the strategy.

For those reasons, the vision should connect the objectives of the firm to the personal values of its members. That's why truly effective expressions of vision do not refer to purely financial targets or shareholder value. Frankly, shareholder value is too abstract and impersonal to inspire the rank and file. However, by tapping into personal values, to use Peters's and Waterman's terminology, you can "achieve extraordinary results through ordinary people."[12]

Public visions typically fall into one of four types:

1. Targeting.
2. Common enemy.
3. Role model.
4. Internal transformation.

Targeting Visions

A targeting vision states a concrete goal. An excellent example is President Kennedy's 1962 challenge to NASA to send a man to the moon and bring him back safely by 1970. Henry Ford's target "to democratize the car" led beautifully into his business definition of making cars for everyone instead of just the wealthiest five percent.

Qualitative targeting visions are more motivational, but quantitative ones are more precise and measurable. Robert Galvin launched two successive targeting visions at Motorola. In 1987, he set an internal, yet customer-driven, target of "six sigma quality" by 1992; that is, fewer than 0.00034 percent of its products would contain defects. As the company approached that target in 1991, he set another target of reducing "cycle time" between order placement and delivery and between product concept and commercialization by 90 percent within five years.

By setting a second target even before the full achievement of the first, Galvin avoided a common problem with targeting visions: What do you do next, after you've reached your target? Lacking a follow-up vision, NASA has floundered ever since it successfully fulfilled its man-on-the-moon mission.

Common-Enemy Visions

Common-enemy visions are powerful motivators. They can mobilize a company just like a war can mobilize a nation. This approach has worked twice for Nike, first in dislodging Adidas from its leadership position in athletic shoes and next in regaining leadership after Reebok took over first place.

In 1979 Yamaha publicly declared its intention to overtake Honda in Japan's motorcycle market. Honda responded with one of the most vivid common-enemy visions ever—"We will beat, squash, slaughter Yamaha." Honda's employees did just that, and within the year, Yamaha conceded defeat and publicly apologized to the Japanese people for being so arrogant as to think it could beat Honda.

One of the problems of common-enemy visions is the enduring mind-set they can create. After Nike defeated Adidas, the company had no enemy and drifted, allowing competitor Reebok to sneak into first place. Only then, with a new enemy, did Nike become reenergized and regain the lead. Nike seems to respond best when there is an enemy. Pepsi's seemingly eternal vision of beating Coca-Cola has brought it a U.S. market share almost equal to Coca-Cola's, but the never-ending warfare has destroyed U.S. profits for both soft drink makers. Mindlessly applied, common-enemy visions can cause people to forget that the purpose of business is to maximize one's own profits and not to beat a competitor.

Role-Model Visions

Small, young companies with high aspirations frequently adopt a role-model vision, which provides guidance on corporate culture as well as strategy. The role-model vision of Giro Sport Design, a startup bicycle products company, is "to be a great company by the year 2000—to be to the cycling industry what Nike is to athletic shoes and Apple is to computers." This conveyed some important and motivating messages—Giro would be innovative and it would allow both employees and customers to achieve their full potential.

During the early 1980s, the real estate firm Trammell Crow set out to become "the IBM of the real estate industry." With that vision, the company strove to become a strong number one through customer service and also be a great place to work. This vision points to a danger with role-model visions—which is the role model itself. Clearly, Trammell Crow's vision was more appropriate and inspiring in the early 1980s than in the early 1990s.

Internal-Transformation Vision

Internal transformation is often the vision of an older company in need of rejuvenation. GE is a classic case. After a targeting vision of becoming number one or two in all its businesses during the first half of the 1980s, Jack Welch articulated an internal-transformation vision of becoming "a big company/small company hybrid," which he explained as follows:

> In addition to the strength, resources and reach of a big company, which we have already built, we are committed to

developing the sensitivity, the leanness, the simplicity and the agility of a small company.[13]

Welch set out to eliminate the "tentacles of bureaucracy" and to institutionalize specific antibureaucratic processes and values as part of the company's structure and culture.

The Public Strategy

The public strategy section of the mission statement further explains and amplifies the vision. Inspiration and motivation are still the keys, but the public strategy is also explanatory. It states the objectives of the organization and outlines its strategy, wrapping them up in the values and behavioral norms of the organization.

The public strategy can take either of two forms:

1. A "vivid description," which may be best for smaller and younger organizations.
2. A traditional statement of objectives, strategies, and responsibilities—a typical approach of large, established organizations.

The Vivid Description

The vivid description usually paints a compelling picture of an ideal future. It should present "a vibrant, engaging, and specific description of what it will be like when the mission is achieved," Collins and Porras suggest. "It provokes emotion and generates excitement."[14] Again, the example of Giro Sport Design:

> The best riders in the world will be using our products in world-class competition. Winners of the Tour de France, the World Championships, and the Olympics Gold Medal will win while wearing Giro helmets. We will receive unsolicited phone calls and letters from customers who say, "Thank you for being in business; one of your helmets saved my life." Our employees will feel that this is the best place they've ever worked. When you ask people to name the top company in the cycling business, the vast majority will say, "Giro."[15]

A "vivid description" such as this is not only a statement of business definition and generic strategy, it also helps define and reinforce the corporate culture. That makes it especially valuable to a young company whose culture is in the early formative phases.

Traditional Approach to Public Strategy

"Traditional" does not mean "uninspiring," for motivation is still the goal of a traditional public strategy. In simple, straightforward language, it should capture the spirit of the organization, impel every member to higher levels of accomplishment, and give them guidance on how to reach their objectives.

Whereas the vivid-description approach really hits hard on the ideal future, traditional mission statements often focus on responsibilities to those who have a stake in the success of the organization, usually referring to several sets of stakeholders:

- *Customers*, who are frequently viewed as the central reason for the company's existence.
- *Employees*, who tend to be recognized as the highest priority, since they are the means for achieving all the other ends and, besides, are the primary target of the mission statement.
- *Stockholders*, with profits and free enterprise often positioned as necessary means to more motivating ends. Sometimes, stockholders are listed last.
- *Suppliers*, *wholesalers*, and *retailers*, who are frequently referred to as "partners."
- *Society*, the broader community, as the mission statement often explicitly recognizes active community involvement and environmental responsibility.

The Johnson & Johnson mission statement, Exhibit 8.4, is couched totally in terms of its responsibilities to its stakeholders, in this order: customers and users, suppliers and distributors, employees, communities, and stockholders.

Traditional public strategies usually discuss (1) purpose and objectives, (2) strategy, and (3) values.

Purpose and Key Objectives.   Purpose is usually stated as the reason the organization exists. Objectives are what the organization intends to achieve within a more limited period of time—such as market share and financial goals and international expansion targets.

The Scientific Press's mission statement, shown in Exhibit 8.5, focuses on purpose. About half of the statement is devoted to purpose, the other half being its strategy for achieving the purpose.[16,17]

The mission of The Scientific Press is to publish books and software that meet the common needs of higher education, industry, and students.

Educational institutions and educational publishers tend to isolate themselves from the needs of business and government. This isolation can lead to an artificial educational experience. For instance, to cite a familiar example, statistics and quantitative methods are often taught in ways largely unrelated to actual business practice.

We believe that the gap between academia and the world of work is a consequence of traditional publishing practice. Educational publishers listen to colleges and universities but rarely to industry or students. We at The Scientific Press see a tremendous opportunity in developing a publishing strategy attuned to all three elements in our market. Above all, we want students and managers to tell us what they need.

How do we make this strategy work in practice?

We try to find products developed in industry, products such as AMPL, developed at AT&T Bell Labs; GAMS, developed at the World Bank; and SUPERTREE, developed at Strategic Decisions Group. We produce low-cost, fully functional educational versions of these products and market them along with their commercial versions to both business and the schools. In this way, students can master a tool that will continue to serve them well once they graduate, and businesses can hire employees already familiar with important analytical tools. Conversely, we also seek educational products that industry can use, products such as MARKSTRAT 2, developed at INSEAD, and ADSTRAT and VALUEWAR, both developed at The Wharton School.

In a sense, this catalog is a progress report on how well we are accomplishing our mission. Of course, you're the real judge of that. We welcome your input.

Exhibit 8.5   Mission statement of The Scientific Press, Inc.

Strategy. Strategy—how the organization intends to realize its purpose and achieve its goals—includes key aspects of its business definition and generic strategy. It explains in some way the business you are in and how you will gain competitive advantage.

BBA, a British textiles company, provides an explicit statement of its business definition and strategy, as shown in Exhibit 8.6.

Values. Frequently, public strategy sections discuss values and behavior standards, reinforcing the strategy and providing guidance on actions. The Anheuser-Busch mission statement, Exhibit 8.7, has a lengthy section on its "guiding beliefs," organized around its products and people, working conditions, and work methods.

A discussion of values is particularly important when there is a significant change in strategic direction. By appealing to the enduring values of the organization and appealing to the pride of employees, you build their commitment to the new strategy.

Bottom-Up Commitment

With the mission statement, you move from strategy development to implementation. So far, the process has been heavily top-down. Effective implementation, however, requires bottom-up participation to gain the commitment of the entire organization. To gain that

---

We shall concentrate in markets where:

  a. The products are in a state of maturity or decline—"Sunset Industries."

  b. The scale of our presence in a market segment will allow price leadership.

  c. The capital cost of market entry is high.

  d. Fragmentation of ownership on the supply side facilitates rapid earnings growth by acquisition of contribution flows.

Source: Andrew Campbell and Laura L. Nash, *A Sense of Mission: Defining Direction for the Large Corporation* (Reading, Mass.: Addison-Wesley Publishing Co., 1990), p. 253.

Exhibit 8.6 Mission Statement of BBA, "Markets" excerpt.

A MISSION STATEMENT FOR
ANHEUSER-BUSCH COMPANIES, INC.

This mission statement clarifies the direction and general goals of
Anheuser-Busch Companies, enabling employees at all levels to better
understand their company and the role they play in its success.
Additionally, by looking beyond any one product or operating company,
this statement provides a reference point from which specific business
strategies can be assessed and progress can be measured.

In the broadest sense, our field of competition is the leisure industry.
Our place in that industry is clear . . .

- Beer is our core business and always will be.
- Other businesses complementary to beer will be needed over the long-
  term to maintain our status as a growth company.

Beer

Our goals are to:
- Maintain our reputation for the highest quality products and services
  in the brewing industry.
- Market our products aggressively, successfully and responsibly. At no
  time will we encourage the abusive consumption of our products, or
  their consumption by minors.
- Sustain and enhance our competitive position within the United States
  through continued market share growth.
- Increase our share of global brewing industry sales through our
  historic emphasis on quality products, and by adapting our marketing
  and distribution expertise to meet the cultural demands of the local
  marketplace.

Diversification Efforts

Our goals are to:
- Broaden the business base of our company and maintain its strong
  growth trends by successfully developing opportunities in the
  entertainment, packaging and food products industries.
- Focus on businesses that permit us to earn a premium on our
  investment by providing superior products and services; that have
  substantial room for financial and market share growth; that
  complement our beer business, and that are compatible with our
  existing coporate culture.
- Rely on technical expertise, investment spending and careful
  management to achieve and maintain the position of low-cost-producer
  in commodity businesses which we have entered to support our
  brewing operations.

Exhibit 8.7   Mission statement of Anheuser-Busch Companies, Inc.

Stakeholders

In discharging our responsibility to the various stakeholders we serve, Anheuser-Busch must translate its business strategies to more specific objectives. Our goals are to provide:

- Our employees at all levels with satisfying and financially rewarding work, and with continuing opportunities for personal development and advancement.
- Our shareholders with a superior return on their investment in our company.
- Our consumers with premium quality products and services that have the highest value-to-cost ratio in their category.
- Our wholesalers with a commitment to our ongoing and mutually beneficial relationship, including opportunities for profitable growth, supporting services and financing.
- Our suppliers with the opportunity for a long-term relationship built on open negotiations to provide state-of-the-art products and services capable of meeting our quality standards at the lowest possible price.
- Our society with an exemplary demonstration of corporate social responsibility and good citizenship in all areas, but with particular attention to the reduction of alcohol abuse through research and education, the protection of our environment, and the full integration of all peoples into the life of our nation.

GUIDING BELIEFS OF THE ANHEUSER-BUSCH COMPANIES

In working together to achieve our mission, the men and women of Anheuser-Busch are guided by a set of shared beliefs that make progress possible. Our task is to strive for constant improvement in making these beliefs a reality.

Our Products and People

We believe in:
- A commitment to quality as the cornerstone of our success.
- Maintaining the highest standards of personal and business integrity.
- Earned pride in our company at all levels . . . in its products and services, its marketing activities, its community responsibility, and in its progressive approach to social and environmental issues.

Our Work Methods

We believe in:
- A sense of urgency and commitment that aggressively seeks to develop every opportunity open to our company.
- Teamwork . . . involving people with a diversity of disciplines to reach decisions that are right, and benefit the entire company.

Exhibit 8.7 (Continued)

- Long-range planning that is based on conclusive analysis of problems at all levels, including sensitivity and dialectic problem analysis.
- Innovation and creativity in all aspects of our business.
- Learning from today's mistakes to build tomorrow's successes.
- Full debate; then all close ranks behind decisions.

Our Working Conditions

We believe in:
- Encouraging all employees to work at their maximum potential.
- Motivating our employees through meaningful work that involves them in appropriate problem-solving and decision-making activities.
- Caring for and standing behind our employees.
- Honesty and the forthright expression of opinions at all levels.

Exhibit 8.7 (Continued)

commitment and to develop a more realistic final strategy, you need to involve all levels and functions of the organization in reviewing and revising the draft of the mission statement. Only then is it "final."[18]

Depending on your organization's size, complexity, and culture, the review process could include every employee or only selected teams from all functional areas and organizational levels.

Comments and suggestions produced in the bottom-up review process should find expression in the final mission statement. If senior management is doing its job and is in touch with employee values and behavior, the final product will be little different from the draft version, and the changes should improve the final version. However, if employees see the review process as a rubber-stamp farce, the whole Cycle 1 process will have been a waste of time.

CONCLUSION

You have now completed Cycle 1 of the Four-Cycle Strategy Planning Process. You have (1) a business definition, (2) a role or strategic objective, (3) a generic strategy, (4) customer and competitor analyses, and (5) a mission statement.

The mission statement is your organization's charter for the next three to ten years. Its power and effectiveness during that time depend mostly on how you and your senior management use it. The key is to *use* it; don't let it die from neglect. It should guide all annual plans and functional strategies and frequently find its way into executive communications, both public statements and private conversations. Tie performance evaluations to it, particularly those of higher-level executives and managers. If the CEO and senior management are truly committed to the vision and strategy, these things should happen naturally and easily.

Now that the strategy is in place, Cycles 2, 3, and 4—annual strategy reviews, bottom-up action plans, and budgeting—implement the strategy that will help you beat competitors in meeting customer wants.

9

DELIVERING RESULTS

Goal Setting and
Three-Cycle Annual Planning

"Before [Michael] Walsh, you could say your results were in the hands of the gods. A good excuse had been an accepted thing at this company." So says a vice president of Tenneco Inc. about his company before Mike Walsh became its CEO.[1]

As the "outsider" CEO who turned around the stagnant Union Pacific Railroad in the late 1980s, Walsh in 1991 again took on the role of an outsider expected to turn around a lackluster performer. One of his first actions was to set higher performance targets for his management team and demand that they meet these targets. All applauded—at first. Some were later stunned when they were called on the carpet for coming up short. They didn't believe Walsh really meant it.

Before Walsh, Tenneco exhibited many of the management failures typical of companies with deeply flawed planning systems. In spite of the formal annual planning processes many of them have, they fail in several critical respects—in setting concrete goals, in providing the resources and programs to achieve them, in holding managers accountable for results, and in rewarding them for delivering on their commitments.

A planning and management system of this sort can be worse than useless, since it provides a veneer of legitimacy to what is in reality a lack of goal-oriented planning. Done right, annual planning produces results and increases the value of the business for all its stakeholders. Done wrong, planning deteriorates into a time-wasting, bureaucratic, and self-deceiving ritual.

Three-cycle annual planning overcomes these failings. It transforms the broad, qualitative strategy of Cycle 1 into quantitative goals and detailed action plans and budgets, as shown in Exhibit 9.1. The process allows a business to keep its long-term strategy fresh, action oriented, and on target. It coordinates and focuses functional and business unit plans. And it moves everyone in the company to contribute at maximum potential toward fulfilling the long-term mission.

This chapter discusses the requirements of goal-oriented planning as they are addressed in the remaining cycles of the Four-Cycle Strategy Planning Process:

- Setting clear, concrete goals.
- Strategic planning in Cycle 2.
- Bottom-up action plans in Cycle 3.
- Budgeting in Cycle 4.

Cycle	Purpose
Cycle 2: Strategic planning	*Review and revise top-down strategy:* • Review environment • Review and revise corporate objectives • Review and revise business unit goals and strategy • Develop three-year plan
Cycle 3: Bottom-up action plans	*Develop functional goals and action plans:* • Consistent with top-down strategy • To meet one- through three-year SBU goals
Cycle 4: Budgeting	*Develop one-year budgets:* • Fund action plans for achieving goals

Exhibit 9.1   Three-cycle annual planning.

OBJECTIVES AND GOALS

A key element of the annual planning process is the setting of goals. All business activities, capacity expansions, and expenditures will flow from the goals, so you have to get them right before you can do anything else right.

Objectives are qualitative or quantitative strategic targets that are set by senior management. By contrast, goals are specific targets to be reached at specified dates in order to realize strategic objectives, as shown in Exhibit 9.2.

Corporate Objectives and Business Unit Goals

All specific goals flow from the corporate strategic objective, the fulfillment of which is their ultimate purpose. Business unit goals derive directly from the objectives and roles established by the corporation. These in turn give direction to functional goals. The relationship between corporate objectives and business unit goals is shown in Exhibit 9.3.

The business should have several specific, quantative goals. William S. Birnbaum argues that there's a six-category hierarchy of goals, culminating in financial results, and that every business should have goals in each category. Shown in Exhibit 9.4 are the categories and the rationale for goals in each.

Whatever the goals, they are not worth much if they can't be implemented and if they are not "excuse-proof." Good goals should be SMART:[2]

- *Specific.* Avoid vague abstractions and platitudes such as "become a leader in our industry" and "become more aggressive marketers." They're meaningless and breed cynicism that undermines commitment.

- *Measurable.* Goals should be stated quantitatively. Avoid vague phrases like "maximize profits." Set a measurable target.

- *Attainable.* Goals must be attainable and realistic as well as challenging. For example, Texas Instruments suffered in the early 1980s because it set unachievably high targets.

	Objectives	SBU Goals	Functional Goals
Definition	Timeless, strategic targets. May be qualitative or quantitative.	Specific targets to be reached at particular points in time, or timeless tactical targets	
Who proposes	Senior corporate management	Senior SBU management	Functional VPs or department heads
Who approves	The board of directors	Senior corporate management	Senior SBU management
Examples	• Maximize shareholder value (profit above cost of capital) • Be number one or two in market share • Increase real sales by 7 percent annually • Reduce real costs by 3 percent annually	• Reduce costs by 3 percent annually. • Achieve a 30 percent market share by 1998 • Achieve a 13 percent return on assets by 1998. • Achieve sales of $100,000 per employee by 1998.	• Reduce energy per 1,000 units by 4 percent annually • Achieve 35 percent share of widgets by 1998 • Achieve 99.9 percent accurate shipments by 1995 • Ship 90 percent of orders within 24 hours by 1995.
Comments	• Objectives, goals, and strategy developed by one level of management provide direction for lower levels. • Each layer of management proposes its own goals, which increases commitment and leads to superior action plans and implementation.		

Exhibit 9.2 Objectives and goals.

	Corporate	SBU
"Evergreen" objectives	• Shareholder value • Measures of financial performance	• Financials • Market share • Costs/productivity • Customer and employee satisfaction
Cycle 1 goals (3 to 10 years)	• Portfolio of businesses (acquisitions, divestments, internal growth) • Diversification/ globalization • Organizational issues (structure, "delayering," management development)	• "Role" (grow, maintain, harvest, divest, or move share or ROI to equilibrium) • Organizational issues
Cycle 2 goals (years 1 through 3)	• Emphasis on sales vs. financial performance • Update to reflect inflation, interest rates, etc.	Quantitative annual goals for 3 to 5 years. (Senior SBU management proposes specific values for each "evergreen" objective for each year.)
Cycle 3 goals (years 1 through 3)	Not applicable	• Each SBU goal is subdivided. • Functional department heads set annual goals for each subobjective

Exhibit 9.3   Corporate and business unit objectives and goals.

- *Results-focused.* You're after results. Avoid activity- or process-oriented goals. For example, "train 50 percent of managers in TQM," while measurable, focuses on an activity. "Achieve 99.9 percent quality within 12 months" is a good goal for TQM, which may require training 50 percent or 70 percent or 30 percent of the managers. The result is what counts.

Category	Rationale for Priority	Examples
Financial	Overarching purpose of business	ROI, earnings growth, capital intensity
Marketing/ sales	Need sales to earn a profit	Market share, sales growth, quality, customer satisfaction
Products	Need a product to sell	Percent of sales from new products
Operations	Need to make a product	Cost reduction, quality measures, speed to market, inventory
Human resources	People run the operation	Sick days, turnover, grievances, removing bureaucracy
Society	Affects all other goals	Meeting legal, ethical, and environmental standards; achieving image/attitude goals

Source: Categories and priorities come from William S. Birnbaum, *If Your Strategy Is So Terrific, How Come It Doesn't Work?* (New York: American Management Association, 1990), p. 128.

Exhibit 9.4   The hierarchy of SBU goals.

- *Time-oriented.* Set deadlines. Otherwise, a goal loses urgency and doesn't command the attention of the manager responsible.

The importance of the M—measurable—cannot be overstated. In a benchmark study of corporate planning, Monsanto Company found that challenging, quantitative, externally oriented goals are a key to effective planning.[3] David Garvin of the Harvard Business School came to the same conclusion in his study of manufacturing quality. In a comparison of Japanese and U.S. manufacturers of room air conditioners, he found that only three of eleven American manufacturing plants set specific annual targets for reducing field failures. These three cut their service call rates by more than 25 percent. The others showed little or no change.[4]

These SMART qualities are the requirements of good goals. To produce commitment and superior implementation, the goal-setting process must meet three other requirements:

1. Development of goals by each layer of management, subject to approval by higher management.[5]

2. Responsibility of a specific individual for implementing each goal.

3. Clear agreement on resources and programs needed for achieving each goal.

Lack of authority, responsibility, and resources has defeated more business goals than any activity of competitors in the marketplace. Just ask Mike Walsh.

One of Walsh's legacies at Union Pacific is an excellent and effective use of goals, as shown in Exhibit 9.5. The range of goals is broad, covering more than financial results and sales growth, and every goal has criteria for measurement, a clear assignment of responsibility, and a baseline against which to compare performance.

The corporation's CEO has the best overall view of the business and should take the lead in setting broad objectives and goals. The CEO determines broad financial targets for all SBUs, approves SBU goals and strategies, allocates corporate resources, makes final decisions on divestitures and acquisitions, and sets goals for corporate-wide programs in such areas as TQM, management development, and manufacturing safety.

The individual SBU heads, however, know more about their respective businesses than anyone at headquarters, including the CEO. Hence, the SBU president should establish the goals and strategies for the unit. This will not result in "low-ball" SBU goals, for a couple of reasons. First, goals must be consistent with corporate guidelines. Second, the CEO has final review and approval responsibility for SBU goals.

Emerson Electric Co. under Chuck Knight is widely regarded as a multibusiness corporation that does a good job of setting goals. Even though Emerson has 40 divisions in eight industries, commonalities in technologies and customers make the corporation manageable. However, Knight avoids trying to micro-manage the divisions and leaves the operations and marketing decisions of these businesses to their presidents. Each of them is responsible for

Business Goals	Measures	Objective Leader	Implementing Responsibility	Baseline		Targets		World Class
				1993	1994	1995	1996	1999
Service quality	• Customer satisfaction • Service failure • On-time performance							
Share growth	Commodity freight revenue							
Financial results	Net income, ROI							
Cost of quality	• Cost of prevention • Cost of quality failures							
Major projects	13 measures							

Safety/claims	7 measures
Cost control	5 measures
Supply effectiveness	6 measures
Asset management	• Locomotive utilization • Car cycle time • Real estate sales
Management effectiveness	• Percentage of goals met • Performance mgmt index • Training effectiveness

Source: Personal communication.

Exhibit 9.5 The Union Pacific Railroad: Effective use of goals.

developing a business definition, goals, and strategy for his or her unit.[6]

Emerson's *corporate* planning then can focus on four broad responsibilities:

1. *Resource and management allocation.* A key corporate responsibility in diversified companies is allocating resources and selecting solid management for subsidiaries. Resource allocation includes acquiring and divesting businesses as well as guiding cash flow goals and investment criteria.

2. *Long-term objectives.* Upon becoming CEO in 1973, Knight set corporate-wide objectives for all SBUs that today remain largely unchanged: Increase sales by 15 percent annually, reduce costs by 7 percent annually, and continuously increase shareholder value (after-tax profit above the cost of capital). Each of Emerson's businesses follows what Knight calls a "best-cost producer" strategy. These goals ensure effective execution of that strategy and profitable growth.

3. *Goal-oriented SBU planning.* Every SBU goes through a one- or two-day planning conference with Knight and the "office of the chief executive." After intensive questioning of assumptions and exploration of alternatives, the plans are revised as needed and approved. The basis for these planning sessions is four tables containing detailed projections of sales and profits. These provide a solid quantitative foundation for goals and strategies.

4. *Monitoring and motivation.* To ensure that SBUs meet their commitments on goals, Knight gets monthly performance reports. Performance is further monitored, and corrective adjustments made, through quarterly meetings of corporate and SBU finance executives. Performance is rewarded through SBU bonuses that are tied directly to achieving the agreed-upon goals.

Both Union Pacific and Emerson Electric have goal-oriented planning processes to produce effective business goals and strategies that support the overall corporate vision and strategy.

─────── **Twelve Reminders on Objectives and Goals** ───────

1. Top management should set "evergreen" objectives that provide a constant compass for business unit direction.

2. The overarching objective of business is shareholder value.

3. Since the key to shareholder value is to beat competitors in meeting customer wants, the highest priority should be customer satisfaction.

4. Goals should reflect the SBU's role: increase ROI, increase share, provide cash, harvest, etc.

5. Goals should be designed to support each key success factor and exploit every major opportunity.

6. Good goals are SMART: Specific, Measurable, Attainable, Results-focused, and Time-oriented.

7. Good goals meet both short-range and long-range needs.

8. Responsibility should eventually be assigned for achieving each objective and programs and resources for achieving it agreed upon.

9. Objectives and goals should be updated each year.

10. Goals should be achieved in a way that builds the organization (not the Billy Martin/Harold Geneen way that produces temporary results). Increase par ROI.

11. All managers should recognize goals as commitments.

12. People should set their own goals. This produces commitment and produces better action plans and implementation.

CYCLE 2: STRATEGIC PLANNING

The most complex and challenging part of the annual planning process is Cycle 2 strategic planning. Cycle 2 planning is to Cycle 1 strategy what a blueprint is to an architect's concept. It turns the long-term strategy into a realistic plan to make the strategy work.

The first requirement of Cycle 2 is to survey the external and competitive environment in order to determine the continuing fit and relevance of the long-term strategy. The second is to review and revise the previous year's quantitative goals and strategy in light of changes in the environment. Finally, one-year and multiyear business plans are produced.

Details of the Cycle 2 process will vary from company to company. For instance, the time horizon of a long-range plan depends on the product development and capacity-planning lead times of the specific industry. Forest products companies have models that plan wood capacity for the 50-year life of a tree. Pharmaceutical companies must plan for the 15 years required to develop and gain government approval of a new prescription drug. Brewers plan for five years, since that is the time it normally takes to site and build a new brewery. Less capital-intensive companies in evolving industries may adopt a planning horizon of only three years or so. Indeed, many companies are moving to a three-year planning horizon to focus on actions and minimize bureaucratic analyses.

In addition, the procedure will vary according to your organization's size and complexity. A large, multi-SBU corporation will require considerably more time than a single-business corporation. Typically, executives in large, complex organizations will need 15 days of time spread over six months to complete the Cycle 2 process. That is because of the necessary interaction between corporate and SBU planning. Exhibit 9.6 outlines the Cycle 2 procedure for a large corporation with multiple products and a few SBUs. Exhibit 9.7 shows that Cycle 2 for a midsize single-business company may only require three days over two months.

On the corporate level, annual planning revolves around three meetings—the corporate objectives meeting, the financial plans meeting, and the long-range planning meeting.

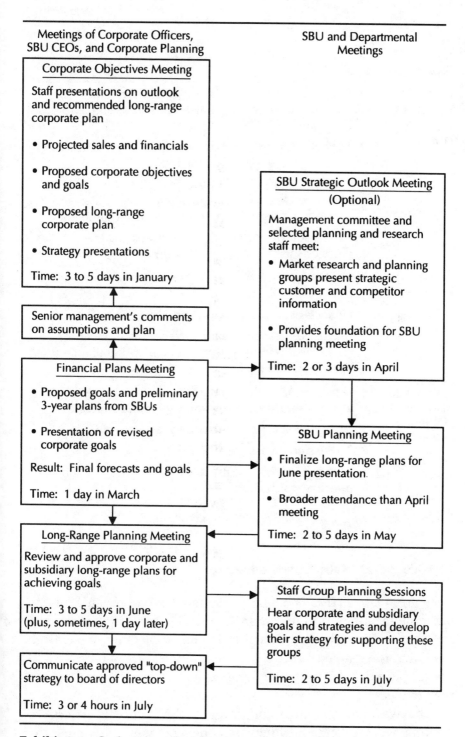

Meetings of Corporate Officers, SBU CEOs, and Corporate Planning

Corporate Objectives Meeting

Staff presentations on outlook and recommended long-range corporate plan

- Projected sales and financials

- Proposed corporate objectives and goals

- Proposed long-range corporate plan

- Strategy presentations

Time: 3 to 5 days in January

Senior management's comments on assumptions and plan

Financial Plans Meeting

- Proposed goals and preliminary 3-year plans from SBUs

- Presentation of revised corporate goals

Result: Final forecasts and goals

Time: 1 day in March

Long-Range Planning Meeting

Review and approve corporate and subsidiary long-range plans for achieving goals

Time: 3 to 5 days in June
(plus, sometimes, 1 day later)

Communicate approved "top-down" strategy to board of directors

Time: 3 or 4 hours in July

SBU and Departmental Meetings

SBU Strategic Outlook Meeting
(Optional)

Management committee and selected planning and research staff meet:

- Market research and planning groups present strategic customer and competitor information

- Provides foundation for SBU planning meeting

Time: 2 or 3 days in April

SBU Planning Meeting

- Finalize long-range plans for June presentation.

- Broader attendance than April meeting

Time: 2 to 5 days in May

Staff Group Planning Sessions

Hear corporate and subsidiary goals and strategies and develop their strategy for supporting these groups

Time: 2 to 5 days in July

Exhibit 9.6 Cycle 2 for a large corporation with a few subsidiaries.

Meeting	Agenda
Corporate objectives meeting (1 day)	• CEO reviews the goals and strategy from last year and materials on how the climate and competitive forces have changed.
	• Marketing head presents base case sales outlook (by product and geographical area).
	• Finance head presents proposed objectives and goals and base case 3-year financial plan (with sales and profit "gaps" between base case and requirements).
	• Discussion of goals and "gap closers" leads to decisions in the meeting or soon after.
Marketing strategy meeting (1 day)	• Marketing head presents goals and 3-year strategy (4 Ps).
	• Finance head presents revised 3-year financial plan.
	• Discussion leads to possible revisions in business goals, final revisions in marketing, and guidance to other department heads.
Long-range planning meeting (1 day)	• Heads of operations, engineering, human resources, etc., present their goals and functional strategies.
	• Finance head presents final 3-year plan with gaps.
	• Discussion closes gaps.
	• CEO summarizes goals, strategy, 3-year plan, and key priorities for the year.

Exhibit 9.7   Cycle 2 for a single-business company.

The Corporate Objectives Meeting

The *corporate objectives meeting* is the most broad-ranging of the planning meetings, and in certain respects the most important. The course of annual planning is set in this initial meeting. It's critical, then, that the tone be right—a goal-oriented process of renewal and not simply a ritual of updating numbers and revising prose from the previous year.

The way you organize and conduct the corporate objectives meeting will depend on your company and your judgment. At minimum, this meeting should include senior corporate officers,

SBU CEOs, and senior managers from the corporate planning department. Its purpose is to create a common view of the strategic situation and to lay the foundation for the final corporate and SBU goals that come a month or two later. Thus, it's a "strategic situation analysis."

The topics discussed at this meeting will cover (1) business and financial conditions and (2) the competitive situation.

The review of *business and financial conditions*, often led by corporate planners,[7] provides an overview of the business and an evaluation of performance measured against long-term goals and strategy. This overview also touches on key issues the company faces, including competitive threats and opportunities and potential candidates for acquisition or divestment. Three-year sales and profits forecasts for the industry, the company, and competitors reveal "gaps" between goals and projections and suggest what strategies you will need to fill the gaps. Not only do these forecasts provide a solid foundation for discussions of customers and competitors, but "running the numbers" always brings a healthy dose of realism to superficially sensible but substantially unworkable plans.

The *climate and competitive forces* review helps you fine-tune your strategies to deal with changes in customer wants. Changes in climate variables cause changes in both competitive forces and customer wants, and detecting these shifts before competitors do allows you to exploit opportunities and to defend against threats.

Demographic trends like an aging population or the growing number of women in the work force have major implications for many industries. Political trends increasingly require quick and energetic responses. U.S. pharmaceutical companies faced fundamental political shifts in their annual planning during the first year of Bill Clinton's presidency.

You should also do a similar competitor analysis to estimate the impact of these forces on your competitors' marketing strategies and their share and profit projections. This will give you insight into which marketing and pricing strategies make the most sense for you.

After this broad review of strategic forces, other staff groups should present other strategically important information. Cyclical companies might hear a detailed economic outlook. A high-tech firm would get a review of technology trends and maybe the three-year plan of the R&D department. Consumer products companies would do well to hear from the market research department about new findings relevant to customer-driven strategies.

You should also hear presentations on critically important SBUs. For example, Philip Morris should always receive a strategic assessment of the domestic tobacco industry. It might also hear from Kraft, General Foods, Miller Brewing, or international tobacco companies if one of them is just starting or just concluding a Cycle 1 strategy process.

On the last day, each corporate officer presents his or her thoughts on strategically critical issues, with the CEO often going last. Corporate officers also should complete follow-up questionnaires which solicit their thoughts on both quantitative items (e.g., economic and sales outlooks) and qualitative issues (e.g., acquisition candidates and SBUs to target for growth). This survey of senior managers' views lets you use their collective judgment and wisdom to balance the corporate planning group's analyses and recommendations.

The Financial Plans Meeting

The *financial plans meeting*, Exhibit 9.8, a mercifully straightforward and short affair of a day or less, includes the same people who attended the corporate objectives meeting. It is based on the senior executive questionnaires from the first meeting and proposed goals from SBU heads. While it leads to a consensus on a preliminary corporate long-range plan, its most important outcomes are SMART corporate and SBU goals. At the end of this meeting, all SBU heads should have clear goals so they can review and revise their strategies.

SBU Planning

SBU strategy is the focus of the last portion of Cycle 2. The first two corporate meetings provided a foundation—the business environment and SMART goals. SBU executives now revise their strategies so they can achieve these goals.

	Corporation	SBUs
Purpose: To establish . . .	• Shareholder expectations • Cost of capital and hurdle rates • Minimum SBU goals	• Role (i.e., build vs. maintain vs. harvest vs. divest). • 1- to 3-year goals for sales, profits, ROI, and costs (which reflect role).
Forecasts	• Address questions raised at the corporate objectives meeting	• 3-year forecasts of industry by segment, company, and competitors.
Financial plans	• Aggregate SBU plans • Establish "gaps" in sales, profits, or ROI	• Preliminary 3-year plans (which include sales, rough budgets, and financials). • Assumptions on prices, costs, productivity, and staffing

Exhibit 9.8 Cycle 2: The financial plans meeting.

When faced with particularly complex issues or large "gaps," an SBU should hold a *strategic outlook meeting* immediately after the corporate financial plans meeting. It allows senior SBU management to address key strategic issues. In situations where such a meeting is necessary, it provides two benefits:

1. Open discussion of key issues is more likely with a small group of senior executives than with a larger group including less-senior people.

2. Clear strategy direction from senior SBU management leads to better functional strategies at the SBU planning meeting to come.

A month before the SBU presents its long-range plan to corporate officers, the SBU head should convene the *SBU planning meeting*. In most respects, this meeting is an SBU version of the corporate objectives meeting, but with a focus on the SBU's situation and needs and its role in the corporate strategy. At this meeting, the

SBU head outlines the current strategy for the unit, the financial expectations of the corporation, the base case financial plan, and the gaps that have to be eliminated. Every functional group should present strategically critical information – opportunities to increase customer satisfaction, ways to reduce manufacturing costs, etc.

The meeting should cover strategic customer and competitor considerations. Market research uncovers changes and emerging trends in customer wants. Sales analysis isolates competitive threats and opportunities. These considerations should be the primary drivers of change in your long-term strategy.

In most cases, this meeting reaches a consensus on goals and strategies. In the first year or two of a new corporate or SBU long-term strategy, however, gaps that have to be filled are large, and this planning meeting can be long, intense, chaotic, and stressful.

Long-Range Planning Meeting

But the stress has just begun. Goals were established earlier in this cycle. Now, corporate management agreement must be forged on the strategy for each SBU for achieving its goals and on ways to close all the gaps. This is done in the long-range planning meeting.

This is usually a three- to five-day meeting, with the SBU plans as the focus. After a review of the corporate goals, financial plans, and gaps, each SBU presents its strategy. These presentations can be very interactive, as senior managers probe and challenge assumptions and projections in the process of convincing themselves that the proposed plan will achieve its goals. There will always be a few sticky issues that require special analyses and additional late night meetings. Often, an extra session needs to be scheduled at a later date to resolve open questions and allow final approval of some of the more troublesome plans.

Staff Group Planning Sessions

At this point, when their "customers" – senior management and the operating units – know their wants, staff groups schedule their planning sessions. Their planning processes will parallel those of the corporation and SBUs. While their functions are not so directly related to market-driven profits and losses, quantification of their goals and strategies is also relevant, for all the same reasons that apply to the rest of the corporation. Their goals also need to be SMART.

CYCLE 3: ACTION PLANS

Cycle 1 generated the architect's vision. Cycle 2 produced the blueprints. In Cycle 3, you call in the contractors and subcontractors to plan and schedule all aspects of the construction. If you've ever actually built a house, you know how important this third phase is to the quality of the final structure and how much of a nightmare it can be if this phase is not done right.

Moving from home building to your strategic planning, Cycle 1 gave you a three- to ten-year role, mission, and strategy. Cycle 2 converted those into quantifiable annual goals and allowed your goals and strategy to evolve. Cycle 3 now produces bottom-up action plans and gets commitment from the people who will make and deliver the goods. Value for all stakeholders is created in each cycle, but none is more critical than Cycle 3, where the process of "constructing" the results starts. Exhibit 9.9 illustrates the process.

As soon as the corporation has approved the SBUs' goals and strategies, each SBU head has a one- or two-hour meeting with his or her department heads. The purpose is to provide direction for developing bottom-up action plans. Top-down SBU goals and strategies are reviewed, including modifications resulting from the corporate long-range planning meeting. The SBU head might also encourage department heads to focus 80 percent of their efforts and budgets during the following year on three to five key issues.

Each functional vice president then has a period of time—three to four months in a large corporation—to pull together his or her function's action plans for implementing the SBU and corporate strategies. This process requires full participation by all levels, with major responsibility falling on managers to propose goals, plans, and cost estimates. Each vice president then puts together an integrated functional action plan and estimates of program costs.

These functional plans next go into the hopper of the SBU action plans meeting in September or October. This meeting will vary in

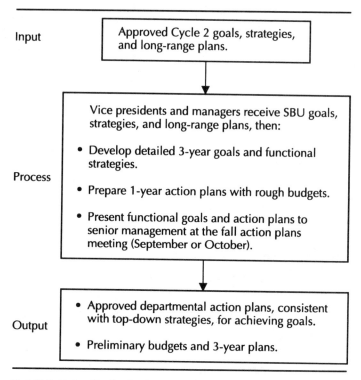

Input	Approved Cycle 2 goals, strategies, and long-range plans.

Process	Vice presidents and managers receive SBU goals, strategies, and long-range plans, then: • Develop detailed 3-year goals and functional strategies. • Prepare 1-year action plans with rough budgets. • Present functional goals and action plans to senior management at the fall action plans meeting (September or October).

Output	• Approved departmental action plans, consistent with top-down strategies, for achieving goals. • Preliminary budgets and 3-year plans.

Exhibit 9.9 Cycle 3: Action plans.

length; a staff unit or small SBU might need only a half day or less. However, major SBUs and SBUs facing strategic changes will need one to five days. The composition of this meeting will again differ from the previous ones. Vice presidents and some lower-level managers will have an opportunity to take part in the presentations. This gives them experience and exposure, and it helps create bottom-up commitment.

After the SBU president again reviews the Cycle 1 strategy and the Cycle 2 goals and long-range plan, the meeting considers each functional action plan—its effectiveness, approximate costs, and the fit between it and the SBU strategy. The meeting resolves conflicts, fills gaps, and forces reality on cost assumptions. If any gaps remain at the end, the SBU and corporate officers work on them until they are eliminated and the SBU has a coherent plan that will move the corporation toward the fulfillment of its mission.

CYCLE 4: BUDGETING

Without the strategies, goals, and plans of the first three cycles, Cycle 4, budgeting, can be one of the most frustrating exercises in business. That's the way it was in the 1950s and 1960s when planning wasn't much more than the "one-cycle" process of bottom-up budgeting. When there's little strategic guidance from the top, budgeting inevitably focuses on eliminating departmental problems rather than on exploiting business opportunities. Department heads jockey for larger budgets, and one of the surest ways of achieving them is by justifying ever-larger departmental bureaucracies. In the end, everybody gets the same percentage increase anyway, and the corporation struggles forward with an unfocused and nonintegrated budget serving as its annual plan.

Contrast that to budgeting in the Four-Cycle Process, as shown in Exhibit 9.10. By the end of Cycle 3, each business has its approved action plans and a good idea of its costs. Budgeting now becomes largely a matter of fine-tuning and of dealing with an occasional surprise. The only involvement of most SBU people is

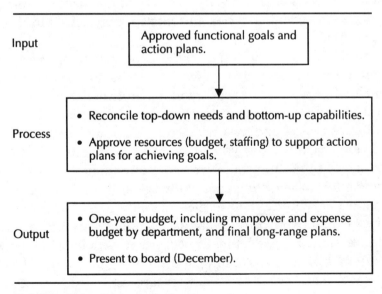

Exhibit 9.10   Cycle 4: Budgeting.

that of completing cost forms. The only meetings are at higher levels, and these too should be mostly routine processes of fine-tuning the SBU budget.

Finally, all the pieces come together at the corporate level in an integrated budget. In good years, the SBU budgets need only minor adjustments to make them consistent with the financial requirements of the corporation. However, sometimes a sudden change in a climate variable or an unexpected move by a competitor between the end of Cycle 3 and the end of Cycle 4 can force major changes in plans and budgets. Some corporations, like Emerson Electric, prepare alternative budgets for such contingencies.[8] This step virtually eliminates surprises and makes the final process much easier. Budgeting has gone from a stressful major effort to a simple and almost mechanical part of the planning process.

CONCLUSION

The Four-Cycle Strategy Planning Process, or at least the *strategy development* and *planning* part of it, comes to an end with the annual planning of Cycles 2, 3, and 4. Exhibit 9.11 summarizes the relationships between planning cycles and management levels in this annual planning process.

Cycles 2, 3, and 4 take you from the development of a vision and mission to the pragmatics of delivering results. While Cycle 1 uses the qualitative tools of strategic thinking, annual planning relies on the quantitative tools of preactive "predict-and-prepare" planning. Quantitative targets and measurements give you control over your organization. They allow you to respond to threats and to take advantage of opportunities. Even more important, people devote time and effort to achieving quantitative goals if their compensation and careers are directly tied to measurable results.

The quantitative nature of annual planning is as critical as the qualitative strategy development of Cycle 1. Academic strategists have ignored preactive planning and planning cycles in the belief that the world moves too fast today for forecast-based "predict-and-prepare" planning to work. What seems an accurate forecast today will be outdated and useless six months from now. This criticism is

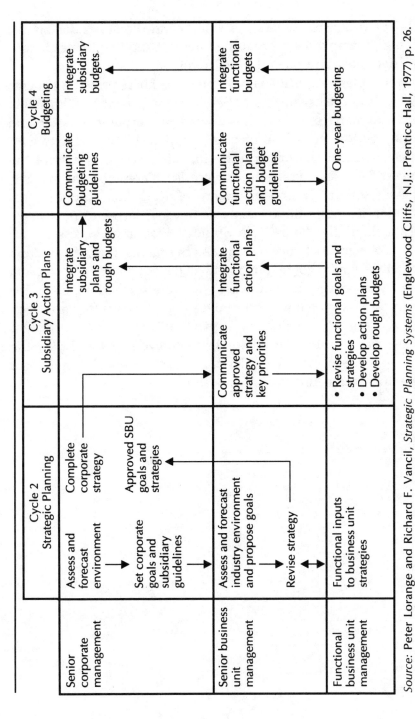

	Cycle 2 Strategic Planning	Cycle 3 Subsidiary Action Plans	Cycle 4 Budgeting
Senior corporate management	Assess and forecast environment → Set corporate goals and subsidiary guidelines → Complete corporate strategy → Approved SBU goals and strategies	Integrate subsidiary plans and rough budgets	Communicate budgeting guidelines → Integrate subsidiary budgets
Senior business unit management	Assess and forecast industry environment and propose goals → Revise strategy ↔	Communicate approved strategy and key priorities → Integrate functional action plans	Communicate functional action plans and budget guidelines → Integrate functional budgets
Functional business unit management	Functional inputs to business unit strategies	• Revise functional goals and strategies • Develop action plans • Develop rough budgets	One-year budgeting

Source: Peter Lorange and Richard F. Vancil, *Strategic Planning Systems* (Englewood Cliffs, N.J.: Prentice Hall, 1977) p. 26.

Exhibit 9.11 Relationships between management levels and the three cycles of annual planning.

valid—but it doesn't negate the value of the forecasts for annual planning. It simply means that the forecasts and the financial plans they drive must be updated more frequently.

Annual planning as it has been presented here provides benefits to all levels of the organization. Senior management has the ability to lead and manage the business toward the corporate mission and to ensure bottom-up commitment and responsibility. Staff and middle managers get the opportunity to influence the course of the business. The clear direction, the precise plans, and the realistic budgets result in far greater quality of work life. And the goal orientation increases the certainty of rewards for performance.

Altogether, the Four-Cycle Strategy Planning Process allows you to take control of your destiny. As the saying goes, if you don't know where you're going, any road will get you there. The problem is, once you arrive you may wish you were somewhere else. The Four-Cycle Process allows you to design a desired future and then map out a route that will get you there. Whether you're driving a Model T Ford in 1911 or a Honda motorcycle in the 1960s, the vehicle you use to get to your desired future will enable you to beat competitors in meeting customer wants.

10

WINNING IN THE REAL WORLD

Top-Down Leadership, Bottom-Up Commitment

Just talk to any CEO. The same one who tells you his or her company is *the* high-quality, low-cost producer in the industry will also try to make you believe his or her company is results oriented from top to bottom. Most like to think so, but few really are. That's the conclusion of Robert Schaffer and Harvey Thomson, who say most companies are more *process* oriented than results oriented. "Most corporate change programs confuse means for ends, process for outcome," they say.[1]

Almost every company today has some sort of continuous improvement process, be it Total Quality Management, Quick Response, Work Reengineering, Diversity in the Workforce, Empowerment, and on and on. Quality *results*, however, have not quite kept pace with the proliferation of programs. A 1991 survey of more than 300 electronics companies revealed that 73 percent had total quality programs, but only 63 percent of these had reduced quality defects as much as 10 percent.[2]

Even the rightly revered and much pursued Malcolm Baldrige National Quality Award in the United States emphasizes process more than results. Quality results account for only 18 percent of the total points in the overall evaluation. "The award gives high marks to companies that demonstrate outstanding quality *processes,*" Schaffer and Thomson write, "without always demanding that the current products and services be equally outstanding."[3]

Winning in the real world of business competition means getting results. In the long run, there is no other way to create lasting value. That point may seem so obvious it is not worth making, but in practice it is more often ignored than heeded.

The Four-Cycle Strategy Planning Process is goal oriented—but it will not produce results if it is treated only as a process. Peter Drucker coined the expression that a plan is worth nothing until it degenerates into action. The Four-Cycle Process carries that thought one step farther: *Action is worthless unless it generates results.* This chapter shows you how to convert a strategic plan into both action and results. There are certain key requirements for doing this:

- Getting the "big picture" right.
- Getting the implementation right.
- Ensuring sound management decisions.

GETTING THE "BIG PICTURE" RIGHT

The first requirement for getting the "big picture" right is to get your strategy right. That's what this book is about. Regardless of the quality of all other elements of your business, you won't win if your strategy is inherently a loser. Some of the lessons from PIMS make this point clear. For instance, businesses with a high-par ROI tend to earn good returns on incremental investments, whereas businesses with a low-par ROI produce poor or negative returns. See Exhibit 10.1. PIMS also teaches that actual ROI moves toward expected or par ROI over time. In other words, you can't make a high-par ROI silk purse out of a low-par ROI sow's ear. An inherently low-par ROI business will deliver poor returns.

Exploit Your Strengths

Exploit your strengths and cut your losses. A strategy that tries to turn around inherently low-par ROI businesses has little chance for success. It reflects the triumph of hope over experience. Even if you

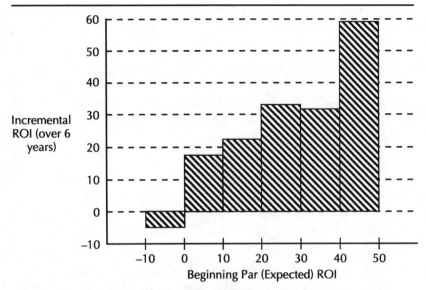

Source: Based on data supplied by the Strategic Planning
Institute through private correspondence.

Source: Based on data applied by the Strategic Planning Institute through
private correspondence.

Exhibit 10.1   Cut your losing businesses and give resources to
your winners.

should succeed, after monumental effort and astronomical expenditures, your previously successful businesses will have withered
from total neglect. You should allocate your capital and management time to the 20 percent of your businesses that produce 80
percent of your profits. Don't spend your time trying to solve
problems. Instead, focus on your opportunities and get rid of the
problems. When Jack Welch became CEO of GE, he devoted his first
five years to getting all his businesses to number one or two in
worldwide market share. Those that couldn't be brought to that
level were soon gone. Welch moved quickly, often against strong
internal opposition, because he knew that if he delayed too long, he
would be stuck with the old, failing strategies. If you don't move to
rid yourself of the previous CEO's baggage within six months or so,
it's yours.

When embarking upon a new Cycle 1 strategy, even if you are
the old CEO, the same principle applies—move quickly to eliminate
weaknesses so you can concentrate on strengths. Otherwise, the

problems will stay with you and sap your ability to implement the new strategy.

The Components of Excellence

Strategy implementation takes place in a context—the "big picture"—in which strategy is just one component. In their famous "7 S" framework, Thomas Peters and Robert Waterman list seven critical components—strategy, structure, systems, style, skills, staff, and shared values. Excellent companies, according to them, consistently focus on all seven areas.[4]

Strategy establishes organizational objectives and the means to achieve them. *Structure* defines clear responsibility and authority to carry out the strategy. *Systems* of information, approval, planning, control, and rewards facilitate decision making and ongoing operational routines. *Style*—common patterns of behavior, managerial control, and leadership in particular—create cohesion and predictability. *Skills* ensure that the company has the core competencies needed to carry out its mission. *Staff*, the people who do the work, excel when the company hires, trains, and assigns the right people to the right jobs and then allows them to exercise their talents fully. *Shared values* keep everyone in the company working harmoniously toward common ends.

Peters and Waterman also found that excellent companies shared a certain set of attributes not consistently present in less than excellent companies:[5]

- *A bias for action.* As Ross Perot told the GM board during his short stint on it: "If you see a snake, kill it. Don't form a committee to study it." Instead of heeding that advice, GM management continued to ponder the snake, which actually turned out to be an Oriental dragon.

- *Close to the customer.* Great companies are relentlessly customer driven. They have an obsession with quality, service, and reliability.

- *Autonomy and entrepreneurship.* Excellent companies encourage leadership and risk taking at all levels, which means they also have a reasonable tolerance for mistakes.

- *Productivity through people.* Excellent companies recognize that bureaucracy stifles people and that real quality and value come from the decisions of people at all levels, not simply through the investment of capital.

- *Hands-on, value-driven leadership.* Senior managers are directly, personally, and persistently involved in the workings of the organization. Excessive bureaucracy is a sure sign that they're not.

- *Stick to the knitting.* Conglomeracy doesn't work. Just look at Exhibit 10.2. Even most related acquisitions don't pay off. Why do most acquisitions fail to pay off? "The answer is simple: managers paid too much for their acquisitions and could not introduce enough operating or financial changes to offset the premiums."[6] Joel Bleeke, et al., give the following characteristics of successful cross-border acquirers:
  - They bought targets in their core business.
  - They seek strong local performers.[7]

- *Simple organizational form, lean staff.* This is necessary if you are going to have all the preceding attributes. In addition, you eliminate the cost of many staff people and all the analyses they demand from line people.

| | 100 Large Company Merger Programs in the United States and the United Kingdom* | | 27 Cross-Border Merger Programs*: International Acquisitions** |
	Small Acquisitions	Large Acquisitions (Over 10% of Book Value)	
Unrelated	38% (N = 16)	14% (N = 35)	N.A.
Related	45% (N = 20)	27% (N = 26)	25% (N = 4)
Core	N.A.	N.A.	61% (N = 23)

*Stephen C. Coley and Sigurd E. Reinton, "The Hunt for Value," *McKinsey Quarterly* (Spring 1988): 29–34.

**Joel Bleeke, et al., "Succeeding at Cross-Border M&A," *McKinsey Quarterly* (1990, No. 3): 46–55.

Exhibit 10.2 Probability of earning at least your cost of capital.

- *Simultaneous "loose-tight" properties.* This means that you have highly centralized core values (e.g., service, quality) but highly decentralized decision making. Wal-Mart, for example, is folksy and loose on the outside but hard as nails on the inside with respect to strategy, core values, and systems.

GETTING THE IMPLEMENTATION RIGHT

Getting the "big picture" right clears the decks for implementation of your strategy. Your concern now becomes (1) implementing the components of the strategy in an order that's logical and effective and (2) doing so day after day with the utmost quality and a continuous improvement program focused on customer satisfaction.

Order of Implementation

An excellent strategy can go down in defeat if its elements are not implemented in the right order. The wrong order can lead to confusion among customers and confusion and resistance among employees. "Ready, aim, fire" usually hits more targets than "ready, fire, aim."

There's no universal right order. It all depends on your specific situation, the nature of your strategy, and just plain common sense. The order of implementation followed by both Anheuser-Busch and Coca-Cola, shown in Exhibit 10.3, reveals one pattern. Both were

Phase	Anheuser-Busch and Coca-Cola
New CEO	Anheuser-Busch in the mid-1970s; Coca-Cola in 1980
New strategy	Significantly accelerate market share through aggressive marketing
Strategy implementation	1. Staff up internally (new senior management and increased marketing)
	2. Transform wholesaler/bottling system
	3. Introduce new products

Exhibit 10.3   Importance of order of implementation in Cycle 1.

clear market leaders and both were facing a challenge from a strong number two—Anheuser-Busch from Miller Brewing and Coca-Cola from Pepsi-Cola. Both saw an opportunity in the situation to protect their leadership positions and to gain market share through aggressive marketing. Their first step was to staff up internally, putting in place a new senior management team—each had a new CEO—and beefing up the marketing function. Next, each transformed and strengthened its wholesaler and bottler network. Only then did they roll out new products and a new marketing mix to customers.

Thus, Anheuser-Busch and Coca-Cola followed one pattern:

1. Staff up for the new strategy.
2. Get your distribution system in order.
3. Then roll out the new strategy.

Jack Welch faced a different set of circumstances at GE when he took over in 1981. Most of the company's businesses had slipped out of first or second place in their markets. The company was guided by inertia and propelled by bureaucratic torpor. GE was facing an imminent crisis whose urgency was not widely perceived or accepted by many of GE's managers.

Welch's strategy was to regain or maintain market leadership for every business. His first step in strategy implementation was to focus on the "hard" elements of his strategy, which required getting rid of any business that could not be brought to first or second place in its worldwide market and to acquire complementary businesses that were leaders. Welch got rid of his losers and developed a coherent group of high-par ROI businesses.

After five years or so of getting the "hard" strategy on track, Welch turned to the "soft" elements of his strategy—the long-term fundamental cultural and structural transformation. His objective was to achieve "the sensitivity, leanness, simplicity, and agility of a small company" so that in the future GE could respond effectively to threats and grasp opportunities. Welch's second stage allowed the high-par ROI businesses to achieve their full potential. If he had attempted to remake the values and culture first or even at the same time, his "hard" strategy could have become bogged down in a quagmire of management and employee resistance.

Thus, GE followed this pattern:

1. Focus on "hard" strategy to achieve the potential for lasting success.
2. Implement the "soft" strategy programs to assure full achievement of potential.

The case of Washington University's Olin School of Business contrasts sharply with that of General Electric. With the support of his board of directors, Welch aggressively implemented a strategy from 1981 to 1985 that wasn't supported by many employees. Such top-down change doesn't work in universities, where a dean needs the support of both the administration and the faculty.

In the late 1970s, the university had made the business school an independent financial unit. At the time, the business school ranked far back in the pack, somewhere below the top 20 in the United States. Its faculty had many good teachers but not top-tier scholars. Its physical facilities were simply awful.

Washington University's chancellor and the business school's new CEO, Dean Robert Virgil, recognized that to succeed as an independent unit, the school had to improve its quality somehow. Virgil's challenge was to lay the foundation for change—to convince various constituents of the need for change, to develop a compelling and credible vision of the future, and to garner political and financial support before moving to implementation.

The key mechanism was a "blue-ribbon" task force of prominent local CEOs, distinguished alumni, and leading academics from around the country, a panel with credibility and clout that would make it easier to get the support and resources he needed. In 1980–1981, this task force put together a challenging but achievable vision for moving the school into the ranks of the nation's best graduate schools of business. To do so, the task force recommended both immediate and critical changes, and in that order: "New facilities is the School's most *immediate* need. . . . Improving the quality of the faculty is the most *critical* need."[8] New facilities would attract additional funds, both of which would attract better faculty and then students. The strategy has worked, and the school has spiraled upward ever since. Its students' GMAT (Graduate Management Admissions Test) entrance scores have increased from an average of 553 in 1982 to 605 in 1992, and its endowment has grown from less than $1 million to over $60 million during the same period.

Both political and strategic needs dictated the order of implementing the school's strategy, which was:

1. Create a consensus on the need for change.
2. Develop a compelling vision.
3. Implement urgent changes.
4. Implement longer-term, more fundamental changes.

There are two important points about the Washington University Olin School of Business story. First, *all* organizations, profit and nonprofit, need strategy. Second, the legitimacy of a strategy for a nonprofit organization is greatly enhanced when it comes from its constituency.

Continuous Improvement

Within the last decade or so, many American manufacturing companies have responded to their declining competitiveness in emerging global markets by changing the way they organize and manage work. The prevailing model was—and still is—command-and-control management, whose theoretical precedents can be found in the American "scientific management" theories of Frederick Winslow Taylor in the early twentieth century and in twentieth century military organizations.[9]

However, the march toward a new style of management in the United States is turning into a stampede, and its triumph seems inexorable, at least in the writings of management gurus. There's a variety of new systems and styles, known as "learning" organizations or continuous improvement (CI) programs. However, they all have certain features in common:

- Each bases decision making on comparative information that is continuously generated.

- Each responds to external forces, in particular the requirement for customer satisfaction.
- Each eliminates or at least lowers functional barriers.

The initial force behind the modern CI movement was quality guru W. Edwards Deming. Long ignored in his own United States, Deming's teachings led the Japanese quality revolution in the 1950s and 1960s. That revolution became the basis for their extraordinary competitiveness in the 1970s and 1980s. His quality program comprised 14 points (see sidebar), 3 of which fully capture the spirit and philosophy of CI:[10]

- Create constancy of purpose for improvement of product and service.
- Constantly and forever improve the system of production and service.
- Break down barriers between departments.

CI can be applied to any of the broad areas of business—finance, manufacturing, marketing, etc. Exhibit 10.4 lists CI programs with different initial focuses, along with the names commonly associated with them. Generally, a company should conduct only one CI program at a time, simply because of the need to keep everyone focused and because of limitations on resources. However, a troubled company might implement both a financial program or information systems program *and* a production or marketing program simultaneously.

Primary Functional Area	Strategic Program
Finance	Shareholder Value
Production	• Total Quality Management
	• Quick Response
Marketing	Customer Satisfaction
Other	Strategic Information Systems

Exhibit 10.4   Continuous improvement programs.

---------------------- **Deming's 14 Points** ----------------------

1. Create constancy of purpose for improvement of product and service.

2. Adopt the new philosophy.

3. Cease dependence on mass inspection.

4. End the practice of awarding business on price tag alone.

5. Constantly and forever improve the system of production and service.

6. Institute modern methods of training on the job.

7. Institute modern methods of supervising.

8. Drive out fear.

9. Break down barriers between departments.

10. Eliminate numerical goals for the work force.

11. Eliminate work standards and numerical quotas.

12. Remove barriers that hinder the hourly workers.

13. Institute a vigorous program of education and training.

14. Create a structure in top management that will push every day on the above 13 points.

As quoted in "A Note on Quality: The Views of Deming, Juran, and Crosby," *Unconditional Quality* (Cambridge, MA: Harvard Business School Press, 1991), p. 24.

===

Whatever their primary emphases, (1) all CI programs are customer driven and (2) all eventually permeate the entire organization by breaking down functional walls. CI programs are "holistic"; they recognize that companies exist to satisfy the wants of customers and that each function is only one step in the total process of customer satisfaction.

Chapter 7 discussed the Customer Satisfaction program. Let's look at two more CI examples and how they work.

Total Quality Management

Total Quality Management (TQM) is certainly the best-known CI program. TQM grew out of statistical quality control of production. Today, TQM encompasses all aspects of the process of satisfying customer wants, from initial design through manufacturing and marketing to after-sale service. In fact, its breadth and its near-universal acceptance could contain the fatal flaw that prevailing orthodoxies tend to develop over time—the original results-oriented accomplishment gives way to process-oriented ritual.

Exhibit 10.5 shows the eight dimensions of quality as defined by David Garvin of the Harvard Business School. Although one or more of these eight dimensions may have greater importance than the others for different products, this list should not be construed as a hierarchy of importance. Each dimension can be critically important. For example, when the Japanese automobile manufacturers entered the American market, the Americans were ahead on performance and durability. However, the Japanese used superiority in conformance to specs and in reliability to take market share.

If any of the eight should be considered most important, it is clearly the last one—quality as perceived by customers—which depends on consistently doing the other seven better than your com-

Views of Product Quality	Dimensions of Product Quality*
Products that work (manufacturing-based view)	• Reliability
	• Durability
	• Conformance to specs
Design excellence (product view)	• Performance
	• Product features
	• Serviceability
	• Aesthetics
Superior satisfaction of needs (marketing concept)	• Perceived quality (long-term customer satisfaction)

*David A. Garvin, "Competing on the Eight Dimensions of Quality," *Harvard Business Review* (November–December 1987): pp. 101–109.

Exhibit 10.5 The eight dimensions of quality.

petitors do. This measure receives 30 percent of the total potential points for the Malcom Baldrige National Quality Award, a far higher weight than any of the other award criteria.

Quick Response

Quick Response focuses on cycle time – everything from turnaround time in filling customer orders to speed of product innovation and development. For some industries, cycle time is critical; for others, it is less so. Exhibit 10.6 lists industry and product characteristics which help determine whether or not cycle time is critical.

Time is key for industries based on fashion, such as clothing. Staying abreast of or even leading the changes in styles can make the difference between success and failure. Industries characterized by new or rapidly evolving technologies need to move fast to adopt the most recent technology. One of IBM's weaknesses in the late 1980s was its slowness, compared to competitors, in bringing out new computer models.

Not everyone needs a short cycle time. The Japanese auto industry in the 1980s moved toward a short model introduction cycle of four and even three years. However, they soon learned that the

Characteristic	Yes If . . .	No If . . .
Product life	Short	Long
Capital intensity	Low	High
Cost of new product introduction	Low	High
Ability to forecast	Low	High
Strategic cost of failure	Low	High
Importance of innovation	High	Low
Examples of industries	High tech, fashion, restaurants, toys, clothing, retailing	Cars, petroleum, heavy manufacutring, beer, real estate

Exhibit 10.6   When is Quick Response a key strategy?

market didn't demand this and that the benefits were not worth the cost. They have now moved back to a longer cycle of about five years. This is not to say that the new-model *development* cycle, as opposed to the new-model *introduction* cycle, should not be shortened. American companies, in particular Chrysler, have been working hard on shortening the development cycle, which should significantly reduce costs and enhance customer-perceived quality.

Quick Response is not a substitute for TQM. After all, the speedy processing of orders for products whose sales are declining because of poor quality gains you little. Once TQM is established, you should move on to a Quick Response program if time is key for your industry.

SOUND MANAGEMENT DECISIONS

Implementation of strategy will be only as good as the quality of day-to-day management decisions, which in turn rely on the quality of information and analysis available to managers. Every effective CI program is based on frequently and regularly gathered information—quantitative information such as "conformance to spec" data and results of customer satisfaction surveys.

Financial Modeling and Forecasting

Information systems, sales analyses, and financial modeling and forecasting systems all support the quality of management decisions. Accounting, financial, and sales data by product line and geographic area are basic. Quality control data, customer satisfaction measures, and competitive costs—yours versus your competitors'—are increasingly essential.

For the longer term, financial forecasting and planning models aid decision making. A model that incorporates major uncontrollable variables as well as controllable ones lets you develop contingency plans for various scenarios. For instance, what would be the effect of a restrictive law or regulation (usually uncontrollable) and how can you counter it through controllable variables? Or what would be the effect of a proposed price increase on sales volumes and market share? Good forecasting models help you answer these questions.

Forecasting is especially critical for the industry leader. Followers mostly react to the decisions of the leader. But to stay in the lead, you must make decisions about the future in some fashion or another. If the methodology must be chosen from among judgment, crystal balls, and quantitative models, choose quantitative models tempered by senior management judgment.

Recurring Decisions: Organizational Routines

Some types of questions and issues come up over and over in the normal course of business—matters like capital expenditure projects and new product evaluations. It's not uncommon for a Fortune 50 company to consider 500 or more major capital expenditure proposals a year. In deciding among these, where similar questions of fact and analysis arise repeatedly, it's best to develop formal organizational routines.

Routines create consistency in the types of information senior managers receive for decision making, thus allowing them to compare the relative merits of the projects. These routines also provide middle managers with a guide for how to get certain jobs done. The alternative is to start the decision-making process from scratch each time. The consequence would be paralysis.

Nonrecurring Strategic Issues: Dialectic Teams

Complex strategic issues, which occur only occasionally, are a different matter. Traditionally, such an issue would be assigned to an operating or staff manager, who then would put together a team to study the issue and come up with a recommendation. This group typically would develop a tentative recommendation after about two weeks and then spend another ten weeks constructing a justification for it, including the requisite "straw man" for the opposing view. Straw men are not known for overly vigorous advocacy of the contrary position.

This approach leaves the CEO and other decision makers at the mercy of the recommending group. Senior managers are under political, time, and complexity pressures that can lead to a decision based on insufficient information and on inadequate exploration of options. The solution: Dialectic teams. Appoint two teams to develop the opposing positions.[11]

With dialectic teams, the straw man gets a brain. The opposing teams present all arguments for and against the proposition. Each team must have complete access to the same information that the other has. Team members put aside any conflicting personal views as they strive to make their case as forcefully and effectively as possible. Both sides conduct the process without political animosity toward each other. The result should be a thorough airing of information and arguments.

This process is justified only for strategically important issues, since it usually takes a minimum of a month and can take three months or more. However, the benefits are worth it. The open debate before senior management, based on thorough investigation by both sides, leads to more objective and effective decisions. Often, the outcome is a blend of the two positions: positive action taken, but with modifications to increase expected payoff and reduce risk.

Questioning Techniques for Complex Decisions

One of the greatest information problems high-level decision makers face is ensuring candor—getting unbiased information, objective descriptions of situations, fair statements of arguments, and honest opinions. There are several questioning techniques you can use to overcome this problem. Harvard historians Richard Neustadt and Ernest May described these techniques as "thinking in time."[12] At Harvard's John F. Kennedy School, Neustadt and May teach "uses of history" to current and potential governmental and public policy decision makers. Their "uses of history" apply to business decision making as well.

The rich historical case material Neustadt and May use to illustrate their critical questioning techniques is too much to summarize here. Instead, listed here are those techniques most useful for probing a business problem and extracting the best judgments and insights from your senior people.

First, there's the matter of accurate understanding of a problem:

- Don't ask, "What's the problem?" Instead, ask, "What's the situation?" The first question gives you the results of someone else's analysis of the situation, however well or poorly done. Moreover, it puts you on the road to considering answers before you really know the questions.

- Ask the journalist's questions: Who, what, where, when, why, and how? Take the "when" back to its beginning. Too often, a problem is brought to the surface only after it's well developed, when the forces that set it in motion are distant and difficult to understand.

- Make lists of what is known, what is unknown, and what is presumed. Don't act on presumptions until they have been thoroughly tested and proven.

Second, after the situation and the problem are clear, you need the best thinking on alternative solutions from your advisors:

- Include all appropriate people. In deciding to approve the Bay of Pigs invasion of Cuba in 1961, President Kennedy received advice from only one branch of the CIA. He was not aware that this branch (covert operations) had not even discussed the proposed invasion with the other two branches, both of which would probably have counseled against it.

- Go around the room. Ask each advisor for his or her judgment. This forces careful counsel and debate. It also leads to commitment to the final course of action and to superior implementation.

- Challenge predictions of outcomes. Ask: "What odds will you give?" or "How much of your own money are you willing to bet on it?"

- Force people to test their own assumptions and conclusions. Ask: "What new facts, if at hand, would cause you to change your presumption? Your decision?"

- Understand your competitors and customers. "Place" them in their natural contexts, both current and past, to understand what makes them tick—to get an idea how a competitor, for example, will react to a competitive attack.

- Select actions appropriate to the situation. If GM executives had asked themselves before they set private investigators onto the tail of auto critic Ralph Nader, "Do we want this to be reported on the front page of *The New York Times*?", would they have taken that course?

Communication and Decision Making

Even if you have the right kind of information, in sufficient quantities, and of the highest quality, it won't do you much good if it isn't used. Good decisions also depend on communicating appropriate information to the right people. And when it comes to sharing information, it's usually better to err on the side of liberality than frugality.

Wal-Mart is famous for its regular weekly practice of sending its executives out across the country to visit stores and evaluate market conditions and trends. Then, every Saturday morning they meet to share information. This information has turned out to be so valuable that today senior management shares the Saturday discussions with all Wal-Mart stores. This additional step means that the meetings lead not only to communication and decision making but also to action on decisions within a few days by all 1,500 Wal-Mart stores. The meetings have become a key component of Wal-Mart's success.

The much-maligned business meeting is greatly underappreciated. Used properly, regular meetings produce significant benefits to managers. The misuse or disuse of them does equal harm. Trying to manage by memos or one-on-one exchanges has inherent drawbacks:

- Confusion, because not everyone will get the same information or the same version of the information.
- Dissension, since consensus is hard to build.
- Disorder, since priorities will not be clear and people will work at cross purposes.

- Inaction and inertia, because the process is bureaucratic and time consuming, and there is an absence of visible and energetic leadership.

By contrast, well-conducted meetings on a monthly or other regular basis that fits your situation can have immense benefits, as shown in Exhibit 10.7. They produce a common perspective on the health or problems of the business, define short-term priorities, and allow midcourse corrections to the annual plan. They reduce paper flow and time-consuming coordination of responses. Oral presentations permit open discussion and quick decisions, and collective participation creates teamwork and counters bureaucratic tendencies.

In senior management meetings led by the CEO, representation of all functional areas ensures the inclusion of appropriate expertise for all topics of discussion. The CEO gets the benefit of the collective experience and wisdom of senior managers, thereby ensuring better decisions and reducing the risk of unwise decisions. And leadership throughout the organization is improved because all senior managers share the same information, understand the same priorities, and hear the same decisions announced.

Agenda Item	Benefits
Routine items: • Sales report • Competitive activity • Operating profit • Production plans	• Keeps management informed on key measures; helps departmental effectiveness. • Allows plan corrections to achieve goals. • Tracking performance uncovers threats and opportunities; promotes a sense of urgency.
Major project results	Demonstrates importance of project and increases likelihood of success.
Special studies	Determine validity; reach agreement on implications, implementation, and next steps.
Tactical issues	Allows quick access to managers and quick response to problems and opportunties.

Exhibit 10.7 Monthly senior management meetings.

Information, knowledge, understanding, and communication—these are critical in the development and implementation of winning strategies. Every chapter of this book has been about *knowledge*—knowing what business you are really in and knowing your customers, knowing the climate and competitive forces that affect you, and knowing when you need a new strategy. It all depends on clear, objective, reliable, and shared information. Company after company in the 1980s let leadership and success turn into business decline because of the failure of intelligence—both kinds. Either they failed to get accurate versions of the fact-based kind of intelligence or they didn't comprehend that information because of a failure of the other kind of intelligence.

BOTTOM-UP COMMITMENT
TO IMPLEMENTATION

In the final analysis, strategy is implemented from the bottom up. Senior management may take the lead in developing strategy, setting objectives, changing or maintaining company culture, and providing overall leadership, but it's the total organization that takes the actions that get the results. Creating bottom-up commitment to the strategy and involvement in implementation is critical to success.

Commitment occurs only when there is an alignment of business values and objectives with personal values and objectives. The Four-Cycle Strategy Planning Process itself forged an initial commitment through the development of a Cycle 1 mission statement and through Cycle 3 action plans. Sustaining that commitment through the monitoring and rewarding of performance is the ongoing responsibility of management.

Monitoring and control mechanisms and incentive systems are subjects for another book. Here, however, a couple of observations about monitoring and control have special relevance to the implementation of long-term strategy.

Monitoring Performance

Monitoring means measuring. Without targets, yardsticks, mileposts, there's no way to know if there's been progress toward strategic objectives. Employees don't know if their performance really makes a difference to strategy implementation. They become confused and anxious, and they eventually disengage themselves. Work becomes "just another job." Commitment goes out the window.

Measurement of performance provides other benefits:

- *Better plans.* Knowing that you expect commitments to be honored leads to more careful analysis and more prudent planning. In the execution of plans, understanding why actual results deviate from the plan allows you to improve your planning in the future.

- *Results.* What gets measured gets done. If people know that their progress will be measured on a regular basis, they will strive to achieve expected results on schedule. Without measurement, a schedule is meaningless.

- *Rewards.* You cannot effectively reward people for performance unless rewards are based on measured and verifiable accomplishments. Otherwise, rewards become subjective. People see them as arbitrary and capricious, perhaps based only on favoritism. Hence, the system of rewards then provides disincentives rather than incentives for excellent performance.

This emphasis on measurement is not to suggest that monitoring should be threatening or oppressive top-down control. Instead, measurement lets everyone know where he or she stands, and that is critical to maintaining commitment.

Rewarding Performance

Performing organizations, as discussed in Chapter 8, are those that focus on the wants of shareowners, customers, and employees. Hence, you should hire and promote people who achieve "hard" objectives (build shareholder value) and who exhibit employee- and customer-driven values in their work. Those criteria have become the basis of the evaluation and promotion of managers at GE, as Jack Welch stated in his letter to shareholders in the 1991 annual report. See Exhibit 10.8.

Performance should be rewarded through both financial and behavioral incentives. While financial incentives tend to emphasize

		Exhibit Employee- and Customer-Driven Values?	
		Yes	No
Meet "Hard" Objectives?	Yes	"His or her future is an easy call. Onward and upward."	"We cannot afford management styles that suppress and intimidate."
	No	"He or she usually gets a second chance, preferably in a different environment."	"Not a pleasant call, but equally easy (as 'yes-yes')."

Exhibit 10.8   General Electric's evaluation and promotion criteria.

desirable long-term achievement and behavioral incentives focus on exceptional one-time performance, both types should be used to reinforce commitment to the strategy and strengthen the alignment between company and individual. That alignment in itself provides the most basic of rewards, the psychic rewards of a quality work life.

Financial Incentives

Financial incentives are especially effective for fostering teamwork and getting employees to identify with the interests of shareholders. The mechanism is simple: stock ownership. The power of ownership is clear with senior management, which is why more and more companies require top executives to own significant blocks of company stock.[13] It works with equal power with other employees, as you can see in the teamwork and spirit of companies like Avis, where employees try harder because they own the company, or the new TWA, where employee ownership has created a palpable and refreshing new spirit of teamwork, commitment, and optimism. Stock options tend to be reserved for upper levels of management, but a stock-purchase plan (or a profit-sharing plan in a private company) ought to be available for all employees.

Behavioral Incentives

Behavioral incentives include all the ego and emotional gratification that comes from recognition, empowerment, pride, respect, and status. They are particularly effective for recognizing one-time achievements. When an employee goes an extra mile to solve a customer's problem, for example, recognize the employee in the company newsletter. Recognizing "heroes" is particularly important when you are trying to reinforce behaviors that support a new Cycle 1.

But don't overlook all-important ongoing behavioral incentives as a regular part of the work environment. Help your employees feel proud of where they work. When the company receives praise from the news media or a public official, publicize that to employees *and* to the local community. Showing respect for individuals in every word and action is a powerful incentive. If it is consistent with your corporate culture, you may wish to eliminate upper management symbols of superiority like the private dining room and the free shoeshine service. Many of these are petty perks that most upper managers won't miss anyway.

CONCLUSION

In late 1992, senior executives of a struggling retail chain sat in a room discussing their many woes. With them was an outsider, who suggested that they might wish to reconsider their strategy, since the rise of a powerful new competitor had fundamentally changed the competitive equation. They listened respectfully, but then told him that they would do fine if only their store managers would meet sales targets. What they really needed, they said, was to put more pressure on the store managers.

Less than a year later, this company declared bankruptcy—no doubt, although the announcement was silent on this, all because of the failure of the store managers. Neither the quality of strategy nor the quality of management seems to have had anything to do with it.

In actuality, superior management is the *only* way to turn around a business decline, the only way to increase a company's long-term growth rate, the only way to achieve long-term objectives. Level changes in price or in advertising, for instance, only produce level changes in sales. But superior management causes the organization to make superior decisions every day up and down the line, and this leads to continual level increases in sales month after month, quarter after quarter, year after year. But superior management is not just a matter of putting the squeeze on your managers. Sometimes that may be part of it. More important, superior management is both a cause and a consequence of superior strategy—strategy that results in intelligent adaptation to change and serves the interests of all stakeholders—shareholders, customers, and employees alike.

Often, superior strategy causes the change. Whether it's Henry Ford's redefinition of the automobile business in the early twentieth century or the long-term "strategic intent" of fledgling Japanese enterprises at midcentury to dominate the world's consumer electronics markets, superior strategy can change the rules and give you competitive superiority.

At other times, external competitive or climate forces change the rules, and you need a new strategy appropriate to the new conditions. Failure to develop one means your eventual decline as competitors fill the strategy void. This is a lesson American automobile makers have learned the hard way. Others should learn from their plight and never forget it.

Whatever the era and whatever the industry, whether you force change or whether change is forced upon you, superior strategy is the only way you will win in the real world—by beating competitors at meeting customer wants.

EPILOGUE
Summary Guidelines and Next Steps

This book ended with some observations about getting results through top-down leadership, sound management decisions, and bottom-up commitment. It was fitting to conclude with the point that no strategy can work—either in its development or implementation—without superior management.

But after ten chapters, a brief recapitulation of the basics of strategy development and implementation would also be useful.

THE BASICS OF
STRATEGY DEVELOPMENT

1. Create your own future by using the qualitative "strategic thinking" tools in Cycle 1. For a turnaround, your Cycle 1 strategy should last three to five years. Otherwise, it should last at least 10 years.

2. "Unfreeze" the organization. Demonstrate the need for a new Cycle 1 strategy by showing that the current strategy will lead to disaster (or at least to performance far below potential).

3. Exploit change. Make sure that your strategy is consistent with the five climate forces and five industry forces.

4. Start with business definition. Produce a breakthrough by creatively defining the four dimensions of customers, wants, mech-

anism, and vertical integration. Focus on opportunities; get rid of problems.

5. Select the appropriate strategic objective and generic strategy. Focus on increasing quality and market share and reducing capital intensity. Make sure you have a clear generic strategy so you don't get caught in the middle.

6. Be customer driven. The key to business success is to beat competitors in meeting customer wants. Develop customer segments that are homogeneous in their wants and their responses to the four Ps of marketing. Use a perceptual map to make sure your segmentation approach makes sense.

7. Do a customer satisfaction survey. Refine your understanding of the wants of each segment and how well you and your competitors meet their wants.

8. Be competitor driven. Understand the laws of business warfare. Use strategic intent to achieve ambitious objectives and avoid war.

9. Use idealized design. Move from complexity to simplicity, release creativity, and develop a vision that excites and motivates. A challenging but achievable vision produces incredible results.

10. Develop a mission statement. Use its development to produce bottom-up understanding, involvement, and commitment. Make sure it focuses on the needs of employees, customers, and shareholders.

THE BASICS OF STRATEGY IMPLEMENTATION

1. Drive implementation with preactive planning techniques. Strategy development requires approaches that are long term, qualitative, and top down. Strategy implementation requires short-term, quantitative, and bottom-up approaches.

2. Use three-cycle annual planning. Make sure meetings are action-oriented rather than process-oriented. Promote interaction and avoid scripted presentations. The decisions made in these meetings are the foundation for decisions throughout the year.

3. Make bottom-up goals and action plans the focus of annual planning. Top management provides broad objectives and strategy. Involvement and commitment arise from people at all levels developing their specific goals and action plans.

4. Use SMART goals. People will find time to achieve *Specific* goals that are *Measurable, Attainable, Results-focused,* and *Time-oriented,* especially if they are evaluated and rewarded based on the results.

5. Use a continuous improvement program. Make sure it is goal-oriented and focuses on customer needs. It will get everyone working toward a common goal and will help reduce functional barriers.

6. Communicate frequently and effectively. Hold monthly meetings. They keep everyone informed and allow quick response to changing competitive realities. Management by memo and one-on-one meetings simply doesn't work as well.

7. Lead as well as manage. Use the leadership techniques from *In Search of Excellence.* Great companies are strong in both the "soft Ss" of style, skills, staff, and shared values and the "hard Ss" of strategy, structure, and systems.

8. Be goal-oriented. Focusing externally on customers and competitors reduces internal politics and produces superior performance.

NEXT STEPS

This book provides a solid foundation for strategy development and implementation. Its approach is logical, and it works in practice. Practitioners really do need to separate strategy development from implementation. They need to recognize that the strategy development tools are very different from the implementation tools. They also need to recognize that the strategy development tools are of greatest use for only a year or so every three to ten years. Most of the time, the less glamorous implementation tools are more relevant to the needs of the organization.

We urge practitioners and academics to build on this foundation in many ways:

- Financial strategy—as well as strategy for R&D, operations, marketing, and human resources—should be included explicitly.

- The best new strategic thinking and preactive planning tools should be included. For example, the book stresses customer satisfaction surveys but omits employee satisfaction surveys.[1] Core competencies,[2] reengineering,[3] and value chain analysis[4] are other prime candidates for explicit consideration.

- The way strategic tools are used will change. For example, I recently discovered that customer satisfaction surveys are a wonderful tool for beginning the strategy development process. Cluster analysis of customer wants leads to identification of customer segments. Analysis of the wants of each segment and how well you and your competitors satisfy those wants leads directly into a customer and competitor-driven business definition.

- Each organization should adapt the framework to meet its own needs based on its culture and its strategic situation. Add, modify, and subtract until the approach works for you.

ENDNOTES

Chapter 1

1. Thomas A. Stewart, "GE Keeps Those Ideas Coming," *Fortune* (Aug. 12, 1991): p. 42, and Noel Tichy and Stratford Sherman, *Control Your Destiny or Someone Else Will* (New York: Doubleday, 1993), p. 14. Most of the information on General Electric in this chapter comes from an analysis of the company's annual shareholder reports from 1979 through 1991 and from the Tichy and Sherman book.

2. Tichy and Sherman, *Control Your Destiny*, pp. 12–13.

3. Ibid., p. 20.

4. Robert Grant, *Contemporary Strategy Analysis* (Cambridge, Mass.: Basil Blackwell, 1991), p. 15. Emphasis his. The discussion of the concept and nature of strategy throughout this chapter draws heavily on Grant's book.

5. See Michael Porter, *Competitive Strategy* (New York: The Free Press, 1980), and Russell L. Ackoff, *Creating the Corporate Future* (New York: John Wiley & Sons, 1981).

6. Ackoff uses *reactive* as in "reactionary," that is, attempting to return to a previous condition by undoing intervening changes between that past condition and the present one. I use the term differently, as in "react to." A reactive company may not be opposed to change so much as being passive in the face of it. It simply responds to external forces instead of acting in advance to control, contain, or channel those forces in a more beneficial way.

7. Ackoff, *Creating the Corporate Future, p. 62.*

Chapter 2

1. Derek F. Abell and John Hammond, *Strategic Market Planning* (Englewood Cliffs, N.J.: Prentice Hall, 1979); Peter Lorange, *Corporate Planning* (Englewood Cliffs, N.J.: Prentice Hall, 1980).

2. See Russell L. Ackoff, *Creating the Corporate Future* (New York: John Wiley & Sons, 1981), pp. 101–103.

3. Michael Porter, *Competitive Strategy* (New York: The Free Press, 1980), p. 4.

263

4. Theodore Levitt, "Marketing Myopia," *Harvard Business Review* (July–August 1960): pp. 45–56.

5. Generic low-cost and differentiation strategies are discussed later in this chapter and in Chapter 5.

6. The four dimensions of business definition are discussed in depth in Derek F. Abell, *Defining the Business: The Starting Point of Strategic Planning* (Englewood Cliffs, N.J.: Prentice Hall, 1980). Abell uses the term *needs* instead of *wants* and *technology* instead of *mechanism*.

7. Virtually every book on business strategy contains some treatment of the BCG matrix. Also see a book of essays by BCG founder Bruce Henderson, *Henderson on Corporate Strategy* (Cambridge, Mass.: Abt Books, 1979), pp. 163–66.

8. Michael Porter, *Competitive Advantage* (New York: The Free Press, 1983), p. 12.

9. Ackoff, *Creating the Corporate Future*, p. 105.

Chapter 3

1. Derek F. Abell, *Defining the Business: The Starting Point of Strategic Planning* (Englewood Cliffs, NJ: Prentice-Hall, 1980), p. 5. Abell provides the four dimensions of business definition used in this chapter.

2. Theodore Levitt, "Marketing Myopia," *Harvard Business Review* (July–August 1960): pp. 45–56.

3. Robert F. Hartley, *Marketing Mistakes* (New York: John Wiley & Sons, 1992), p. 179.

4. See Robert D. Buzzell and Bradley T. Gale, *The PIMS Principles: Linking Strategy to Performance* (New York: The Free Press, 1987).

5. These examples come from William S. Birnbaum, *If Your Strategy Is So Terrific, How Come It Doesn't Work?* (New York: American Management Association, 1990), pp. 112–13.

6. See Arthur A. Thompson, Jr., and A. J. Strickland III, *Strategy Formulation and Implementation* (Plano, Tex. Business Publications, Inc., 1983), pp. 255–57.

7. Michael Porter, *Competitive Strategy* (New York: The Free Press, 1980), Ch. 1.

Chapter 4

1. See the discussion of the business definition of motorcycles in Chapter 3.

2. See Chapter 8 for discussion of motivating missions.

3. Annual goals are discussed in Chapter 9. The term *role*, as used here, refers to the single most important long-term objective.

4. GE and McKinsey & Co. may have been the first to refine the BCG matrix planning approach, but they were not alone. A. T. Kearney, Royal Dutch Shell, and others developed various refinements, all similar to the GE/McKinsey Industry Attractiveness/Business Position matrix.

5. PIMS grew out of a research project initiated by GE in the early 1960s. Top management was continually faced with "hockey stick" forecasts from business

units claiming that incremental investments would produce high incremental returns. In an effort to identify businesses that could benefit from additional management and capital and those that could not, GE's planners sought to develop a regression model to determine the "par" or expected ROI given a business's controllable and uncontrollable variables. This work led to the initial PIMS pilot project at the Marketing Science Institute at Harvard Business School in 1972. In 1975 the Strategic Planning Institute was founded to conduct the ongoing PIMS research.

See Robert D. Buzzell and Bradley T. Gale, *The PIMS Principles: Linking Strategy to Performance* (New York: The Free Press, 1987), Ch. 3, for background and an overview of PIMS. The discussion of PIMS presented here is based on this excellent book.

6. P/Es as reported in *The Wall Street Journal*, May 11, 1994.

Chapter 5

1. Michael Porter, *Competitive Strategy* (New York: The Free Press, 1980), Ch. 2.

2. Previously, the discussion has covered five climate forces and five competitive forces. In this and later chapters, those forces will be subsumed under the four Cs—Company, Customers, Competitors, and Climate. This schema includes those earlier ten forces, and it is simpler to keep in mind. Moreover, it relates more directly to the focus of strategy, which is beating *competitors* in meeting *customer* wants.

3. For a discussion of PLC and its criticisms, see Steven P. Schnaars, *Marketing Strategy, A Customer-Driven Approach* (New York: The Free Press, 1991), Ch. 12.

4. Our concern here is more with long-term business strategy than with product marketing, so the focus is more on company and industry life cycles than on those of individual brands. For the sake of simplicity, a company or industry life cycle is also referred to here as "PLC."

5. See Derek F. Abell, "Strategic Windows," *Journal of Marketing*, (July 1978): pp. 21–25.

Chapter 6

1. See Lee Iacocca, *Iacocca: An Autobiography* (Toronto: Bantam Books, 1984), p. 63, for these quotations. The discussion of the Mustang is based on Chapter 6 of Iacocca's book, which recounts the story of the development of the Mustang.

2. Ibid., p. 65.

3. Ibid., p. 76.

4. See Ronald E. Frank, William F. Massey, and Yoram Wind, *Market Segmentation* (Englewood Cliffs, N.J.: Prentice Hall, 1972), pp. 4–5, for a summary discussion of twentieth-century markets.

5. Ries' and Trout's thinking on positioning is presented in their classic book, *Positioning: The Battle for Your Mind* (New York: Warner Books, 1981).

6. Dennis H. Gensch, Nicola Aversa, and Steven P. Moore, "A Choice-Modeling Market Information System That Enabled ABB Electric to Expand Its Market Share," *INTERFACES*, (January–February 1990): pp. 6–25.

7. For an excellent discussion of geodemographic systems and other sophisticated new market research systems, see David J. Curry, *The New Marketing Research Systems* (New York: John Wiley & Sons, 1993). Chapter 13 discusses PRIZM and other major geodemographic systems.

8. George S. Day, *Market Driven Strategy* (New York: The Free Press, 1990), p. 103.

9. The statistical technique used is called *multidimensional scaling*. The input data could be different types of survey results. For instance, the researchers could ask respondents to *grade* hospitals on a five-point scale (1 = weak, 5 = very strong) on each of the 16 services. Or they could *rank* the hospitals from best to worst on each of the 16 services. See David A. Aaker, Ed., *Multivariate Analysis in Marketing: Theory and Application* (Belmont, Calif.: Wadsworth Publishing Co., 1971), Part 2, particularly the essays in Sec. B., pp. 257–98.

10. Al Ries and Jack Trout, *Positioning: The Battle for Your Mind* (New York: Warner Books, 1981), Chs. 12–13.

11. The perceptual map for cars is changing again. Light trucks (e.g., pickup trucks, minivans, vans, and 4-wheel drive vehicles) represented 43% of the Big 3's car and light truck sales in 1992. Type of car (e.g., sporty cars, traditional family cars, and the various types of light trucks) may be more important for segmentation strategy in the future than the price segments that have dominated product planning since the 1920s.

12. Marketing materials from Maritz Inc., St. Louis, Missouri.

Chapter 7

1. Robert Sobel, *IBM: Colossus in Transition* (New York: Truman Talley Books/ Times Books, 1981) Chs. 11 and 13. Also see "RCA Goes Head to Head with IBM," *Fortune* (Oct. 1970), and "The 250 Million Dollar Disaster That Hit RCA," *Business Week*, (Sept. 25, 1971).

2. The best known of these are Al Ries and Jack Trout in their book, *Marketing Warfare* (New York: McGraw-Hill, 1986). My discussion draws heavily on that book. Also see Robert Durö and Björn Sandström, *The Basic Principles of Marketing Warfare* (Chichester, U.K.: John Wiley & Sons, 1987), and Philip Kotler and Ravi Singh, "Marketing Warfare in the 1980s," *Journal of Business Strategy* (Fall 1980), as reprinted in Roger A. Kerin and Robert A. Peterson, eds., *Perspectives on Strategic Marketing Management* (Boston: Allyn and Bacon, 1983), pp. 67–81.

3. See Col. John R. Elting, U.S. Army, Ret., *The Super-Strategists* (New York: Charles Scribner's Sons, 1985), pp. 323–31.

4. The following discussion of defensive and offensive strategies is based on Kotler and Singh, "Marketing Warfare in the 1980s," in Kerin and Peterson.

5. See "Coca-Cola: A Spurt into Wine That Is Altering the Industry," *Business Week* (Oct. 15, 1979); p. 126; "The Wine War Gets Hotter," *Business Week* (Apr. 11, 1983; p. 61; "Why Coca-Cola and Wine Didn't Mix," *Business Week* (Oct. 10,

1983): p. 30; "Coca-Cola: A Sobering Lesson From Its Journey Into Wine," *Business Week* (June 3, 1985); p. 96; and "How Gallo Crushes the Competition," *Fortune* (Sept. 1, 1986); p. 24.

6. Ries and Trout, *Marketing Warfare*, p. 31.

7. Kotler and Singh, "Marketing Warfare in the 1980s," in Kerin and Peterson, p. 75.

8. The concept of "strategic intent" was brilliantly developed by Gary Hamel and C. K. Prahalad in "Strategic Intent," *Harvard Business Review*, (May–June 1989): pp. 17–30. This discussion draws heavily on this article.

9. For a discussion of Savin's entry into the photocopier market, see George L. Farr of McKinsey & Company, "Developing New Game Strategies," a talk at the American Marketing Association's 1983 Strategic Planning Conference, Chicago, April 19, 1983.

10. Hamel and Prahalad, "Strategic Intent," p. 24.

11. Ibid., pp. 23 and 25.

12. This is a trademarked credo for *The Real World Strategist*, a strategy newsletter published by James Fullinwider and the author.

13. See C. K. Prahalad and Gary Hamel, "The Core Competence of the Corporation," *Harvard Business Review* (May–June 1990); pp. 79–91, for a discussion of core competencies and the example of NEC.

14. Magid Abraham and Leonard Lodish, *Advertising Works: A Study of Advertising Effectiveness and the Resulting Strategic and Tactical Implications* (New York: Information Resources, Inc., 1989), p. 1.

15. Robert Axelrod, *The Evolution of Cooperation* (New York: Basic Books, 1984), pp. 27–69.

16. Michael Porter, *The Competitive Advantage of Nations* (New York: The Free Press, 1991), pp. 69–89.

Chapter 8

1. One of the best works on mission statements is James C. Collins and Jerry I. Porras, "Organizational Vision and Visionary Organizations," *California Management Review* (Fall 1991): pp. 30–52. Comments on mission statements in this chapter rely heavily on that article.

2. Ibid., p. 31.

3. Andrew Campbell and Laura L. Nash, *A Sense of Mission: Defining Direction for the Large Corporation* (Reading, Mass.: Addison-Wesley, 1990), p. 6.

4. John P. Kotter and James L. Heskett, *Corporate Culture and Performance* (New York: The Free Press, 1992), pp. 4–5. This book informs in all remarks about corporate culture in this chapter.

5. Ibid., p. 7.

6. Ibid., pp. 142–43.

7. Ibid., p. 106.

8. This discussion of core values and beliefs draws heavily on Collins and Porras, "Organizational Vision and Visionary Organizations," pp. 35–38.

9. See Thomas A. Falsey, *Corporate Philosophies and Mission Statements* (New York: Quorum Books, 1989), Ch. 3, and Campbell and Nash, *A Sense of Mission*, Ch. 6.

10. Collins and Porras, "Organizational Vision and Visionary Organizations," p. 38, say it should "guide an organization for at least 100 years."

11. Russell Ackoff, then of the Wharton School, developed the idealized design approach, which he has applied to dozens of organizations, including some of America's largest corporations. Ackoff's *Creating the Corporate Future* (New York: John Wiley & Sons, 1981) presents his theory of interactive planning; Chapter 5 deals with idealized design. Ackoff, et al., *A Guide to Controlling Your Corporation's Future* (New York: John Wiley & Sons, 1984) is a "how to do it" guide to interactive planning. Michael Hammer's concept of "reengineering" is similar to idealized design. See Hammer, "Reengineering Work: Don't Automate, Obliterate," *Harvard Business Review* (July–August 1990): pp. 104–12.

12. Thomas J. Peters and Robert H. Waterman, Jr., *In Search of Excellence* (New York: Harper & Row, 1982), p. 239.

13. Quoted by Collins and Porras, "Organizational Vision and Visionary Organizations," p. 46.

14. Collins and Porras, "Organizational Vision and Visionary Organizations," pp. 46–47.

15. Quoted by Collins and Porras, "Organizational Vision and Visionary Organizations," p. 49.

16. Unfortunately, its purpose is not as eloquently and effectively presented as it could have been. The opening paragraph is too heavy on products and customers, with a vague reference to the purpose ("meet the common needs"). This company has a powerful purpose of bridging "the gap between academia and the world of work." This should be stated in the opening sentence.

17. The Scientific Press has a very effective marketing use for its mission statement. This one was reprinted as a message to customers in its product catalog.

18. At Johnson & Johnson, the half-century-old credo is never final. It has undergone continuous scrutiny and occasional revision. It's been subjected to a series of "challenge meetings" in which managers were asked to challenge the relevance of its statements of values. It is communicated continually in annual reports, management conferences, performance reviews, and any number of other ways. It is the foundation of an ongoing program that surveys every employee on how well the company is performing against the standards stated in the Credo. See Campbell and Nash, *A Sense of Mission*, pp. 140–56.

Chapter 9

1. See *The Wall Street Journal*, Mar. 29, 1993, p. A1, for an account of the late Mike Walsh's transformation of Tenneco.

2. These criteria for good goals, but not the SMART acronym, are based on Arthur A. Thompson, Jr., and A.J. Strickland III, *Strategy Formulation and Implementation* (Plano, TX: Business Publications, Inc., 1983), p. 27.

3. Private communication, 1993.

4. David A. Garvin, "Quality on the Line," *Harvard Business Review* (September–October 1983): pp. 65–75.

5. Peter F. Drucker argues for the importance of people proposing their own goals. See his *Management: Tasks, Responsibilities, Practices* (New York: Harper & Row, 1973), p. 438.

6. See Charles F. Knight, "Emerson Electric: Consistent Profits, Consistently," *Harvard Business Review* (January–February 1992): pp. 57–70, for his account of "what makes Emerson tick."

7. Corporate planning departments are generally support groups for CEOs. Hence, a planning group's proposed long-term plan obviously will reflect considerable input from the CEO. If the planners have done their job, they will also have kept in close touch with the SBU heads and will incorporate input from those executives.

8. Knight, "Emerson Electric," p. 65.

Chapter 10

1. Robert H. Schaffer and Harvey A. Thomson, "Successful Change Programs Begin with Results," *Harvard Business Review*, (January–February 1992): p. 80.

2. Ibid., pp. 81, 84.

3. Ibid., emphasis added.

4. See Thomas J. Peters and Robert H. Waterman, Jr., *In Search of Excellence* (New York: Harper & Row, 1982), pp. 9–12, for a discussion of the "7 S" framework.

5. Ibid., pp. 13–16 and most of the rest of the book.

      Some of the "excellent" companies studied by Peters and Waterman have turned out to have had less than sterling business performances since 1982. This simply shows that the real world of business is dynamic and that winning in it takes constant effort and attention. There are no guarantees.

      In the first place, even an excellent company can suffer setbacks. Digital Equipment, for instance, ran afoul of a fundamental market shift when advances in PCs severely eroded the market for their minicomputers.

      In the second place, excellent companies can change for the worse, especially if they let success go to their heads and become internally focused. IBM's case makes the point that you must focus on *all* of the seven Ss; IBM failed to adapt both its strategy and corporate culture to fundamental changes in climate and competitive forces. Time will tell if it still has the stuff of excellence.

6. Stephen C. Coley and Sigurd E. Reinton, "The Hunt for Value," *McKinsey Quarterly* (Spring 1988): p. 30.

7. Joel Bleeke, *et al.*, "Succeeding at Cross-Border M&A," *McKinsey Quarterly* (1990, No. 3): p. 46.

8. Washington University, *Report of the Business Task Force* (St. Louis: Author, 1982).

9. Marvin R. Weisbord, *Productive Workplaces* (San Francisco: Jossey-Bass, 1991), gives an excellent overview of the evolution of management theory since Frederick Taylor.

10. As quoted in "A Note on Quality: The Views of Deming, Juran, and Crosby," *Unconditional Quality* (Cambridge, Mass.: Harvard Business School Press, 1991), p. 24.

11. Russell Ackoff deserves credit for the concept of dialectic teams. See Russell L. Ackoff and Elsa Vergera, "Creativity in Problem Solving and Planning: A Review," *European Journal of Operational Research* (Vol. 7, 1981), pp. 1–13.

12. Richard E. Neustadt and Ernest R. May, *Thinking in Time: The Uses of History for Decision Makers* (New York: The Free Press, 1986).

13. See, for instance, "Buy or Bye," *The Wall Street Journal* (Apr. 21, 1993): p. R9.

Epilogue

1. The importance of people to organizational performance is the theme of Jeffrey Pfeffer, *Competitive Advantage Through People: Unleashing the Power of the Work Force* (Boston, Mass: Harvard Business School Press, 1994).

2. C. K. Prahalad and Gary Hamel, "The Core Competence of the Corporation," *Harvard Business Review* (May-June 1990): pp. 79–91.

3. Michael Hammer and James Champy, *Reengineering the Corporation: A Manifesto for Business Revolution* (New York: HarperCollins, 1993).

4. Michael Porter, *Competitive Advantage* (New York: The Free Press, 1985).

INDEX

Note: Page numbers in italics indicate illustrations.

A

Abell, Derek F., 23
Ackoff, Russell, 13–14, 43, 195
Action-oriented planning, as factor in effectiveness, 20
Action planning, bottom-up, 229
Action plans (Cycle 3), 229–230, *230*
Administration, as principle of business warfare, 157
Advantage, layers of, 173–174
Advisors, questioning techniques for, 251–252
American Express, business definition of, 71–72, *72*
Anheuser-Busch
  business role of, 96
  mission statement of, *206–208*
  and order of implementation, *240*, 240–241
  and segmentation, 137
Annual planning, three cycles of, 233
Attack
  in business war, 156
  of undefended segments, 172
Auto industry
  and disequilibrium, 87–88

Auto industry (*Cont.*)
  and flank-positioning defense, 159–162
Axelrod, Robert, 181

B

Basic shared values, in corporate culture, 188
Behavioral incentives, 256–257
Behavior norms and patterns, in corporate culture, 188
Behaviors, and segmentation, *136*, 137
Benefits-sought segmentation, 138–139
Big-company competition, increase in, 4
Birnbaum, William S., 213, 216
Bleeke, Joel, 239
Boston Consulting Group (BCG)
  Growth/Share matrix, 35, 77, *78*
Bottom-up commitment
  to implementation, 254–257
  and mission statement, 205–208
  and success, 235–258
Bottom-up planning
  in Cycle 3, 45, 229
  as factor in effectiveness, 19

271